The Professional Songwriter

Louis Anthony deLise

The Professional Songwriter

Songwriting, Recording and Making Money with Your Music

Bocage Music Publishing, LLC
Cherry Hill, NJ USA

© 2019 Louis Anthony deLise. All rights reserved.

No part of this publication may be reproduced, stored in a retrieval system, or transmitted, in any form or by any means—graphic, electronic, or mechanical, including photocopying, recording, taping, or information storage and retrieval systems, or otherwise—without prior written permission of the publisher except in the case of brief quotations embodied in critical reviews and certain other noncommercial uses permitted by copyright law.

Bocage Music Publishing, LLC
83 Park Drive
Cherry Hill, NJ 08002
www.BocageMusicPublishing.com
856-616-2867
info@BocageMusicPublishing.com

Ordering Information:
Special discounts are available on quantity purchases by corporations, associations, and others. For details, contact the publisher at the address above.
Sole distributor for Europe and Asia: United Music & Media Publishers BVBA, www.ummp.eu.

ISBN-13: 978-0-578-56092-2 (Paperback)
ISBN-13: 978-0-578-56125-7 (Electronic)
Library of Congress Control Number: 2019011811

Printed in the U.S.A.

Publisher:	Bocage Music Publishing, LLC, Cherry Hill, NJ, USA
Editor, Production Editor:	Theresa deLise
Copy Editor:	Kathy Parsons
Interior and Cover Designer:	Caffeinated Brew Arts
Research Assistant:	Elizabeth deLise

Printing History:
August 2019: First Edition. (A revised edition of the work previously published as *The Contemporary Minstrel*.)

For Jonathan, James, and Elizabeth

Contents

Chapter One.	**Melody, Rhythm and Harmony** 1
	Study, Analysis and Listening 2
	What Is a Melody? 3
	Intervals 4
	Rhythm 14
	Harmony 17
	Exercises 39

Chapter Two.	**Song Forms** 45
	A Reason to Analyze 46
	Analysis: Musical Forensics 47

Chapter Three.	**Single Period Form** 49
	History of "Amazing Grace" 52
	Analysis of "Amazing Grace" 53
	The Lyrics of "Amazing Grace" 64
	Some Critical Comments about "Amazing Grace" 65
	Musical Arrangement and Record Production of Single Period Songs 68
	Other Songs in Single Period Form 71
	Exercises 72

Chapter Four.	**The Blues Form** 73
	The Earliest Blues 74
	Call-and-Response 75
	Blue Notes 76
	Color Chords in Blues 76
	Lyrics for Blues Songs 77
	Twelve-Bar Blues Form 78
	Sixteen-Bar Blues Form 82
	Other Songs in Blues Form 84
	Exercises 85

Chapter Five.	**Verse/Chorus Form** 87
	The Verse in Classic Verse/Chorus Form 87
	The Verse in The Twenty First Century Verse/Chorus Form 89
	The Chorus in Verse/Chorus Forms 91
	Exercises 108

Chapter Six.	**Twentieth-Century Bar Form** 111
	History 112
	The Harmonic Motion of the Periods 115
	The Title is the Hook 116
	A Bridge Provides Contrast 116
	Variations 122
	Other Songs in Twentieth-Century Bar Form 125
	Exercises 127

Chapter Seven.	**Pop Song Binary Form** 129
	Harmonic Motion and Cadences 130
	Delayed Lyrical Conclusion 131
	Other Songs in Pop Binary Song Form 136
	Exercises 137

Chapter Eight.	**Lyrics** 139
	The Most Important Link to the Listener 139
	One Big Thought Said Plainly 140
	Lyrics, a Composite of the Writer's Experience 142
	The Subject of Your Song 142
	Something to Write About 143

	The Prosody of the Lyrics Must Match the Rhythm of the Melody	146
	Rhyming and Other Poetic Devices Used in Lyrics	147
	Exercises	151
Chapter Nine.	**Reasons to Write, Methods to Monetize**	**153**
	A Reason to Write	153
	Songwriting as a Business	156
	Developing Your Practice	164
Chapter Ten.	**A New Paradigm**	**177**
	The Cast of Characters	179
	Building Your Team	179
	Recipes for Success	186
	Some Final Thoughts	205
Chapter Eleven.	**Coda**	**207**
	Appendix	**209**
	Scales	210
	Scales in Comparison	212
	Common Chord Symbols	214
	Common Chord Progressions in Minor	217
	Common Chord Progressions in Major	219
	Glossary	**221**
	References	**235**
	Music Examples (cited in order of appearance)	235
	Periodicals	237
	Texts	238
	Interviews	239
	Websites	240
	Index	**241**

List of Tables

Table 1:	Interval Names	5
Table 2:	Interval Quality	6
Table 3:	Modifying Intervals	7
Table 4:	Diatonic Scale Degree Formal Names	18
Table 5:	Labeling Conventions	48
Table 6:	Rhyme Scheme of Amazing Grace	64
Table 7:	Title Placement Based on Form	147
Table 8:	Possible Patterns for a Four-Line Lyric	150

List of Examples

Example 1:	Musical Alphabet (Beginning Here on C)	4
Example 2:	Perfect Intervals of the C Major Scale Plus Augmented 4th	6
Example 3:	Major Intervals of the C Major Scale	6
Example 4:	Minor Intervals of the C Major Scale	6
Example 5:	Naming Intervals and Enharmonic Equivalence	7
Example 6:	Treble Staff Names of Lines and Spaces	9
Example 7:	C Major Scale	9
Example 8:	C Natural Minor Scale	10
Example 9:	C Harmonic Minor Scale	10
Example 10:	C Melodic Minor Scale, Ascending and Descending	10
Example 11:	"The Girl from Ipanema"	13
Example 12:	Essential Rhythm for "Take Five"	15
Example 13:	Essential Rhythm for "Money"	15
Example 14:	Essential Rhythm for "Promises, Promises"	16
Example 15:	Diatonic Triads	17
Example 16:	Quality of Triads	19
Example 17:	"Your Cheatin' Heart"	20
Example 18:	Chord Symbols Commonly Found in Lead Sheets	21
Example 19:	"The Lead Sheet Song"	22
Example 20:	Chord Chart for Blues in Slash Notation	23
Example 21:	Chords in Inversions	24
Example 22:	Shared Chord Progressions	25
Example 23:	"Here, There and Everywhere"	26
Example 24:	"Piano Man"	27
Example 25:	Chord Symbol and Roman Numeral Analysis for "Piano Man"	27
Example 26:	"Wake Me Up When September Ends"	28
Example 27:	"Bristol Stomp"	29
Example 28:	"Blue Moon"	30
Example 29:	"Carolina in My Mind"	31
Example 30:	"World Without Love"	31
Example 31:	"All of Me"	32
Example 32:	"What a Wonderful World"	33
Example 33:	Bass Movement in "Carolina in My Mind"	33
Example 34:	"Autumn Leaves"	34
Example 35:	"Dindi"	35
Example 36:	"The Days of Wine and Roses"	36
Example 37:	"Yesterday"	36
Example 38:	"Gone With the Wind"	37
Example 39:	"I Should Care"	37
Example 40:	"I Only Have Eyes for You"	38
Example 41:	V—I CADENCE	50
Example 42:	Time Signature, Counting, and Tempo	54
Example 43:	Complete Periods with Phrases and Sub-Phrases Marked	56
Example 44:	Common Pentatonic Scales	58
Example 45:	Melodic Contour	59
Example 46:	Four Sub-Phrases a^1, a^2, b and a^3	61
Example 47:	Proposed New Setting of Lyrics for "Amazing Grace"	66
Example 48:	Graphic Analysis of Joseph Renzetti's Arrangement of the Song, "Sunny"	69
Example 49:	The Blues Scale	76
Example 50:	Twelve-Bar Blues Chord Progression in C Major	77
Example 51:	"Backwater Blues"	79

Example 52:	Opening Of "Backwater Blues" Showing the Flat Seventh	80
Example 53:	Eight Measures of "Backwater" Without A²	80
Example 54:	Lyrics for "Backwater Blues"	81
Example 55:	Variations on the Blues Chord Progression in Sixteen-Bar Blues	83
Example 56:	Lyrics from "I Just Called to Say I Love You"	92
Example 57:	Lyrics from "The Gambler"	94
Example 58:	"How Sweet It Is" Pentatonic Collection	96
Example 59:	Partial Phrasal Analysis of "How Sweet It Is"	96
Example 60:	Melodic Analysis of Phrase IIB of "How Sweet It Is"	97
Example 61:	Phrasal Analysis of "At the Hop"	99
Example 62:	"You've Got a Friend" Verse/Chorus with Bridge	101
Example 63:	First Seven Measures of "You've Got a Friend" Chorus Plus Pickup	103
Example 64:	B-Phrase of Period II as Pre-Chorus	104
Example 65:	Overview of "Roar"	105
Example 66:	Major Pentatonic Melody of "Roar"	106
Example 67:	"Shake It Off"	106
Example 68:	Phrasal Analysis of "Jeremy"	107
Example 69:	Leadsheet Analysis of "Jeannie with the Light Brown Hair"	114
Example 70:	Harmonic Motion and Formal Design of "Wake Me Up When September Ends"	117
Example 71:	Harmonic Motion and Formal Design of "My Funny Valentine"	119
Example 72:	Moving to Key Other Than Relative Minor for the Bridge	121
Example 73:	Introductory Verse of "My Funny Valentine"	123
Example 74:	Codetta of "Yesterday"	124
Example 75:	Codetta of "My Funny Valentine"	124
Example 76:	Twentieth-Century Bar Form Template	126
Example 77:	Pop Song Binary Form Template	130
Example 78:	Lyrics "The Days of Wine and Roses"	131
Example 79:	Lyrics "Here's That Rainy Day"	132
Example 80:	Lyrics "My Romance"	133
Example 81:	Harmonic and Phrasal Analysis "The Days of Wine and Roses"	134
Example 82:	Lyrics to "We Didn't Start the Fire"	140
Example 83:	Leadsheet for "Nick and Me"	145
Example 84:	Opening Line of "A Fine Romance"	146
Example 85:	Opening Line of "My Romance"	146
Example 86:	Some Words That Rhyme	148
Example 87:	Polysyllabic Rhymes	149
Example 88:	Sample Split Agreement	187
Example 89:	Solicitation Letter (sent via USPS or e-mail)	201
Example 90:	Permission Request Postcard	202
Example 91:	Permission Request E-mail	203

About the Author

Louis Anthony deLise is an award-winning composer, record producer, arranger and conductor. His compositions for soloists and ensembles have been recorded and are often performed worldwide. His arranging and conducting work appears on albums alongside that of many of the world's top pop artists including, Carlos Santana, Sheila E., Wynonna Judd, Kanye West, CeCe Winans and Paul Shaffer.

Louis deLise was arranger and conductor for Robert Hazard (writer of "Girls Just Wanna Have Fun") and Grammy® winners Patti LaBelle and Halestorm in concert performances and recordings. He arranged and conducted on two albums for Miss LaBelle: *Timeless Journey* and her number one hit, *The Gospel According to Patti LaBelle*. deLise was producer, arranger and songwriter for William DeVaughn's hit album *Figures Can't Calculate*.

Additional songwriting, composing, arranging and producing credits include albums and singles on EMI, Vanguard, Def-Jam, Centaur and CBS record labels.

Dr. deLise served on the Theory and Compostion Faculties of the Boyer College of Music and Dance, and Rowan University. He maintains an active career as composer of concert music published by Metropolis Music Publishers and ALRY Publications.

His flute concerto *Salone del Astor* won the National Flute Association's "Newly Published Music Competition" for 2019.

He can be reached through his website at: *www.LouisAnthonydeLise.com*.

Preface

Making up songs to sing has been a human activity since beyond memory. It's an inborn ability. Still, the Internet is filled with self-proclaimed songwriting gurus who author books, give seminars, and otherwise claim to have the secret sauce for success. I make no such claim. *The Professional Songwriter* is a study of the *craft of songwriting* and the *business of music* as it is presently practiced.

Songwriting is a widespread hobby. In my work as a record producer, musical arranger, and college professor, I have worked with many amateur songwriters who were business owners, physicians, carpenters, physical therapists, and schoolteachers. They all shared a passion for making up songs. While this book can be helpful for the ambitious amateur, it was specifically created for the aspiring *professional songwriter:* a creative who makes their living writing songs on demand and on schedule; works in several musical styles; plays well with others; and is competent in business.

As a text on both the musical craft and the business of songwriting, *The Professional Songwriter* assumes only the most basic of musical knowledge. In the opening sections, I include a distillation of the essential information I have presented many times in first-year music theory classes. Thus, I have purposely excluded much of the technical jargon and details of music theory in favor of the *practical* information songwriters really need.

I have seen first-hand how the spark of an idea in the hands of an expert can be crafted into a raging musical success. I have also seen promising careers tragically spiral downwards because of unfortunate business decisions. My hope is that *The Professional Songwriter* will provide you the knowledge you need to craft great songs, exploit them in the marketplace, and protect your intellectual property.

Writing songs can be fun. With much work, careful planning, dedicated study, and smart decision-making, it can also be profitable. I wish you all the best in your quest to become *The Professional Songwriter* you want to be!

Acknowledgements

This book would never have materialized had it not been for the indispensable assistance of two remarkable and wonderful women, both of whom I have the honor of loving: my daughter, Elizabeth; and my wife, Theresa. Thank you for the care, respect, and integrity you each have brought as you helped research, edit, and design this text.

Theresa, thank you, especially, for the many, many hours you have devoted to helping me birth this and all my other "projects."

Special thanks to the persons who proofread drafts of this text: James Clark; Maria Elena Contreras, D.M.A.; James M. DeLise, Ph.D.; Jonathan A. DeLise; Michael Angelo Grassi; Lora Lawrie; and Suzanne Zlotnick.

Thank you to my colleagues who have graciously taken the time to share their expertise for this book: William DeVaughn; Bobby Eli; David Ivory; Lori Landew; Esq.; Joseph Renzetti; Bernard Max Resnick, Esq.; Stephanie Seiple; Allen Slutsky; Jonathan Sprout; and Tess Taylor.

In looking again at the lists of the generous folks who have loaned to me their expertise, I am truly humbled to observe the years of training and education, the number of advanced degrees, gold and platinum records, Grammy awards and nominations and even an Oscar. Thank you, my friends.

Introduction

I believe the key elements to writing good songs are an understanding of song form, an ability to create harmonies that have direction, the ability to craft an interesting melody that captures and holds the listener's attention, and to set a lyric to a melody so that the meaning of the words is clear and even enhanced.

An inspired idea is a wonderful gift, but its impact will remain blunted unless it is crafted into a unified expression with both musical and lyrical direction. To accomplish the goal of unified expression—a song with a beginning, middle, and end—songwriters need to know stuff. Indeed, today's songwriters need to know many more things than songwriters had to know in years gone by.

Songwriters need to know some things about *music theory*, like how chords are formed, how chords progress from one to another, and how they coexist, support, and spawn melodies. That is why I present aspects of music theory in Chapter One and throughout the book as I discuss various other aspects of the songwriting craft.

I believe that aspiring professional songwriters need to know about the most commonly heard song forms. That is why in Chapters Two through Seven, I introduce and explain the standard song forms including several twenty-first century variations. In addition to discussing lyric writing in the chapters I devote to the various song forms, I devote all of Chapter Eight to the study of lyric writing.

Songwriters need to know about *business*, it is after all called *The Music Business*. That is why I spend all of Chapters Nine and Ten discussing the songwriting business as it is presently practiced. I include in Chapter Nine a discussion of some of the many ways songwriters can use their craft to make an income. You will discover that, along with the better-known avenues for songwriting success, I introduce several less obvious and seldom discussed markets for songs. I include in this chapter an introduction to the publishing business, music for film, and I explain licensing and royalties.

In Chapter Ten, I present an overview of today's "do-it-yourself" music world. I introduce some of the tools songwriters will need to become *music entrepreneurs*. I explain self-publishing, copyrights, forming a record company, working with sub-publishers, and building your team of music industry professionals. Finally, I present two *recipes for success*; two blueprints you can follow to exploit your songs.

In addition to knowing about compositional technique, lyric writing, and business, songwriters now need to have a working knowledge of the *recording business*. While demonstration records are still useful (and today, easier, and less expensive than ever to make), success in the songwriting business is inexorably connected to being able to produce *master-quality* records or be aligned with someone who can. A thorough study of the recording craft is outside the scope of this textbook. I recommend you consider buying studio time at a professional studio so you can see first-hand how records are made; you watch as many on-line videos about recording technique as you can; and you buy some inexpensive, computer-based recording equipment so you can "get your hands dirty" and learn the craft.

New in the Third Edition

I have generally expanded and updated the information in the book. This is especially true of the chapter on Verse/Chorus song form and the chapters on the songwriting business. I have also refined, updated, and expanded both the Appendix and the Glossary, and created a companion playlist of the examples presented in the text. Look for the *Professional Songwriter Playlist* on Apple Music and Spotify.

In addition, I have included several new interviews with music business professionals. These will be found mostly in the later chapters of the book and are identified as, "The *Real* Music Business 101."

Studying with a master musician-tutor remains an important part of any aspiring musician's training, and one I highly recommend. There are talented and knowledgeable music educators the world over. There are also many charlatans and pretenders masquerading as music business mavens. Songwriters who are seeking a tutor will do well to carefully research the prospective teacher's record of success, including label releases, publications, and how their other mentees have fared in the music business.

Aspiring songwriters are today very fortunate to have at their disposal very low-cost or free access to original high-quality recordings of just about any composition. I sincerely encourage all songwriters to carefully listen to the examples cited in the book. Thoughtful listening to the work of master songwriters in all genres is, along with analyzing, emulating, reengineering, and studying with a good musician, a key factor in learning the songwriting craft.

Louis Anthony deLise, D.M.A.
Cherry Hill, New Jersey, USA
8 August 2019

Chapter One

Melody, Rhythm and Harmony

It's quite amazing! Even though music surrounds us at every turn, even though we "know what we like when we hear it," it is almost impossible, even for musicians, to explain succinctly what it is that makes a particular composition resonate with us. We hear, remember, and sing along with the songs, symphonies and jingles that wash over us each day, but what is it that causes this music to stick in our memories?

Some music endures for centuries. "Shenandoah," "Silent Night," "Amazing Grace," "Ode to Joy," "'O Sole Mio," "On Top of Old Smoky," "Beautiful Dreamer," "Londonderry Air," and "Happy Birthday" are compositions that remain popular even though all were crafted many years ago. And remember, each of these was introduced at a time when there was no mass audio communication.

Of course, it is the **melody** that has kept these songs popular for generations. It is not the song's **production** that we whistle as we work, and it is not a singer's performance that makes these songs timeless. It is the song's melody that we remember. What about the lyrics? Well, a catchy turn of phrase is also likely to be remembered. But words that are sung to a melody are statistically more likely to be remembered (therefore, the existence of jingles).

> **Note**
> For most of us, describing why one melody works and another one does not is like explaining why we like vanilla ice cream rather than strawberry, or why blue is our favorite color.

In this chapter, I will offer some insight into what makes melodies endure and how you can go about refining your melodic gifts. I will share with you my thoughts about why some melodies have become part of the fabric of our lives. I will accomplish these goals through a thoughtful analysis of some exceptional music. Our careful examination of the techniques that great songwriters have employed will furnish guidelines for your personal songwriting.

The idea of melody making evolved from speaking. The songs of birds and other animals likely influenced early melody making. The anthropologist and ethnomusicologist, Steven Feld, found that the Kaluli people of the Southern Highlands Province of Papua New Guinea believe that human speech is for utilitarian purposes, whereas bird song (interpreted by humans as weeping, poetry, and song), is for conveying feelings. It is easy to imagine melody then as the human form of bird song: a heightened form of speaking, especially when one considers that normal speech also occurs in rhythm with the speaker's voice rising and falling in pitch. Rhythm and pitch changes supply interest, variety, and emphasis in both speech and melody.

Study, Analysis and Listening

I am always stunned to meet people who aspire to create their own songs but know little or nothing about music. These folks think that their ambition alone will somehow provide them the wherewithal to create a hit song or two.

> **Note**
> In my recording and performing career, I have never met anyone who alleged that his or her musical prowess was stymied by having formally studied music.

It's not that one needs to be an expert performer or music theorist to write a hit, rather you need to be expert in *something*. For instance, in my professional experience of working as a music arranger and record producer, I have worked with folks who possess very little formal musical knowledge, who haven't been expert performers or trained composers, but who were, perhaps, expert listeners. Through their listening, and singing along as they listen, they have discerned what it is that makes music work. They might not be able to articulate in musical terms why they do what they do, but they are able to intuit how to take the germ of a musical (and perhaps lyrical) idea and successfully shape it into a fully formed song. They hone their melodic gifts by listening and singing along to music that others have composed. Listening and singing along to famous songs is foundational for a songwriter's musical education.

Studying the material presented here will yield an additional level of professionalism, as will studying with an experienced master musician. I have met many competent singers, instrumentalists, and aspiring songwriters who had honed their craft through study with a music professional.

What Is a Melody?

A melody is a coherent horizontal series of single tones that floats above the **harmony** and is anchored by the **rhythm** and **meter**. In a pop song, the melody carries with it the short narrative of the song's lyric.

Melody is distinct from harmony in that the pitches used to create harmony occur as vertical simultaneities. It is distinct from rhythm in that the sounds making up a melody are pitched: the frequencies of a melody are clear, regular, and stable enough to be heard as something other than noise.

The duration of both pitches and silences in a melody's horizontal tones as they occur in time is integral to how impressive the melody will be, and therefore how it will be recognized as special and memorable.

For the gifted songwriter, creating a potent melody is an intuitive act. The creative act is a mysterious process where the composer, drawing on a thorough knowledge of chord patterns and melodic gestures, hears in her inner ear, and then commits to paper or recording, what the world will laud as beautiful. Indeed, knowledge fuels intuition. An expert songsmith will have a command of **harmonic motion** (chord progressions), **melodic gestures** (the implied meaning of a melody), **melodic contour** (the shape of a melody—how it goes higher and lower), **form** (how **phrases** are managed), and **development** (the way composers manipulate important musical material). Obtaining this knowledge is necessarily a matter of study, analysis and listening.

It is easy for most of us to recognize a melody when we hear one. The **pitches** and rhythm of a melody are a shape that takes us on a journey. From the beginning, we listeners and performers ride a melody's crests and troughs, curving high and low from one emotion to another until expectation leads finally to resolution at the melody's end.

In the following sections, I will introduce components of melody, including its supporting players, harmony (individual tones that are sounded together or in proximity), and rhythm (the patterns of sounds and silences that flow through time). The words melody and harmony are often adjectives used to describe a kind of rhythm. We will see in our discussion of harmony, that **chords** also move from one to the next in rhythmic and specific ways.

Intervals

The distance between any two pitches of a melody (or two pitches in any other musical context) is called an **interval**.

> **Note**
> The interval between any two keys separated by one intervening key is a whole

Intervals are measured and named in a few ways. First, by simply counting the scale steps that an interval covers. For instance, to measure the interval from C up to G, you would use the **musical alphabet** (A, B, C, D, E, F, and G) to count five scale steps: C, D, E, F, and G. Thus, C up to G is *some kind* of fifth since it encompasses five musical alphabet letter names.

The smallest interval used in Westerns music is the half step or **semitone**. Half steps are found between any two adjacent notes on the piano keyboard (Example 1).

Example 1:   Musical Alphabet (Beginning Here on C)

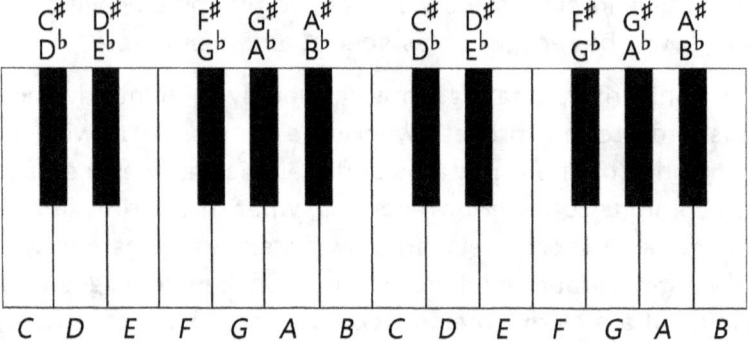

The white keys of the piano keyboard are called the natural keys. They correspond to pitches represented by the seven letter names of the musical alphabet. If you begin on any white key and then count up or down eight keys, you will have traveled an interval of an **octave**. The letter name of the note an octave above or below your starting pitch will always have the same letter name. Start on a D and count up eight keyboard notes and you will arrive at another D. The two D's are said to be an octave apart. Listeners perceive notes to the right of the keyboard as being *higher* in pitch and those to the left as being *lower*. The frequency of the pitches increases as we travel up the keyboard and decreases as we go down the keyboard to the left.

Quality

Musicians ascribe quality to **intervals** by using one of five qualifying adjectives in their description. Intervals are deemed to be perfect, major, minor, diminished, or augmented depending on the number of **semitones** contained in the interval. See Table 1 for a chart of intervals measured in half steps.

The intervals of a fourth, fifth and octave are called **perfect intervals**. The intervals of a second, third, sixth, and seventh are called **major**.

When perfect intervals are made smaller by a half step, they become **diminished intervals**. When a major interval is reduced by a half step it becomes a **minor interval**. A minor interval reduced by a half step becomes a diminished interval. Both perfect and major intervals if made larger by a half step become **augmented intervals**.

> **Note**
> Intervals must be named in two respects: the number of steps between the two pitches and the quality—major, minor, diminished, or augmented.

Table 1: Interval Names

Semitone (half steps)	Interval Names (with alternates)
0	Perfect Unison (Perfect Prime)
1	Minor Second (Half Step)
2	Major Second (Whole Step)
3	Minor Third
4	Major Third
5	Perfect Fourth
6	Augmented Fourth (Diminished Fifth)
7	Perfect Fifth
8	Augmented Fifth (Minor Sixth)
9	Major Sixth
10	Minor Seventh
11	Major Seventh
12	Perfect Octave

The distinctive sound quality of each interval is significant. You will find it an important and helpful skill to be able to identify intervals by ear. Like all skills, being able to name the intervals you hear, sing, and play can be developed through drill.

Interval quality is abbreviated as in Table 2.

Table 2: Interval Quality

Interval Quality	Abbreviation
Major	M
Minor	m
Perfect	P
Augmented	A or +
Diminished	d or °

Within one octave of a major scale, one will find these intervals: perfect prime (unison), major second, minor second, major third, minor third, perfect fourth, perfect fifth, major sixth, minor sixth, minor seventh, major seventh, perfect octave and the augmented fourth. See Example 2, Example 3, and Example 4, below.

Example 2: Perfect Intervals of the C Major Scale Plus Augmented 4th

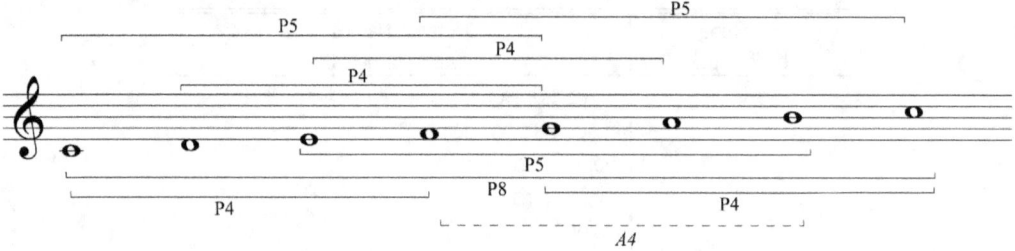

Example 3: Major Intervals of the C Major Scale

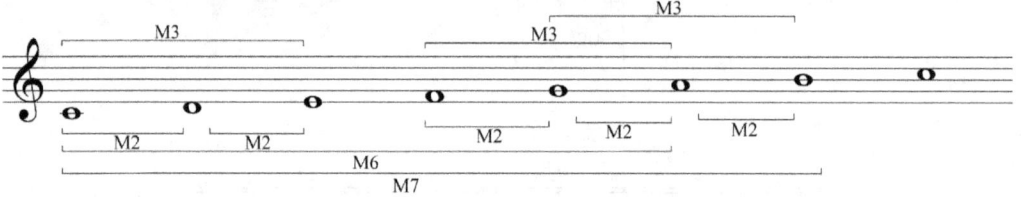

Example 4: Minor Intervals of the C Major Scale

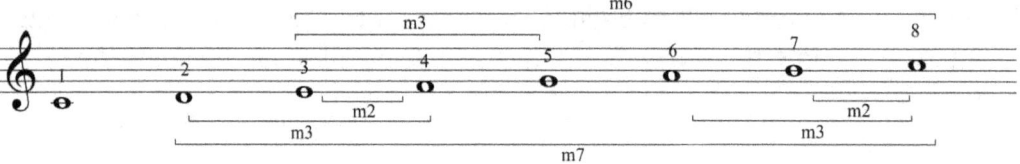

Modifying Intervals

Returning to our previous example, the interval of C up to G, we can also count the semitones in the span. Using the piano keyboard as a guide, you can count seven half steps. Table 1 indicates that an interval spanning seven half steps is a *perfect fifth*.

If in a composition we decided to sound an interval going from C up to G-flat (G♭), we will have an interval that is one half step smaller than a perfect fifth. Using Table 1, we can see that an interval spanning six half steps is either a *diminished fifth* or an *augmented fourth*.

Because we called the pitch G♭, the interval will be identified as a diminished fifth. If we write the interval as C up to F-sharp (F♯) counting four musical alphabet letter names, we would call this an augmented fourth. Table 3 shows the names of intervals as they are modified by adding or subtracting half steps.

Table 3: Modifying Intervals

-2 half steps	-1 half step	Starting Interval	+1 half step	+2 half steps
-	Diminished	Perfect	Augmented	-
Diminished	Minor	Major	Augmented	-
-	Diminished	Minor	Major	Augmented

Enharmonic Equivalence

Pitches that represent the same frequency and are named differently are said to be **enharmonically equivalent**. Musicians will choose to use one name over the other depending on the musical context. In the previous example, F♯ and G♭ are enharmonically equivalent. On the piano keyboard, they are the same key. Some examples of enharmonically equivalent intervals are shown in Example 5.

Example 5: Naming Intervals and Enharmonic Equivalence

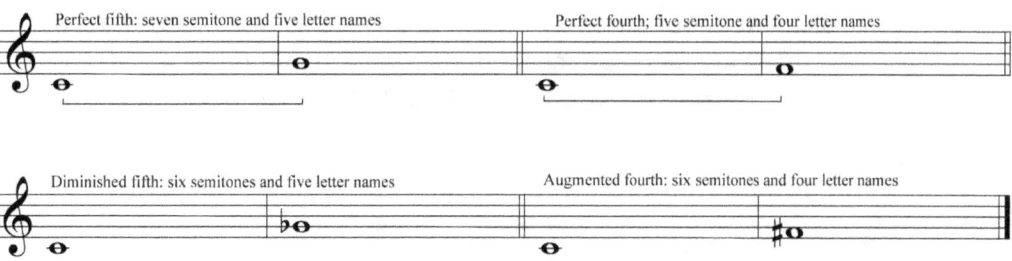

Additional Naming Conventions

Intervals of up to a perfect octave (twelve half steps) are considered **simple intervals**. Intervals greater than an octave are called **compound intervals**. Compound intervals include *elevenths* (an octave plus a fourth), *thirteenths* (an octave plus a sixth), *tenths* (an octave plus a third), and *ninths* (an octave plus a second). Compound intervals will also be perfect, major, minor, diminished, or augmented depending on the number of semitones contained in the interval added to the octave. For example, an augmented fourth added to an octave will yield an augmented eleventh.

Melodic and Harmonic Intervals

Intervals that occur in succession (horizontally) are called **melodic intervals**. Those that occur simultaneously (vertically) or in rapid succession, are called **harmonic intervals**. Melodic intervals are, of course, fundamental to melody writing just as harmonic intervals are the basis for forming the chordal underpinning of tunes.

In other cultures, musicians use smaller intervals, like quartertones. Some pop singers, especially jazz and blues singers, purposely sing intervals that are smaller than half steps to produce **blue notes**. Other perhaps less skilled singers and instrumentalists have been known to perform quartertones, but not on purpose...the subject for another discussion and beyond the scope of this text!

Treble Staff

Note

Evolution of the G-clef.

The examples in this book are almost all written on a treble staff. Staves offer a convenient graphic representation of the sounds used in music. The treble staff uses a treble clef, also called a G-clef, that defines the second staff line as the pitch "G." To be precise, this is G4, the fifth above middle C (also called C4). Using the musical alphabet, one can easily determine the names of the rest of the staff's lines and spaces. The spaces are named F, A, C, and E; the lines of the staff are named E, G, B, D, and F.

Melody, Rhythm and Harmony

There are several other clefs used in music, but the treble clef will serve our purposes.

Example 6: **Treble Staff Names of Lines and Spaces**

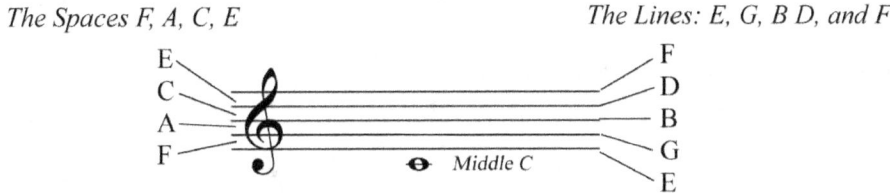

Scales and Keys

Pitches can be organized into special collections called **scales**. There are several scales in common use. Each is defined by the arrangement of the half and whole steps it contains. The most commonly used scales in Western music are the **major scale** and the **minor scale**. The minor scale is used in three varied forms: **natural minor**, **harmonic minor,** and **melodic minor**. The formula for the interval relationships of a major scale is shown in Example 7.

The white keys of the piano offer a convenient memory aid for the major scale formula. The eight keys from C up to the next C are arranged in precisely the half step and whole step formula used to construct major sales.

Example 7: **C Major Scale**

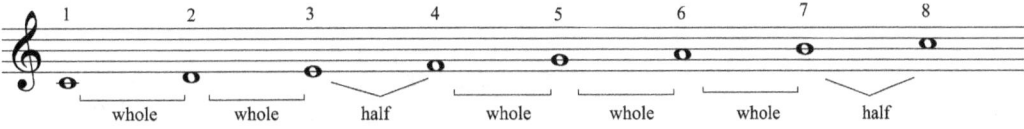

Major scales can be replicated in either direction, ascending or descending, using this same whole step/half step formula. More important perhaps, using the major scale formula of half and whole steps you can build a major scale starting on any of the twelve pitches.

Minor scales come in three forms. You can find the scale formula for the natural minor scale (Example 8) by playing all the white keys on the piano from A, to the A an octave above, and observing the half step and whole step locations. The harmonic minor and melodic minor forms incorporate **chromatic alterations** and are demonstrated in Example 9 and Example 10, respectively.

Example 8: **C Natural Minor Scale**

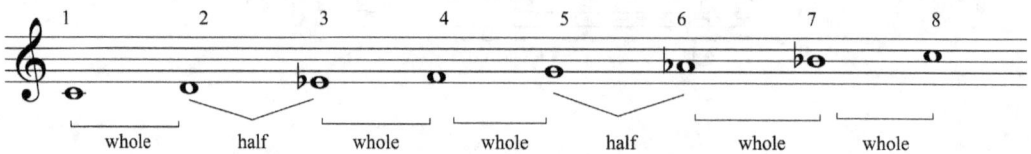

Example 9: **C Harmonic Minor Scale**

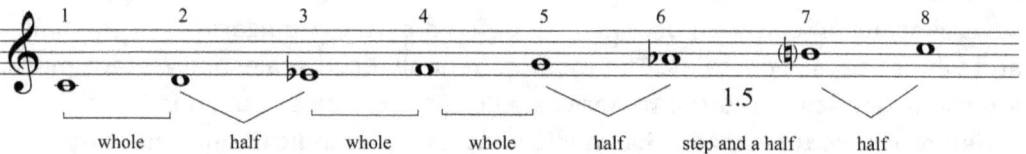

Example 10: **C Melodic Minor Scale, Ascending and Descending**

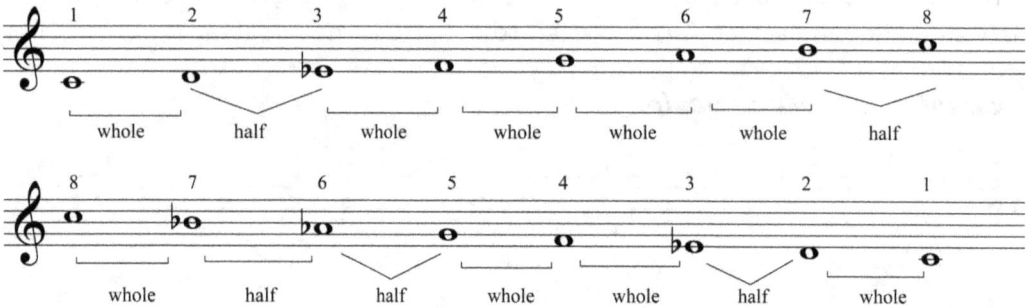

Scales are named by their first degree or pitch. The major scale demonstrated in Example 7 begins on the pitch C and follows the interval formula for a major scale. It is therefore called a *C major scale*. A piece of music, or a section of a piece of music, that primarily uses the pitch collection of a single scale is said to be *in the key of* that scale. Thus, a song that primarily uses the pitch collection of the C major scale is said to be *in the key of C major*.

Chromatic Collection

In our Western culture system of music making, the octave is divided into twelve pitches that are equidistant from one to the next: they are each a semitone apart. The twelve pitches of the octave when considered together are the chromatic collection. Played in succession, they form the **chromatic scale**.

Composers (including songwriters) tend to use scales made up of seven notes, represented by the diatonic white notes on the piano, or five notes (**pentatonic scale**), represented by the five black keys of the piano. They use the twelve pitches of the chromatic scale collection as possible pitch choices but mainly use scales that feature a combination of whole steps and half steps.

A remarkable exception to this tendency of avoiding chromatic scales for pop song melodies is "Midnight Sun," written by Lionel Hampton (1908-2002), Sonny Burke (1914-1980) and Johnny Mercer (1909-1976). It was written initially as a jazz "head" by Messrs. Hampton and Burke with lyrics later added by Mr. Mercer. In "Midnight Sun," the writers take the melody through nearly an entire chromatic scale within the first two-and-a-half measures! (The 1957 recording by Ella Fitzgerald is well worth the listening.)

> **Note**
> A "head" is a melodic phrase that becomes the basis for improvisation. It is played literally the first time and improvised upon thereafter.

Other Scales

There are many other scales used in Western popular songs. These include the **Dorian**, **Phrygian**, **Lydian**, **mixolydian**, and **Aeolian** modes. The term "mode" is applied to the six scales that originated in the Catholic Church of the Middle Ages and were inspired by the music theory of ancient Greece. Again, the piano keyboard offers a helpful visual aid in learning and remembering the formulas for these scales. The formula for the Dorian mode is found by playing and visualizing the eight diatonic notes from D to D. The notes from E to E represent the Phrygian mode. The Lydian collection formula is found in the white notes from F to F; mixolydian, from G to G; and Aeolian, from A to A. Note that the Aeolian mode contains the same pitches and ordering as the natural minor scale. See the Appendix for examples.

Consonance and Dissonance

Intervals are further characterized as being either **consonant** or **dissonant**. Consonant intervals are major and minor thirds, perfect fifths, and major and minor sixths. All seconds, sevenths, fourths, and the augmented and diminished versions of fifths are considered dissonant. In his excellent music theory text, *The Complete Musician*, the theorist Steven G. Laitz gives us an additional refinement. Dr. Laitz calls perfect octaves and perfect fifths, **perfect consonances**. Major and minor thirds and major and minor sixths are **imperfect consonances**.

Although consonance and dissonance are to some extent in the ear of the hearer and a function of acculturation, some music theorists believe that humans possess a genetic predisposition to sounds we consider consonant or dissonant. In his book, *This is Your Brain on Music*, Daniel J. Levitin notes that infants show a preference for consonance over dissonance. Dr. Levitin proffers that an appreciation for dissonance generally evolves later in life as one matures. This might be true, nevertheless, many listeners develop little tolerance for dissonant melodic and harmonic intervals. Instead, they experience dissonant melodies and dissonant chords as unpleasant. Like musical context, cultural context is a key factor in developing aural perception. The perceived unpleasantness of dissonance may well be why so few Alban Berg or Ornette Coleman tunes have broken into the *Billboard* magazine "Hot 100."

The concept of what we perceive as consonant or dissonant musical sounds has evolved over the centuries. Further, we might hear the same sounds as consonant in one context and not in another. In this way, the perception of an interval's relative consonance or dissonance is a function of its musical surroundings.

Let's listen to the interval of the major seventh. The interval of a major seventh, for instance the interval of middle C to the B-natural (B♮) above it, is heard as very dissonant. The inversion of the major seventh, the minor second (middle C to the B♮ a half step below it) is also heard as a biting dissonance in our Western culture. However, when sounded along with the pitches of a major triad to form a **major seventh** chord, this interval sounds quite pleasant, enough so that it is used continually in popular music, including as the concluding chord of many songs.

Melody, Rhythm and Harmony

Listen, for instance, to the song, "Garota de Ipanema" ("The Girl from Ipanema"), written by composer, Antônio Carlos Jobim (1927-1994), and lyricists, Vinícius de Moraes (1913-1980) and Norman Gimbel (1927-). This song is thought to be the second most recorded song in history after John Lennon (1940-1980) and Paul McCartney's (1942-), "Yesterday".

The underlying harmony of the first measure of "The Girl from Ipanema" is a major seventh chord. Coincidentally, like the Beatles' song, "Yesterday," the melody of Mr. Jobim's song begins on the second degree of the scale, but unlike "Yesterday," the melody of "Ipanema" does not resolve downward to the first degree of the scale, as would be customary. Instead, it floats down to the seventh degree of the scale, also known as the **leading tone**.

Most startling to classically trained ears, instead of resolving upward to the first degree of the scale (as all good leading tones are supposed to do), Mr. Jobim moves the melody back to its starting point, scale degree 2, as shown in Example 11.

Example 11: **"The Girl from Ipanema"**

Rhythm

The word **rhythm** has a few meanings. In a general way, rhythm refers to musical sounds and silences that are systematically arranged in patterns of relative duration over time. The term rhythm can also be modified by the adjectives "melodic" and "harmonic."

The word rhythm is, of course, also used to mean the recurring patterns played by the rhythm section (the drummer, bassist, guitarist, and pianist) to undergird the other instruments in the performance of a pop song. The rhythms played relate to historic or current dances, including the fox trot, waltz, salsa, cha-cha, twist, shuffle, and so on.

Melodic Rhythm

In the context of a melody, a pattern of musical tones and silences heard flowing over the constant of time is called the song's **melodic rhythm**.

Harmonic Rhythm

Chords also progress in patterns over time. This pattern is referred to as the **harmonic rhythm** or **chord progression**.

Pulse or Beat

The time referred to in the previous definitions is a series of consistently regular pulses that are gauged against clock time. This is the **beat** or **pulse** to which dancers dance or soldiers march.

Tempo

The speed at which the beats unfold is referred to as **tempo**. Tempos can and normally do vary from the start of a composition to its end, but in pop music mostly remain very consistent. Tempo is measured precisely when expressed in beats per minute (bpm). Alternately, tempo may be indicated more vaguely by using descriptive words like *adagio* (slowly) or *presto* (quickly).

Meter

Beats are organized into manageable groups of two or three (or their multiples), to form units called measures (known colloquially as "bars"). The beats of a measure are generally characterized as accented or unaccented, with the first beat almost always accented. Pop songs are mostly composed in four beats per measure, but sometimes are developed in three beat measures, like the song, "Someday My Prince Will Come," or twelve beat measures, like "Can't Help Falling in Love." The composition "Take Five," made famous by Dave Brubeck and composed by Paul Desmond (1924-1977), is written using measures with five beats.

Example 12: Essential Rhythm for "Take Five"

In addition to commonly being written in four-beat meters, most songs use just one meter from beginning to end. The song "Money," made famous by Pink Floyd and written by Roger Waters (1943-), is a great exception to both tendencies.

"Money" is composed for the most part with seven beats in each measure. But it also *changes* meter several times throughout the song. (The song goes to a different meter in measures nine and ten and, in the recording, for the guitar solo.)

Example 13: Essential Rhythm for "Money"

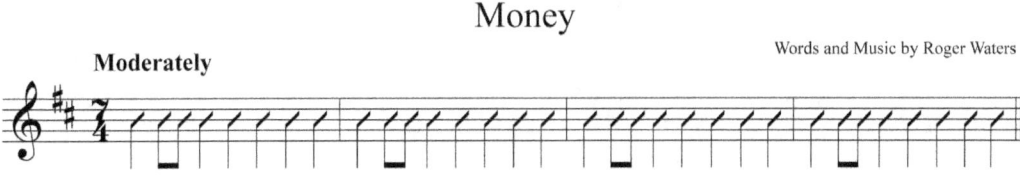

The undergirding meter of a song is an important glue that holds the song together. In a recording this meter can translate into what I call the essential rhythm or groove.

The composer, Burt Bacharach (1928-), working with lyricist Hal David (1921-2012), made rapid and multiple meter changes a regular feature of his writing. The title song for their musical, *Promises, Promises* is a good example. This very successful song moves quickly from one meter to another throughout. The essential rhythm of "Promises, Promises" is also the rhythm of the melody—the melodic rhythm (See Example 14).

Example 14: Essential Rhythm for "Promises, Promises"

Harmony

Melodies of pop-style songs exist in a mutually dependent relationship with an underlying harmony. Harmony in this instance refers to the chords that accompany a melody. You hear harmony underpinning melodies in recorded pop songs. The chords played on the guitar or piano, sounded in the string and horn section, or sung by the back-up vocalists generally supply the harmony in recordings.

The word "harmony" is also used to mean the back-up vocals that often accompany a lead vocal in a pop recording or concert performance.

Building Chords

The term **chord** is the name given to three or more pitches arranged vertically and sounded more or less simultaneously. When all the chord tones are sounded at once, the chord is called a **block chord**. When the chord tones are sounded in rapid succession, but heard as part of the same musical unit, the chord is said to be **arpeggiated** or a broken chord.

Three-note chords made by stacking thirds one on top of another are called **triads**. Chords with four pitches stacked in thirds are called **seventh chords**. When chords are made up strictly of scale tones, they are called **diatonic chords**. Example 15 shows the diatonic triads one can construct using only the notes of the C major scale.

Example 15: Diatonic Triads

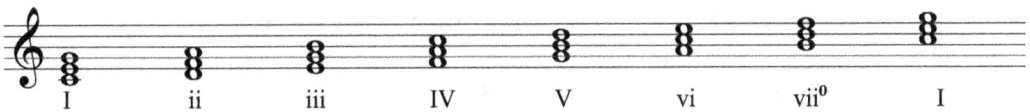

Naming the Parts of a Chord

The notes of chords are called chord voices or simply, voices. The note upon which a chord is built is called the **root**. The third above the root is called the *third* or chord third. The *fifth* above the root is the chord fifth or simply, the *fifth*.

Naming Chords

Chords are named for their root and for their quality. In this context, quality refers to the sound quality ascribed to the chord. The kinds of thirds used and the order in which they are used determines the quality of a chord.

As you have seen, musicians often have developed multiple ways to express the same musical thought, characteristic, or principle. This is the case with chords. In addition to naming chords using the root and the chord quality, chords can be described according to their function, or the scale degree upon which they are constructed. The degrees of the scale are numbered and named. A handy chart in Table 4 shows the scale degree and its formal name.

Table 4: Diatonic Scale Degree Formal Names

Diatonic Scale Degree	Formal Name
1	Tonic
2	Supertonic
3	Mediant
4	Subdominant
5	Dominant
6	Submediant
7	Leading tone

A chord built on the first degree of the scale, where scale degree 1 is the root of the chord, can be called a **tonic triad**. A triad built on scale degree 2 is called a **supertonic triad**, and so on.

We can use Roman numerals as a shorthand method to describe chords. Uppercase Roman numerals will be used to mean major chords (e.g. V); lowercase Roman numerals (e.g., vi) will be used to mean minor chords. Diminished chords are indicated using small numerals and the degree sign (e.g., vii°). Augmented chords are symbolized in this method by using a numeral and a plus sign (e.g., V+).

Building a Major Triad

Placing a major third above the root and a minor third above that creates a major triad. A major triad built on C will contain the pitches C, E and G. Put another way, the interval between the chord root and the chord third is a major third. The interval between the chord third and the chord fifth is a minor third. The interval between the root and the chord fifth is a perfect fifth.

Building a Minor Triad

A minor triad is constructed by placing a minor third above the root and a major third above that. Put another way, the interval between the root and the chord third is a minor third. The interval between the chord third and the chord fifth is a major third. A minor triad built on C will contain the pitches C, E♭, and G. The interval between the root and the chord fifth is a perfect fifth.

Building a Diminished Triad

A **diminished triad** is constructed by placing two minor thirds, one above the other. A diminished triad built on C will contain the pitches C, E♭ and G♭. The interval between the root and the chord fifth is a diminished fifth in a diminished chord.

Building an Augmented Triad

An **augmented triad** is constructed by placing two major thirds, one above the other. An augmented triad built on C will contain the pitches C, E and G♯. The interval between the root and the chord fifth is an augmented fifth in an augmented chord.

Example 16 shows triads of each quality all built on the root, C.

Example 16: Quality of Triads

Using the naming rule above, the chords in this example are called: C major (C), C minor (Cm), C diminished (C°), and C augmented (C+).

The Primary Triads

Tonal music, the term used to describe music based primarily on diatonic chords and melodies, ascribes special importance to three of the chords used to harmonize major scale or minor scale melodies. Called **primary triads** or **primary chords**, these are the chords built on the tonic (I), the subdominant (IV) and the dominant (V) degrees of the scale.

The one chord (I), the four chord (IV), and the five chord (V), as musicians sometimes call them, are often heard as the pillars of a composition. It is quite possible to create very successful songs using just these three chords.

The songwriter and singer, Hank Williams (1923-1953), made thorough use of the three primary chords in many of his hit songs. Williams uses only primary chords in the first sixteen measures of his song, "Your Cheatin' Heart," (Example 17).

Example 17: *"Your Cheatin' Heart"*

Chord Symbol Notation

In Example 17, the harmony is expressed using chord symbols. Chords are represented in sheet music for popular songs using a shorthand method called **chord symbol notation**. Chord symbols indicate the root of the chord, the quality of the chord, any added color tones, and what chord member is to be played in the bass (the lowest pitch in a chord voicing).

Added Notes

The three primary chords form the essential underpinning of many blues songs, hymn tunes, and many pop and rock songs. I write "essential" because songwriters often modify the primary chords by adding other **color tones**, like sixths, sevenths, and seconds to the basic chords. Added notes change the sound of chords, but in popular music the chord's function is generally not changed by the addition of color tones.

Added notes are indicated as a number that represents the interval between the root of the chord and the added note. For instance, a sixth added to a C chord will be represented as C6. A musician seeing this symbol will sound a C major triad, with the interval of a diatonic (major) sixth added above the root. In other words, she will play the pitches C, E, G, and A, the added 6th above the bass. Most commonly, one will see a seventh added to a chord. This means to add the interval of a minor seventh above the root. In a C7 chord the pitches C, E, G, and B♭ would be sounded. A capital letter alone tells one to play a major chord in root position with no added notes.

In Example 18 some chords are expressed in multiple ways.

Example 18: Chord Symbols Commonly Found in Lead Sheets

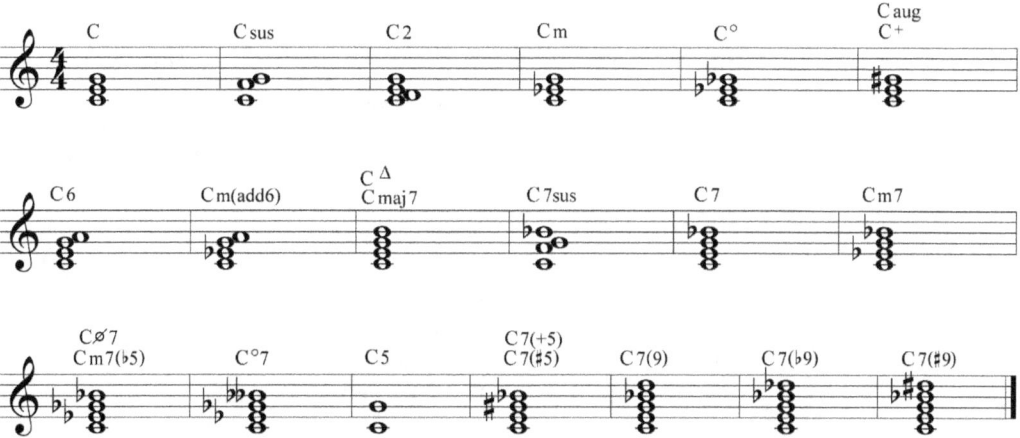

Lead Sheets

A **lead sheet** (or fake sheet) is a simplified manuscript for representing music. The typical lead sheet will feature the song's melody written on a treble staff, the lyrics of the song, and the harmony notated in chord symbol notation. The lead sheet will show the tempo and style of the song. It should also include the names of the composer, lyricist, and copyright owner. See Example 19.

Example 17 shows the Hank Williams song, "Your Cheatin' Heart", written as a lead sheet.

Example 19: "The Lead Sheet Song"

A **chord chart** is even more utilitarian. It shows the simplified rhythm of the chord changes in slash notation. Musicians use slash notation and the associated chord progressions as they improvise accompaniments.

Melody, Rhythm and Harmony

Example 20: Chord Chart for Blues in Slash Notation

Example 20 is written using **slash notation**. Slash notation shows only the essential underlying rhythm of the harmony without indicating pitches, accents, or groove.

Example 12, Example 13 and Example 14 use a varied form of slash notation called rhythm notation which is used to express subtleties of groove and accents in the harmonic rhythm.

> **Note**
> Blues songs can also use only primary triads!

Chord Progressions: Harmonic Motion

Chords are a melody's support system, the musical frame upon which the melody is woven. Chord movement helps give direction and energy to a melody.

Chords move from one to another in goal oriented and often predictable ways. The predictability of chord progressions is the result of tone tendency, goal orientation and conditioning. Tone tendency, simply put, is the likelihood that a pitch will move in one direction or another based on its position in the scale and expectations generated because of conditioning: we have heard scale degrees move in a particular way before and therefore expect that they will do so again.

In pop-style songs, chord progressions are governed by the tone tendency of the lowest voice of a chord, the *bass*, forming what musicians call a **bassline**.

> **Note**
> Does this mean that the chord progressions of all songs are predictable? No, it does not. In fact, one goal of good songwriting is to create unique chord patterns that are still in pop style.

The goal of nearly all chord progressions in tonal music is to come to rest at the end of a piece on the tonic harmony. In the meantime, between the beginning of the song and its end, the movement of chords from one to another helps propel a song to its conclusion.

It's All About the Bass: Basic Chord Movement

In pop-style songs, chords progress from one to another based on patterns of root movements established by the songwriter. Chord root movement patterns are most often scalar (they follow a scale or part of a scale either up or down), based on root movements by fourths (e.g., roots moving from D to G to C), movement by thirds (e.g., thirds falling from C to A to F to D), or frequently some combination of these.

> **Note**
>
> Chords are said to be arpeggiated when the members of the chord are played in rapid succession.

Scalar root movement is obvious on its face: The chord roots simply ascend or descend following the pattern of a scale or part of a scale. The movement of chord roots by fourths mimics the very important progression of the dominant chord (V) to the tonic chord (I) that is found as the concluding progression of so many songs. Falling thirds or ascending thirds root movement follows chord arpeggiation or partial chord arpeggiation.

Inversions

When a chord is presented with its third, fifth or seventh in the bass, it is said to be inverted. In a triad, when the root is in the bass, the chord is in *root position*, when the third is in the bass, it is in *first inversion*, when the fifth is in the bass, it is in *second inversion*. In a seventh chord, when the seventh is in the bass, the chord is said to be in *third inversion*. Example 21 shows the described chord inversions. Chord inversions allow songwriters to compose more interesting and intricate basslines than they otherwise could by using chords in only root position.

Example 21: Chords in Inversions

C major triad in root position	C major triad in first inversion	C major triad in second inversion	C7 in third inversion
C	C/E	C/G	C7/B♭

Often Heard Chord Progressions

Many chord progressions have become standard. We hear them all the time in lots of different and successful songs. Chords that skillfully move in a non-standard progression, if not perceived as a mistake, will be titillating, and heard as interesting.

As a beginning songwriter, I thought it was "cheating" for one to borrow a chord progression from another song. But, it's not! Employing commonplace chord progressions as a starting point for a new melody and lyric is a regular practice among great songwriters. And eventually, with diligence, experimentation, and creativity you will come up with your own convincing new chord progressions.

Consider the opening chord progression, the melody, and the success of two songs: "This Masquerade," with words and music by Leon Russell (1942-2016) and "My Funny Valentine" by composer, Richard Rodgers (1902-1979) and lyricist, Lorenz Hart (1895-1943). The success of both songs is undeniable. Both are considered by critics and musicians to be pop music gems. Both have been recorded many, many times. Yet, both songs use the *very same* chord progression in their opening four measures.

Example 22: Shared Chord Progressions

"My Funny Valentine" and "This Masquerade"

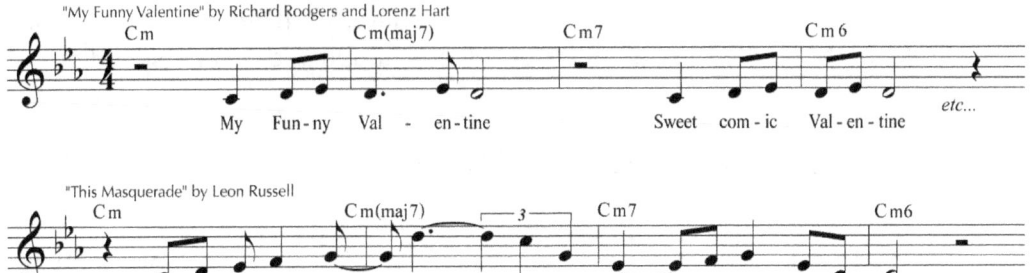

Intertextuality refers to the influence one piece of art has on another. In music, composers often use the work of other composers, not to steal from, but as models for their new and original work.

In his seminal book on **intertextuality**, *Intertextuality in Western Art Music*, Michael Klein writes:

> The frontiers of music are never clear-cut: beyond its framing silence, beyond its inner form, it is caught up in a web of references to other music: its unity is variable and relative. Musical texts speak among themselves.

I suggest you try using some of the following often-heard chord progressions as starting points for your new songs. In the hands of good songwriters, even stock progressions can be combined, varied, and reworked in wonderfully creative ways to produce fresh sounding accompaniments for newly composed melodies and lyrics. Often-heard chord progressions will not be experienced as clichés if used in thoughtful and creative ways.

Note that many of the often-heard chord changes that I am about to present can be combined.

In the following examples, you will find both chord symbol notation and Roman numeral analysis. For now, we'll look at chord progressions in major keys. Some common minor key chord progressions are included in the Appendix.

Scalar Ascending: I—ii—iii—IV

The great Beatles song, "Here, There and Everywhere," written by John Lennon and Paul McCartney, features a beautiful melody supported by an ascending scalar chord progression.

Example 23: *"Here, There and Everywhere"*

Melody, Rhythm and Harmony

In Example 23, the roots of the associated harmony progress through the first four degrees of the G major scale

Scalar Descending: $I-V^6-IV^6-I^6_4-IV-I^6-ii$

"Piano Man," (Example 24) by the composer Billy Joel (1949-), employs a bassline that descends through an entire major scale. Mr. Joel uses chords in inversion to create a more interesting bassline than he would have had he used the same progression in root position.

Example 24: "Piano Man"

Inverted chords are written in sheet music with a slash. For example, G/B indicates to the musician that the G chord is in first inversion, with the B (the third) in the bass. Classical musicians write first inversion chords with a "6" superscript (e.g. V6).

In Example 25, the descending bassline is shown both in the bass staff and through the chord symbol notation along the top of the treble staff. Remember, G/B means a G chord with a B in the bass; F/A means F chord with the A in bass; and so forth.

Example 25: Chord Symbol and Roman Numeral Analysis for "Piano Man"

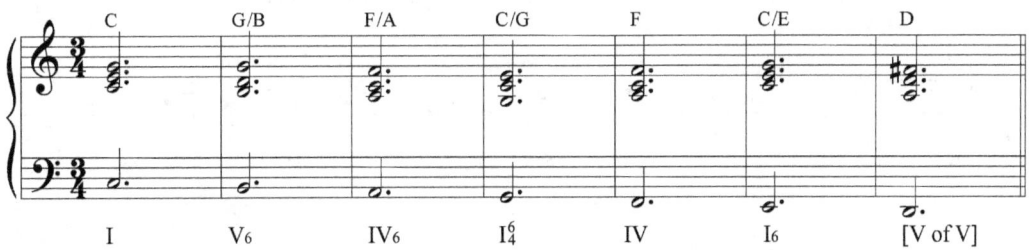

"Wake Me Up When September Ends" (Example 26) was written and released in 2005 by the band, Green Day. It was written as a collaborative effort by the band. The band's lead singer, Billie Joe Armstrong (1972-), created the lyrics.

Like Billy Joel's "Piano Man," "Wake Me Up When September Ends" was also written using a descending scalar bassline. The writers of this song chose to harmonize their descending bassline differently than did Billy Joel. During the first five measures of the song, Billie Joe Armstrong and his co-writers create a bassline that descends from the tonic, through the leading tone and submediant, to the dominant and then to the subdominant, all the while sounding a G **power chord**.

Notice the new chord symbol featured in this song: G5. This indicates that a power chord should be sounded. Power chords are **dyads**, two-note chords made up of the root and fifth (a triad minus the third). The power chord/dyad in "Wake Me" is composed of G and D.

In measure six, the creators of "Wake Me Up When September Ends" sound a **chromatic harmony**. A chromatic harmony is one that does not normally exist in the key of the song. In this case, the chromatic chord, Cm, is borrowed from the parallel minor key, G minor. The subdominant of G minor is Cm. Using borrowed chords is a common feature of pop music. Another name for this practice is **modal mixture**. The most frequently borrowed chords include the minor chord on the fourth scale step (as in measure six of "Wake Me Up When September Ends"), the major chords built on the flat sixth and the flat seventh scale steps.

Example 26: "Wake Me Up When September Ends"

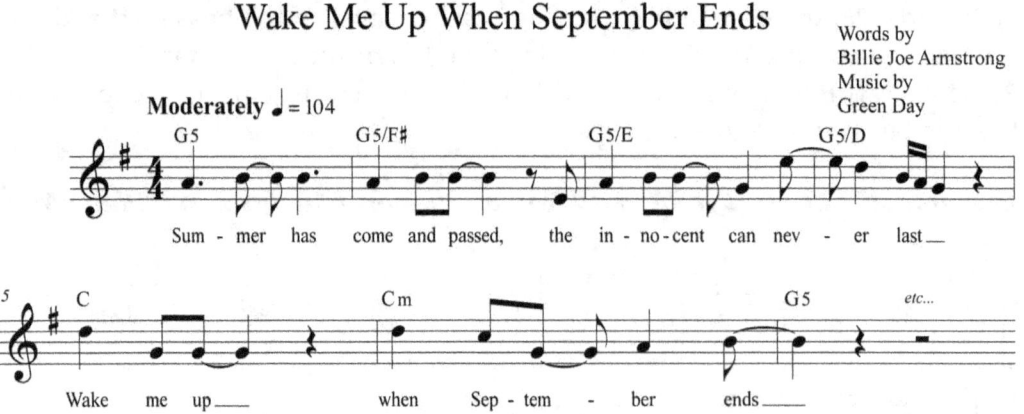

Falling Thirds: I—vi—IV—V

The root motion of the chord progression I—vi—IV—V outlines an arpeggiated subdominant triad that resolves to the dominant. In C major, the pitches found in the subdominant triad are F, A, and C. The root movement of the chord progression I—vi—IV (C—A—F) outlines the subdominant triad in reverse order.

Because the IV chord leads nicely to the dominant harmony, in this case, G, the progression I—vi—IV progresses very convincingly to V. The progression of subdominant (IV) to dominant (V) to tonic (I) is very strong and an essential progression in tonal music. We have seen this progression before, in the song, "Your Cheatin' Heart" (Example 17). You'll see this progression again, and again, and again!

"Bristol Stomp" (Example 27) is one of many songs from the 1950's and 1960's that used the I—vi—IV—V chord progression as its foundation. It is a song that made it to number two on *Billboard* magazine's "Hot 100". A 1961 recording of "Bristol Stomp" by The Dovells sold over a million copies. Kal Mann (1917-2001) and David Appell (1922-2014) wrote this early pop hit.

Example 27: "Bristol Stomp"

Falling Thirds, Varied: I—vi—ii—V

One chord can substitute for another if the two chords have at least two pitches in common. For example, in the key of C major the subdominant chord is F. It is composed of the three pitches, F, A, and C. The supertonic chord, Dm, is made up of the pitches, D, F, and A. The two triads share the pitches F and A; therefore, one chord can substitute for the other.

Using the concept of chord substitution, we can easily modify the falling thirds progression, I—vi—IV—V, to become I—vi—ii—V. This progression might be slightly more potent than the original I—vi—IV—V because it incorporates an additional root movement by fourth, ii—V. The progression of ii—V, supertonic to dominant, is very important and is found in many songs.

"Blue Moon," (Example 28) written by composer Richard Rodgers and lyricist Lorenz Hart uses the progression I—vi—ii—V for the first six measures of each of the first two eight-measure phrases (measures one through six and nine through fourteen).

Example 28: "Blue Moon"

The progression, I—vi—ii—V, can also occur at the end of a phrase. The songwriter James Taylor (1948-) ends each verse of his song, "Carolina in My Mind," (Example 29) with this chord pattern.

Melody, Rhythm and Harmony

Example 29: "Carolina in My Mind"

Rising Thirds: I—III7

In the previous progression, the I chord moves directly to vi. The tonic (I) can also progress to the submediant (vi) by moving through the submediant's dominant. In this progression, I moves to III7, which functions as V7 of vi. Here, vi becomes a **temporary tonic** and III7 its dominant. In this progression, III7 is considered a **secondary dominant**, a dominant for a temporary tonic. Using secondary dominants is a very helpful way to move to almost any chord and to prolong a phrase.

Here is how songwriters John Lennon and Paul McCartney use the progression I—III7—vi in their song, "World Without Love." In Example 30, the tonic, C, moves to III7 (E7) and then to vi (Am). Note that the I—III7—vi progression is followed immediately by a falling thirds movement. In measures three and four, vi7 (Am7) moves to IV (F). Here, a **passing tone** in the bass connects the two chords and produces a smooth transition. Passing tones are tones that move stepwise to embellish the movement between two chord tones or two melody notes.

Example 30: "World Without Love"

The song "All of Me," (Example 31) by Gerald Marks (1900-1997) and Seymour Simons (1896-1949), was introduced in 1931 and has become a standard that has been recorded many, many times. Mr. Marks and Mr. Simons use the same ascending third bassline as is found in "World Without Love."

The bassline moves from scale step one, to scale step three, and then to scale step six. But in this case the writers harmonize scale step six as a dominant-seven chord that leads at the end of the phrase to ii.

Example 31: *"All of Me"*

Let's dig a little deeper...

To analyze the harmonic progression of this warhorse, I'd like to work backwards. Let's start at the end of the first eight-measure phrase.

The first phrase ends in measure eight on a Dm chord. To arrive at the Dm, the writers precede it with its dominant-seven chord, A7. Working backwards again, we can now view the A7 as a *target* chord and see that its dominant-seven chord, E7, precedes it. Once the harmony is lifted to E7, it is easy to progress upwards repeatedly by fourths. As we have seen before, root movement by fourths is important and ubiquitous in pop music. We'll see many examples as we proceed.

Let's look at another kind of upward moving root movement by thirds.

Rising Thirds: I—iii—IV (V⁷ of vi)

The long-lived hit song by George David Weiss (1921-2010) and Bob Thiele (1922-1996), "What a Wonderful World," (Example 32) begins with the chord progression I—iii—IV. Here, the goal is to move the harmony from the tonic (F) in measure one to the subdominant (B♭) in measure two. The goal is achieved by passing through the mediant (iii). As we analyze more songs, notice that the goal of many chord progressions is a primary chord, often IV (or a substitute), that then moves to V, and ultimately to I.

Example 32: "What a Wonderful World"

By now, you will have noticed that the progression of the chord root often, but not always, provides the bass movement for a song.

Here is another example where the composer creates momentum by moving the bass through an inverted form of a chord. In Example 33, from James Taylor's "Carolina in My Mind," the bass moves from a root position tonic chord (F) to a tonic chord in first inversion (F/A) to reach the IV chord. This follows the same bass movement as "What a Wonderful World," but substitutes a I6 chord for iii.

Example 33: Bass Movement in "Carolina in My Mind"

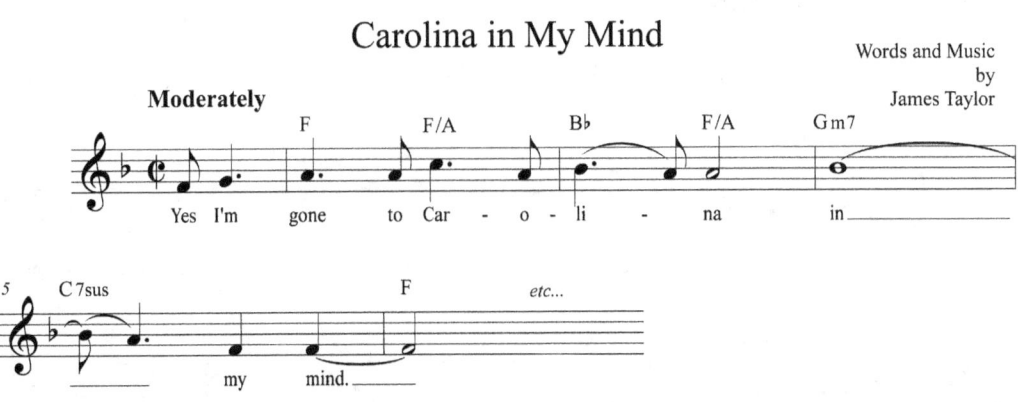

Progression by Fourths, Mimicking ii—V—I

Let's take another look at chord progressions by fourths. Following is a song that features chords whose roots progress by fourths. You could say this is its raison d'être, since we're looking at a pop song from France.

Introduced in the 1946 film, *Les Portes de la Nuit*, "Autumn Leaves" began life as, "Les Feuilles Mortes." The music is by the composer Joseph Kosma (1905-1969), with the original French lyric by Jacques Prévert (1900-1977). Johnny Mercer wrote the English lyric.

The composers of "Autumn Leaves" use the modal mixture technique that we earlier saw used by Green Day. They begin in B♭ major with a ii7—V7—I progression. Next, they move to a ii7—V7—I progression in G minor. They connect to two ii7—V7—I progressions by using another progression by fourth (B♭—E♭—A).

Note that in G minor, the supertonic chord is diminished. In this song, a minor seventh interval is added above the root of the supertonic. In pop music lead sheets, this sonority is labelled as a m7(♭5).

In other words, a chain of fourth progressions harmonizes the entire first eight measures of "Autumn Leaves"! Viewed another way, one can think of every third chord as a temporary tonic preceded by a ii—V progression (e.g., Cm7—F7—B♭maj7, where B♭maj7 functions as a temporary tonic).

A temporary tonic, or **key-of-the-moment**, is a harmony that serves momentarily as a tonic-like target and a point of resolution.

In pop music, chord roots often move in fourths. I—IV, ii—V, V—I are all common chord progressions.

Example 34: "Autumn Leaves"

Melody, Rhythm and Harmony   35

Falling to Seven

The song, "Dindi," (Example 35) by composer Antônio Carlos Jobim, with the English lyric by Ray Gilbert (1912-1976), and the Portuguese lyric by Aloysio de Oliveira (1914-1995), contains a chord progression that moves from I (E♭) to ♭VII (D♭) in the first two measures. The immediate effect is startling, because the harmony built on ♭VII is so foreign to the tonality of the home key. Things calm down a little when the composer takes us to the temporary key of the subdominant (A♭) in measure four (the B♭m to E♭ is ii—V in the key of A♭).

Example 35: "Dindi"

"The Days of Wine and Roses," (Example 36) written by composer Henry Mancini (1924-1994) and lyricist Johnny Mercer, won the Academy Award for Best Original Song in 1962. Like "Dindi," it begins with a progression from the tonic to the ♭VII. However, instead of returning to the tonic (F), Mr. Mancini uses ♭VII (E♭) as a passing chord in his move to the secondary dominant chord (D7) of ii (Gm).

I see the E♭7 as a dominant preparatory chord (what classical musicians call a misspelled German augmented sixth harmony) that leads to D7, which acts as V7 of Gm.

Example 36: "The Days of Wine and Roses"

Now, we turn our attention back to Messrs. Lennon and McCartney. Their song "Yesterday" (Example 37) begins on the tonic harmony (F) and in the second measure moves to a minor chord built on the seventh degree of the scale (Em). We quickly learn that Em is functioning as ii in the key of D, the target of the chord progression.

Example 37: "Yesterday"

Beginning on Something Other Than I

Not all songs begin on the tonic harmony. When a composer chooses to begin a song with a harmony other than the tonic, he establishes a sense of ambiguity. The listener does not know clearly from the beginning what key he is experiencing. The tension this ambiguity creates is released only when the tonic is finally sounded.

In Example 38, the standard "Gone With the Wind" by composer Allie Wrubel (1905-1973) and lyricist Herb Magidson (1906-1986), the tonic of E♭ major is not heard until the second measure, where it is the resolution of a ii—V—I progression.

Example 38: "Gone With the Wind"

Similarly, "I Should Care," (Example 39) by Sammy Cahn (1913-1993), Alex Stordahl (1913-1963), and Paul Weston (1912-1996), begins with a ii—V—I progression that is extended by a kind of **deceptive cadence**.

A true deceptive cadence is one where V resolves to vi instead of I. In this song, V does not resolve to I in measure two. It resolves to iii as a substitute for both I and vi. The ii—V—I progression is finally resolved in measure four with an **authentic cadence** (V—I).

By beginning on the supertonic and then prolonging the resolution to the tonic Messrs. Stordahl and Weston create tension and ambiguity. Perhaps the composer wanted to create a sense of being unsettled to underscore the sarcasm of the lyric, "I should care, I should go around weeping."

Example 39: "I Should Care"

The great songwriting team of Harry Warren (1893-1981) and Al Dubin (1891-1945) created a similar effect with their 1934 song, "I Only Have Eyes for You" (Example 40).

It begins on the supertonic, but moves to V7 of ii, and then back to ii, to begin a series of three iterations of ii—V. The tonic is finally sounded for the first time in measure five. By beginning on ii (Dm) and following it with the dominant of ii (A7), Mr. Warren causes us to feel that we are hearing a song that is in the key of D minor. This sense is unfulfilled when he returns us to Dm and then follows up with several playings of Dm to G7, ii—V—ii—V—ii—V—I (finally!). The sense of mystery and wonder that is expressed in the lyrics is underscored by music that is not obviously grounded in a sense of key.

Example 40: "I Only Have Eyes for You"

Songs with Few Changes

Many, many songs whose melodies are supported by only a few chords have become very successful. They derive their momentum, drive, and interest from something other than a series of interesting chord changes. It might be a compelling lyric, a driving bassline, or, in the case of a record production, a particularly compelling **rhythm track** and sensational performance by a lead vocalist. Whatever it is, these songs have become commercially successful even though they possess very little harmonic variety.

"Chain of Fools," by Don Covay (1938-) with a hit record released by Aretha Franklin, is composed of one chord: Cm. The hit song, "Be Thankful for What You Got," with a hit record made by its writer, William DeVaughn (1947-), has only two chords, F#m and Em. Finally, the song "American Woman" by the Canadian group, The Guess Who, is built around one chord, an E chord. Released with great success in 1970, the song was an improvised jam by the band's members, Randy Bachman (1943-), Garry Peterson (1945-) and Jim Kale (1943-) with lead singer Burton Cummings (1947-) ad-libbing the lyrics. The compelling lyric and Burton Cummings' powerful delivery, along with a propulsive rhythm powered by a driving bass riff, helped make this song a commercially successful record.

Exercises

Example:

Given:

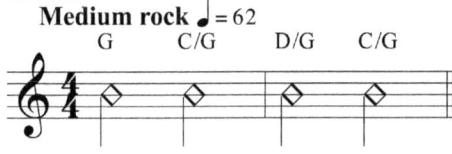

Compose a new melody for each of the chord patterns provided. Be sure to keep in mind the tempo (indicated as beats per minute) and the style. Your final melody should fit exactly the style and tempo indicated.

One method for creating a new melody over given chord changes is to create a simplified melody using just chord tones. Do this in your first draft.

First draft

In the first draft, write a very simple melody that is composed of chord tones only.

Second draft

In the second draft, elaborate your melody by adding passing tones.

Exercise #1

Given:

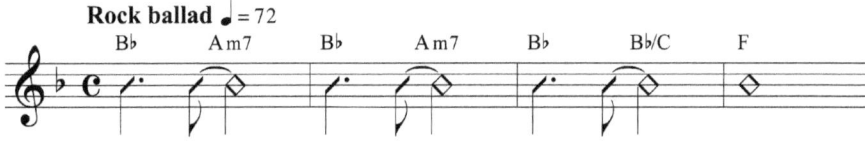

First draft:

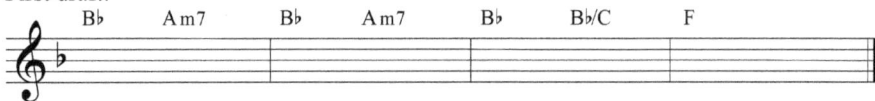

Second draft:

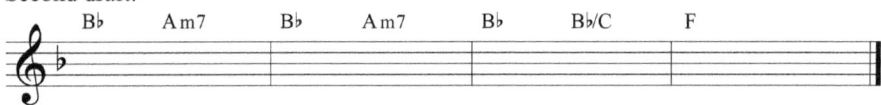

Exercise #2

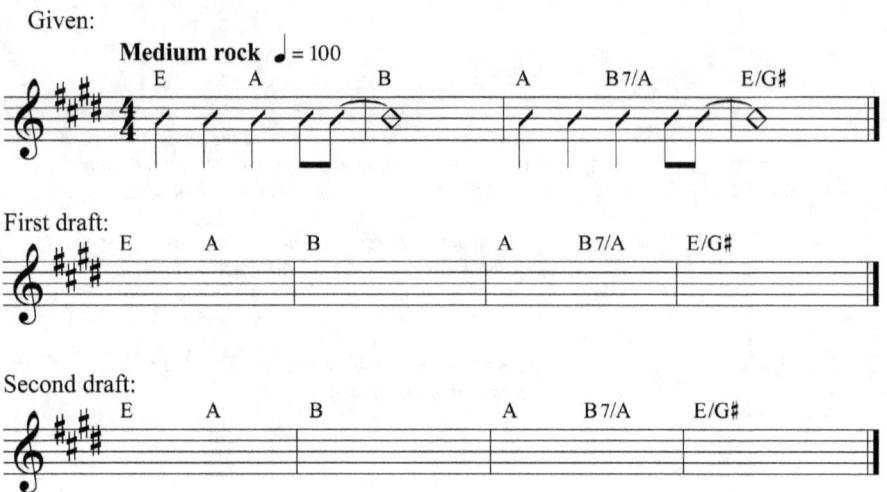

The given phrases in Exercises #1 and #2 are written using *rhythm notation*. Rhythm notation shows where the chords change and indicates the rhythm of the accompaniment without showing exact voicings or countermelodies. Musicians use rhythm notation, slash notation, and the associated chord progressions to improvise accompaniments.

Exercise #3

Given:

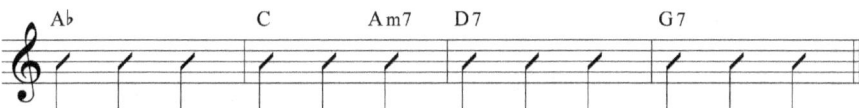

First draft:

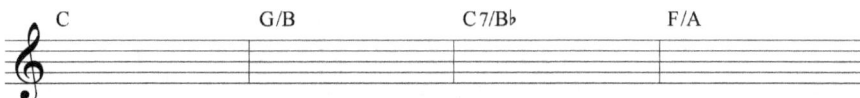

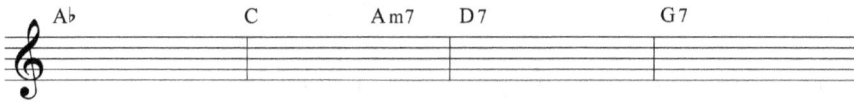

Second draft:

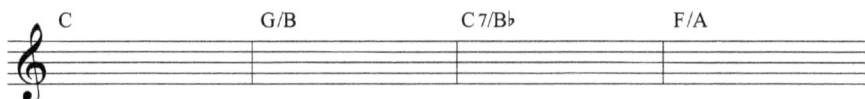

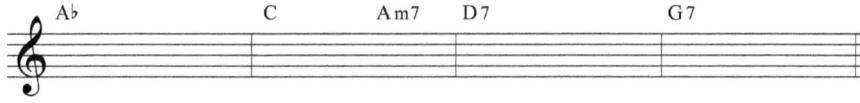

Exercise #4

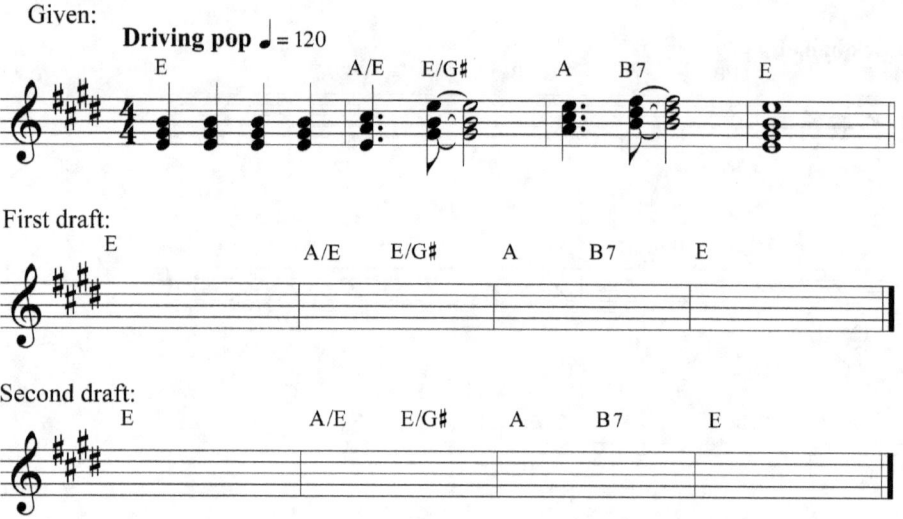

Exercise #5

Create an 8-measure chord progression using two of the 4-measure chord progressions presented in this chapter. Next, create a melody that works (and sings) well over your new 8-measure progression.

Exercise #6

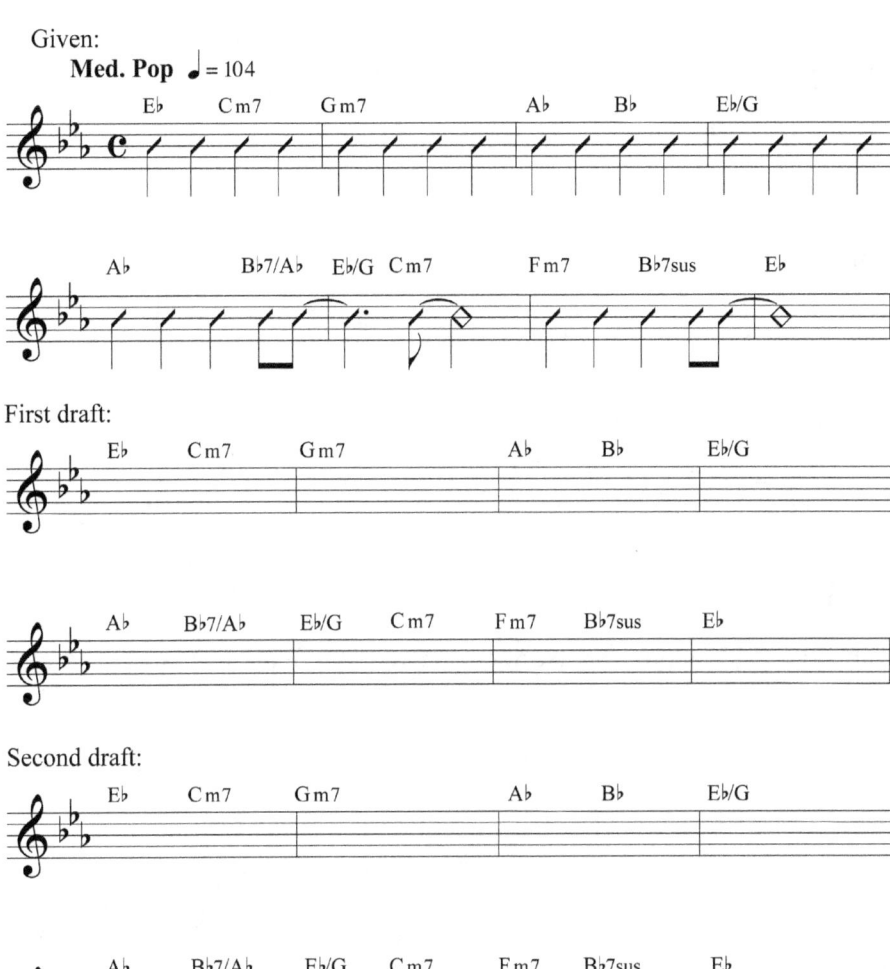

Exercise #7

Second draft:

Exercise #8

Express the chord progressions for Exercises #5 and #6 using Roman numerals.

Chapter Two

Song Forms

Good songs, like all successful works of art (and most other things in our lives), are constructed according to a formal plan. For instance, a shirt is recognized as a shirt only if it meets some basic criteria. All shirts need to have accommodation for the arms and the neck of the wearer, and they typically cover most or all the torso.

At a basic level, the formal plan for a song is something like this: A song is a collection of words that express a singular thought in a lyrical manner. The lyrics are sung to a melody that is almost always supported by a harmony. While generally accurate, this description is not very helpful or instructive.

It is more useful to have specific information about how the smaller sections of a song's music and lyrics are built up, connected, repeated, and modified.

In Chapter One I introduced elements of music theory that one needs to know to work as a professional songwriter. I included scale formulas and demonstrated how to construct several of the chords that are commonly used by contemporary songwriters. I also included examples of some of the chord progressions that are often found in pop songs.

In the next several chapters, I will explain how those musical elements are used by composers to create songs. I will introduce the song forms that are most frequently used by contemporary pop songwriters in their work. I will explain how lyrics are most effectively set to music and how chords are used to undergird melodies and propel songs forward to a successful finish.

In Chapter Three I present **Single Period Form**. In Chapter Four, I offer details about a special Single Period Form called **The Blues**. In Chapters Five, Six and Seven, I present the three standard **Double Period** Song Forms—**Verse/Chorus Form**, **Twentieth-Century Bar Form**, and **Pop Song Binary Form**.

All these forms are well represented in the popular literature of the nineteenth, twentieth and twenty-first centuries. They endure! Indeed, I present examples from at least the past one-hundred thirty years and analyze many including several very recent releases.

As we learn about song form, I introduce additional music theory material including a few new scales, chords, and some musical terminology.

A Reason to Analyze

As we analyze songs, we answer questions about the architecture of the separate parts, how the sections are formed, how the parts work with each other, and perhaps why the composer made the choices he did.

The specific questions we answer include:

- How long is each section?
- How many sections are there?
- In what order do the sections appear?
- Are they repeated, and if so, are they varied as they recur?
- How is the melody harmonized?
- What is the form of the lyric?
- Do lyrics recur and if so, are they repeated exactly?
- Are there rhymes?
- Where do hooks happen?

In the first chapter I spent a lot of time discussing chords and presenting commonly used chord patterns. In my years of teaching songwriting, I have found that students often find it difficult to develop chord patterns that *progress*.

Why spend so much time learning about song forms? Because *these are the blueprints that successful songwriters use to build their songs*. Songs are not just a matter of inspiration. They are good ideas molded into a memorable shape that is easily understood. The formal designs for songs work and are effective, however chord patterns and song forms are adaptable.

Music is dynamic and resilient. One can choose to compose new songs that precisely follow the standardized forms and use the common chord progressions, or one can use the formal blueprints and standard chords as mere starting points. Either way, you will be well served to understand what you are constructing.

I believe you will discover that music is often about repetition, but it is just as often about novelty, allure, and variation.

Knowing what great songwriters did to create their great songs will percolate through your songwriting in quiet and hard to discern ways. My hope is that you will be influenced in your decision-making by modeling your choices after those made by the writers of the songs you analyzed, that you would incorporate into your songwriting the techniques you observe in the songwriting of others.

We begin...

Analysis: Musical Forensics

Musical analysis is a kind of "musical forensics." Through musical analysis we develop an understanding of the structure of a piece of music (its form), how the various parts of melody, harmony, rhythm, and lyrics interact with each other, and how those parts are presented, repeated, and transformed. Once we have analyzed a composition, we can develop a theory of how it works. Then, we can create our own new works by imitating the principles we have learned.

> **Note**
> Phrases in music are roughly equivalent to sentences in language.

We will identify the smaller sections of the melody (its **motives** and **phrases**), the shape of the melody (melodic contour), and examine how pitches of the melody relate to each other and to the harmony. We will also explore various aspects of rhythm: melodic rhythm, harmonic rhythm, groove, tempo, and meter.

Labeling Conventions in Musical Analysis

All the components of a song can be labeled to aid in our analysis and discussion. I use these labeling conventions:

Table 5: Labeling Conventions

Component	Label Type	Example
Periods	roman numerals	I, II, III, etc.
Phrases	capital letters	A, B, C, etc.
Sub-phrases	lowercase letters	a, b, c, etc.
Phrases that recur with variation	Superscript or parenthesis	A^1, A^2, or B (like A), and so on.
Sub-phrases that recur with variation	superscript	a^2, a^3 and so on.

Chapter Three

Single Period Form

We begin our journey of with a thoughtful look at the Christian hymn, "Amazing Grace."

The sixteen measures that make up "Amazing Grace" can be considered a **musical period** or simply, a period. Thus, the song we know as "Amazing Grace" is a single period song. Songwriters model their construction of song periods after those found in the music of the **Classical Period** (music that was popular from about 1750 through 1825).

In pop-style songs, as in longer compositions, a period is defined as two musical phrases that work together to convey to the listener a complete musical statement. A musical **phrase** is a unit of artistic expression that is roughly analogous to a clause in language. Phrases always conclude with a harmonic and melodic cadence, a kind of musical punctuation. A cadence is a harmonic progression that creates in the listener a sense of partial stop or full stop. Some cadences require no further resolution and sound final. Other cadences create only a pause in the flow of music and encourage the listener to follow the music as it proceeds to another phrase.

Songs in popular style are typically composed using phrases that are of an even number of measures: 2, 4, or 8 measures long. Phrases may be divided into smaller units of measures called **sub-phrases**.

> **Note**
>
> The term "phrase" is defined variously to mean a unit of music that is usually four to eight measures long and that expresses a more or less complete musical thought, or that which can be sung in one breath. If nothing else, music theory is imprecise.

The first phrase of a period ends with a **cadence** that punctuates the phrase but creates in the listener an expectation that there will be more music to come. In classical music and in lots and lots of pop music, the **chord of resolution** at the end of the first phrase will be a dominant chord (V or V7). This type of non-ending cadence that resolves on the dominant is called a **half cadence**. In pop music, other chords of resolution might possibly substitute for the dominant chord.

The second phrase of a period ends conclusively. The cadence here resolves on a tonic chord. In Classical music the harmonic progression at the cadence point will be dominant (V or V7) to tonic (I). A cadence that progresses from dominant to tonic is called an **authentic cadence** (also called a **full cadence**). An authentic cadence is the strongest cadence in tonal music.

> **Note**
> Break some rules! John Lennon and Paul McCartney created the most recorded song in popular music, "Yesterday." Its first two phrases are each seven (not eight) measures long!

Composers, including songwriters, play with and rely on half and full cadences to help keep listeners engaged because they produce a sense of incompleteness followed by completeness.

Musical phrases are generally complementary in that they work well together and lead from the first phrase to the second to form a unified statement. The complementary phrases of a period are sometimes called an **antecedent phrase** and a **consequent phrase** or as a question and answer.

Example 41 demonstrates two cadences, a **perfect authentic cadence,** and a **half cadence**. The perfect authentic cadence progresses from V (or V7) to I with both chords in root position where the chord of resolution has the tonic in the highest voice.

Example 41: V—I CADENCE

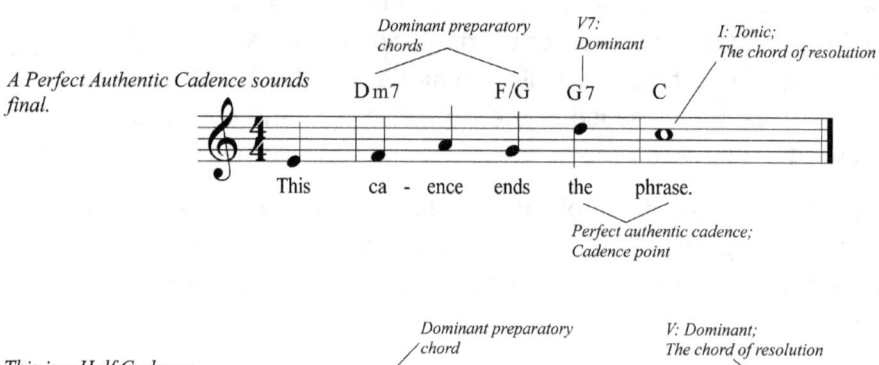

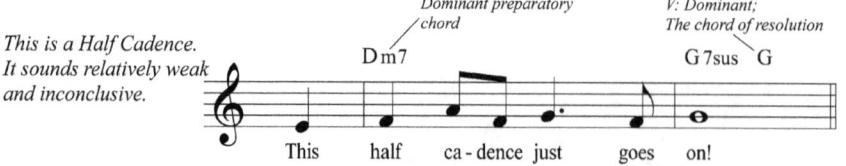

There are a few other commonly used cadences, including the **Plagal cadence**, and the **deceptive cadence**. A Plagal cadence moves from IV—I and is commonly called the "Amen Cadence" as it is often used at the end of Protestant hymns to accompany the singing of the word, "Amen." Deceptive cadences generally move from V—vi.

In the perfect authentic cadence example, the entire two measures, plus the pick-up note, E, can be construed as a cadence. The Dm7 and the F/G chords serve as **dominant preparatory chords**, as they help establish the harmonic move to the dominant chord, G7. The C chord is the chord of resolution, the goal of the harmonic motion. There is also a melodic cadence as the pitch "B," resolves to the pitch "C." Note that the conclusion of this melodic phrase coincides with the conclusion of the lyrical phrase.

The half cadence resolves melodically on scale step five and harmonically on the dominant harmony leaving the listener hanging in suspense and wanting to hear more.

In the concert music of the Classical Period, the periods were often sixteen measures long, made up of two eight-measure phrases. The phrases are, in turn, often made up of shorter phrases or sub-phrases of four measures each. Periods can in turn be joined together to form longer compositions.

Single Period Form is sometimes called by other names, including **strophic form**. A strophic form song is one where all the separate lyrics are sung to a single melody. In strophic-style lyric setting, the melody is repeated with very little variation from verse to verse.

History of "Amazing Grace"

"Amazing Grace," is, according to the American music historian, Gilbert Chase, "without a doubt the most famous of all the folk hymns." It is estimated that "Amazing Grace" is performed about 10,000 times each year and has been recorded hundreds of times. The lyrics and the melody began as separate works that were joined together several years after they were created and after each had enjoyed years of individual celebrity and use.

The melody and harmony of "Amazing Grace" began life as a tune called, "New Britain." In 1831 "New Britain" appeared in a musical anthology called the *Virginia Harmony* and was attributed to a man named James P. Carrell (1787-1854). Some, however, attribute an earlier version of the tune to Charles Spilman and Benjamin Shaw who wrote the anthology, *Columbia Harmony* (also called the *Pilgrim's Musical Companion*), published in 1829. It is, in fact, unclear who composed "New Britain." It is possible that Mr. Carrell and the others did not compose the tune, that they were simply transcribing a **folk melody** whose authorship was undetermined.

Folk tunes, folk melodies, folk hymns—any music described as being *folk* is a piece whose composer and or lyricist are unknown and lost to time.

Folk music is that which has come down to us through the years. It is part of an oral tradition and is passed from one generation to the next. Because the composer or composers of "New Britain" are not known, the credits on the song are most often listed as "Anonymous."

The English poet and clergyman, John Newton (1725-1807), wrote the text of "Amazing Grace" and included it, without musical accompaniment, as part of a sermon he delivered at the church in England where he preached. The Reverend John Newton's poem was first published in 1779 in a collection called *Olney Hymns*. Written by Rev. Newton and his writing partner, William Cowper (1731-1800), it included several hymns and the text to a sermon by Rev. Newton entitled, "Faith's Review and Expectation". The sermon is the text of the song that became known for its opening line: "Amazing Grace."

When Rev. Newton introduced his now-famous words, he might have given "Amazing Grace" a choral recitation in a tradition called **lining out**. This is where the leader reads a line and the congregation repeats it in unison or where the leader sings a line that is then repeated.

John Newton's sermon became very popular. Over the years, musicians made many settings of Reverend Newton's text by joining the words he wrote with existing or newly composed songs. Someone put "Amazing Grace" together with the "New Britain" tune sometime during the 1830's. This successful pairing has endured ever since.

Analysis of "Amazing Grace"

In dissecting a song, in addition to looking at its musical form, harmonic motion, melodic contour and melodic rhythm we will want to include in our analysis the song's **lyrical form**, **prosody** and **rhyme scheme** .

We will begin our analysis of "Amazing Grace" with general observations and then move to the details. As we continue with our analysis, I will introduce some new terms that you will be useful in your work going forward.

The Meter of "Amazing Grace"

"Amazing Grace" is composed in 3/4 meter. Music occurs in time that is measured by beats, an even succession of metrical pulses like the sound that is made when soldiers march. Beats are grouped in patterns of strong and weak pulses. Most songs are characterized by the regular recurrence of these groupings of weak and strong beats. These patterns are the song's **meter**.

In music notation, one complete occurrence of one such pattern is called a **measure**. The meter of a song or a section of a song is given as a fractional number called a **time signature** or meter signature. A time signature is placed at the beginning of a composition or section thereof. The denominator of the time signature shows the basic note value of the meter (what note value receives the basic beat of the piece). The numerator equals the number of note values in a measure (how many beats are found in each measure).

In Example 42, we see the 3/4-meter signature of "Amazing Grace" which indicates that the quarter note receives the beat (the basic pulse) and that there are three beats in each measure.

Musicians count the beats of the measure, often subdividing them so they can keep the pulse even, and to know where they are in the music. For instance, in 3/4 one will count, "one, two, three" or "one and two and three and." In 3/4 meter, we will experience a strong pulse on "one" followed by two weak pulses on "two" and "three".

Example 42: Time Signature, Counting, and Tempo

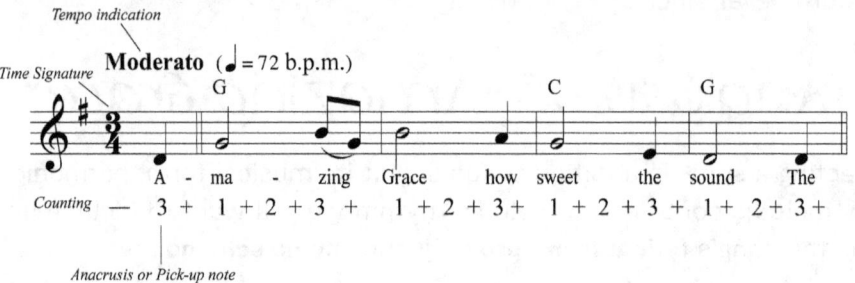

There are several other time signatures commonly used in pop music. These include 2/2, 2/4, 4/4, 5/4, 6/8, 7/8, 9/8 and 12/8.

Tempo

Some composers use words like slowly, **moderato,** or **andante** to communicate an approximate tempo for a composition. Other composers choose to supply performers with precise directions about the speed of their tune. To be precise these composers will use a formula like ♩ = 72 bpm, where the abbreviation bpm means "beats per minute". Note that Example 42 and Example 62 demonstrate both ways to indicate tempo in sheet music.

Metrical Accents in Music

The first beat of the measure (the downbeat) of all commonly used meters, 2/4, 3/4, 4/4, 5/8, 6/8, receives the primary accent. In compound meters such as 4/4, 5/8 and 6/8, a secondary accent is experienced. In 4/4, the secondary accent falls on the third beat; in 5/8, the secondary accent is on either the third or the fourth beat; in 6/8, the secondary accent is on the fourth beat.

Also called an **anacrusis**, a pick-up note occurs before the first metrically strong beat of a musical phrase. An anacrusis can also be a group of notes. Pick-up notes are generally heard as propelling the music forward to the downbeat. In "Amazing Grace," the pick-up note is sung to the "A" of the first "A-maz-ing."

Why is it Important to Know about Musical Accents?

Language and music share some characteristics. For songwriters, one of the most important of these is that they are both sounds that occur in time and in rhythm. As we speak, we place more or less stress on one syllable or another. The stresses in our speech correlate to the accents experienced in music, so when setting lyrics to music it is important that the musical accents line up with the lyrical accents. If the accents do not correspond, the listener may not easily perceive the words and the meaning of the lyrics might be lost. Lyrics that flow in a rhythmically natural way will always be more easily understood and remembered.

Phrasal Analysis of "Amazing Grace"

"Amazing Grace" is very regular in its phrasal structure. It is composed of two eight-measure phrases. Each phrase is made up of two four-measure sub-phrases. Together, the two eight-measure phrases form one sixteen-measure period. See Example 43.

> **Note**
> Amazing Grace" is composed of sixteen full measures, Plus a pick-up note!

A musical phrase that moves harmonically from tonic to dominant is called an **opening phrase**. The tension that is created in the listener by this musical inconclusiveness is important and encourages the listener to continue listening.

The "A" phrase is an antecedent, or question phrase. It ends inconclusively with a half cadence on V7 leaving the listener wanting an answer. The "B" phrase gives us that answer and is the consequent phrase. It ends conclusively with an authentic cadence of V7—I. The lyrics for this phrase, and all subsequent phrases, conform to the antecedent and consequent scheme of the music.

Note that the melody for the opening phrase and the last half of the closing phrase are very similar. The last four measures of the closing phrase are in fact a variation of the first four measures of the opening phrase. This kind of melodic construction helps to unify the composition by creating what are commonly called "bookends." Notice also that the melodic rhythm established in the first two measures of the song, recurs at the beginning of each subsequent four-measure sub-phrase.

Be sure to take the time to study the details in Example 43. Notice that reading music for analysis is different than reading for performance.

Example 43: Complete Periods with Phrases and Sub-Phrases Marked

Establishing the Key

The melody of the first phrase (A) begins with an anacrusis on scale degree five. The first strong beat of the melody of the A-phrase is a tonic, scale degree one, that is supported by a tonic harmony (the I chord).

By sounding the dominant on the pick-up note and the tonic on the first strong beat of the melody, the anonymous composer of "New Britain" firmly announces the key center of the song. Our example is in the key of C major.

Establishing a key is important. Key centers are hinted at by the melody but are reinforced as they are harmonized with a dominant (V chord) and tonic (I chord).

By establishing the key early in the song, the composer essentially declares that she will follow several conventions. Most of these revolve around how she will choose melody notes and how she harmonizes the melodies she chooses. Establishing a key and adhering to the tenants of the tonal system is the norm in popular music but breaking with tradition and flouting rules might create interest and is sometimes desired.

> **Note**
> I always find it interesting to wonder what came first—the chord progression or the melody?

Melodic Analysis

The composer of "Amazing Grace" uses just five pitches to create the melody. In the key of C major the pitches are: C, D, E, G and A. This set of pitches is special and, when arranged within an octave, they are called a **pentatonic scale**. After major scales, composers most often use pentatonic scales to create pop melodies.

The name *pentatonic* is derived from the Greek words for five ("pente"), and tone ("tonic"). There are several pentatonic scales. The most common is the **major pentatonic** scale.

The interval formula for the major pentatonic scale follows exactly the arrangement of the black keys of the piano beginning with G♭. There is a whole step between the first and second, and second and third degrees of the scale, a minor third between scale steps three and four, and a whole step between the fourth and fifth degrees.

The interval formula for the **minor pentatonic** scale also uses the black keys of the piano as its basis but begins on the E♭. The scale begins with the leap of a minor third (thus the name) followed by two whole steps and then, between scale step four and five, another leap of a minor third.

It is very convenient to use the black keys of the piano keyboard to remember the scale formula for the pentatonic scale. Alternately, picture a major scale without the fourth and seventh degrees.

Pentatonic scales are found in folk music all over the world. Theorists suggest that pentatonic scales are so ubiquitous because they lack dissonance. There are no minor seconds or sevenths, and no **tritones** (the interval of an augmented fourth or diminished fifth). These intervals are heard as dissonant in all cultures.

As with other scales, pentatonic scales can be transposed. They can be built up beginning on any pitch by maintaining the scale formula of intervals between pitches. The formula for the pentatonic scale is shown in Example 44.

Example 44: Common Pentatonic Scales

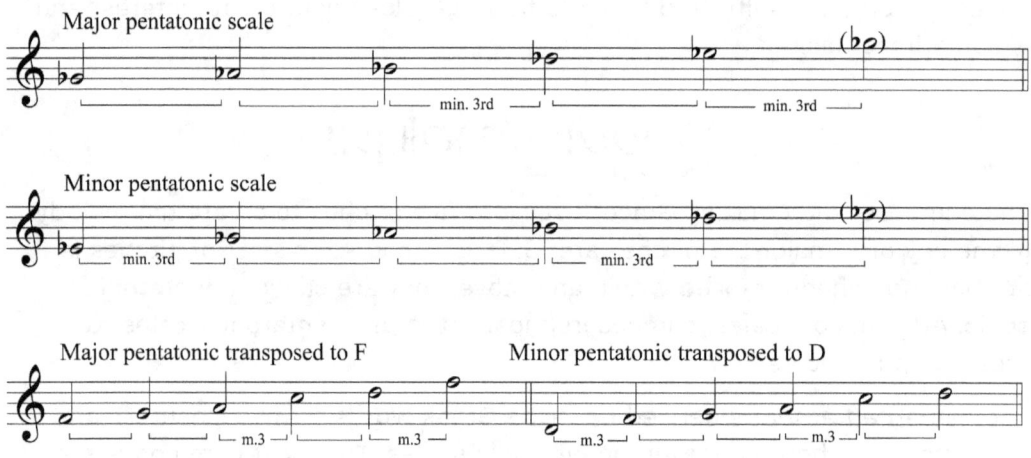

The Shape of the Melody

All melodies have a shape. This shape is its melodic contour. A simple drawing using arches can represent the melodic contour of a song.

Let's look back to Example 43. The melody of the first eight-measure phrase (A^1) ends in measure eight on scale degree five. This is the climax of the first full phrase.

The melody of the second eight-measure phrase (B) begins on scale degree five. This phrase also begins with an anacrusis on scale degree three on the word, "I" of the phrase, "I once was lost..."

In "Amazing Grace/New Britain," the B-phrase serves to complete the A-phrase.

In our example the melody begins on a low G (on the pick-up note), moves through the first phrase to a high G (scale step five in measure eight) and gradually, during the second phrase, resolves back down to a C (the tonic pitch in measure sixteen).

The first four-measure sub-phrase (a¹) returns in slightly varied form as the concluding four measures of the B-phrase. The second half of the B-phrase is a repeat of the opening material. By repeating a varied version of sub-phrase a¹ and ending it with a very final-sounding authentic cadence, the composer creates a palpable sense of completeness. The listener has heard the opening sub-phrase end up in the air. Now, in its varied repeat, they hear the end of the story.

In summary, during each verse the hymn "Amazing Grace" (in terms of its melody and harmony) begins calmly, increases in perceived tension, and then resolves back to a place of rest.

Graphing the Melodic Contour

If one were to draw an arch to graphically represent the direction of the melody, one would have the apex of the arch correspond with the word "me" in the first line of the text, "Amazing Grace, How sweet the sound that saved a wretch like me!" From that point in the song, having created a heightened sense of tension, the composer gradually brings the listener to a point of relative rest at the end of the B-phrase during the singing of the lyric, "I once was lost, but now am found, Was blind, but now I see." Example 45 illustrates the melodic contour just described.

It is very common for songs to engender in the listener a sense of building tension that is released by the end of the song.

Example 45: Melodic Contour

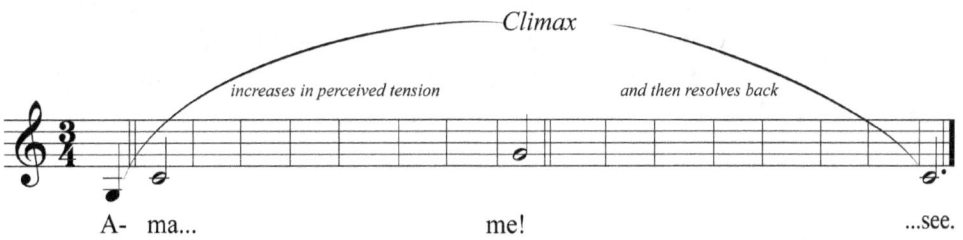

Melodic Development

When a composer concocts a great melodic hook, she repeats it over and again. However, exact repetition causes boredom so when a composer repeats a hook, she often, but not always, varies it. Creating changes to a melody over a musical span of time is called **melodic development**.

The composer of "New Britain/Amazing Grace" uses this concept of development (or varied repetition) with great results (Example 46). For instance, the opening of the second phrase (measure nine with its pick-up) contains the same music as the opening of the first phrase (measure one with its pick-up). However, the music is varied: it is **transposed** up a third. In other sections, the composer of "New Britain" repeats musical material almost exactly.

The first sub-phrase is the same as the second sub-phrase, except that the first phrase ends on scale step five down the octave. The second phrase ends on scale step five up the octave. In our example, sub-phrase one ends on a low G while sub-phrase two ends on a high G.

The second four-measure sub-phrase, a^2, is like a. Again, the sub-phrases begin the same, but end differently. The first two measures of the sub-phrases are the same. Only the third and fourth measures are different.

The last sub-phrase, a^3, is almost an exact repeat of the first sub-phrase, a^1. Again, a^3 begins exactly like the first sub-phrase, but ends differently to make it a closing phrase. (It ends on a tonic chord.)

Play through the four sub-phrases of "Amazing Grace" as they are listed in the next example. Play one, pause for a few seconds and then play the next. Notice the similarities between the four sub-phrases. Notice that sub-phrase a^3 begins exactly like sub-phrase a^1 but ends differently. Sub-phrase a^3 ends with a final sounding cadence in both the melody and the accompanying chord.

While the development of the melody in this song is modest, it does clearly demonstrate techniques you can readily employ in your writing. Notice during your regular listening when a songwriter uses the technique of development.

In the next chapter, I will introduce another song form that mimics the formal structure of the sub-phrases of "Amazing Grace": a^1, a^2, b, a^3. Called Twentieth-Century Bar Form, it was the most popular form of the twentieth century. It is the form of many songs in the standard literature of American and European popular music.

Single Period Form

Example 46: Four Sub-Phrases a¹, a², b and a³

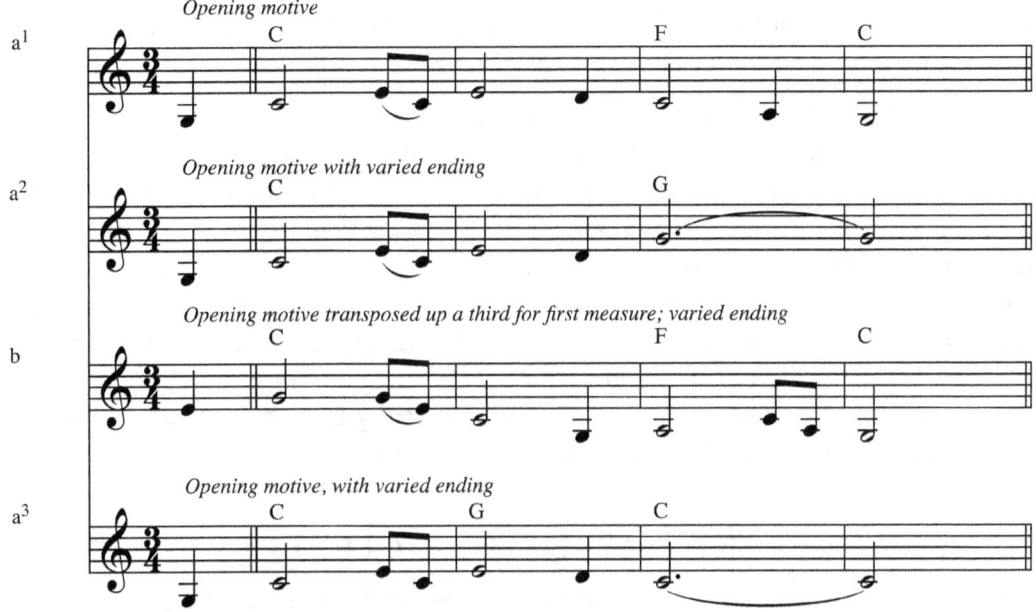

Melodic Hooks

All successful songs have **lyrical hooks** and **melodic hooks**. The main lyrical hook and the main melodic hook usually occur together.

The term hook, as used in pop music (especially recordings), refers to any short lyrical phrase (as short as a word or two) or any short melodic fragment. In a musical arrangement, a hook might be:

- a distinctive lick played by the rhythm section, like the opening of the Dave Brubeck Quartet's 1959 recording of "Take Five" written by Paul Desmond,
- a distinctive instrumental lick that recurs often, like the ascending six-note line played on the electric guitar in the Temptations' 1964 recording of "My Girl" written by Smokey Robinson (1940-), and Ronald White (1939-1995), or
- an unusual instrumental sound, like Anthony Jackson's bass guitar (modified with a phaser effect by recording engineer, Joseph Tarsia) on the 1973 recording of "For the Love of Money" written by Kenneth Gamble (1943-), Leon Huff (1942-), and Anthony Jackson (1952-).

A musical hook could be an unusual vocal sound, like Frankie Valli's voice on any of the records he made with his band, the Four Seasons.

Hooks, whether instrumental or lyrical, serve to draw listeners into a composition or recording. Hooks are clues that help the listener remember a song and act as a memory trigger. One needs to hear but a little bit of a musical hook to be reminded of the entire song or recording.

Music theorists call the principal melodic hook of a song (or longer composition) a **motive**. The principal musical motive of "Amazing Grace" is its opening lick, the music to which the words "A-ma-zing Grace" are set. Like all motives, this one is rhythmically impressive. It has a precise and distinctive rhythm (a quarter note upbeat followed by a half note and two eighth notes). Like many motives, it outlines the underlying harmony. The initial statement of the principal motive of "Amazing Grace" sounds all the pitches of the tonic harmony. As demonstrated in Example 46, the opening motive in "Amazing Grace" recurs four times in slight variation, occurring on different pitches or being completed with slight, but important, changes.

Motives Unify Songs

Melodic motives, and their modified repetitions, unify songs. A listener is introduced to a melodic lick, hears it again and again (accepting its slight variation as they listen), and, as is the case in "Amazing Grace," hears it repeated at the end of the song with a strong, final cadence. The listener learns the motive, learns to trust the songwriter as he repeats the motive in variation, and then accepts the song or part of the song as complete when the songwriter repeats it one last time, ending this time with the harmonic shorthand of an authentic cadence, alerting the listener that this means, "the end."

Harmonic Analysis

"Amazing Grace" can be harmonized very satisfactorily using just the three primary chords: tonic, subdominant, and dominant (I, IV and V). (Chords built on the other degrees of the scale are regarded as secondary chords. A chart of all the diatonic chords is presented in Example 15.)

"Amazing Grace" begins with an authentic cadence that firmly establishes the tonality of the piece. The anacrusis is harmonized with the V7 chord and the downbeat, with the tonic. The opening eight-measure phrase ends with a half cadence. In measures seven and eight, both the melody, ending on scale degree five, and the harmony, ending on the dominant, create a sense that the song is not yet over. There needs to be a concluding phrase to bring the listener back to a resting point on the tonic in the melody and the harmony.

The second phrase begins on a tonic harmony and ends on a tonic harmony. A phrase that begins and ends on a tonic harmony is called a **circular phrase**.

Reharmonization

Arrangers desirous of creating an original version of a well-known song often use a technique called reharmonization. Reharmonization involves the replacement of certain chords with others that the arranger deems to be more appropriate for the assignment at hand. The subject of **chord substitution** is complicated in its depth of possibilities. In brief, as mentioned previously, one chord can often substitute for another if both chords share at least two chord tones. This method is not foolproof since it does not take into consideration the movement of the chord roots and how that motion sounds against the melody. I encourage the reader to listen to my choral arrangement of "Amazing Grace," *Amazing Grace: A Choral Fantasy (www.ummpstore.com)*, to hear at least one arranger's take on how an old "chestnut" can be souped-up.

Reharmonization is an important topic. If mastered, it can help you write more interesting songs.

The Lyrics of "Amazing Grace"

"Amazing Grace" has five or six verses of lyrics (depending on the edition one uses) that are each sung to the same melody. Songs like this, where the melody remains the same while the lyrics change from verse to verse, are said to be strophic. Single Period songs are normally strophic. Strophic songs are especially useful in telling stories or, as is the case with historic hymns, educating illiterate congregants about the Bible.

The lyrics in "Amazing Grace" follow a consistent rhyme scheme of ABAB. This simple rhyme scheme helps to make Reverend Newton's poem memorable. Each four-measure phrase of the melody ends with a word that is rhymed. In the first verse, the rhyming words are: *sound* and *found*, *see* and *me*.

Table 6: Rhyme Scheme of Amazing Grace

Verse One	Rhyme Scheme
Amazing Grace, how sweet the sound	A
That saved a wretch like me!	B
I once was lost but now am found;	A
Was blind, but now I see.	B

I have now written (and you have read) quite a lot about just sixteen measures of music! Determining what makes a great song great takes some significant detective work, but you will find the results of those efforts to be extremely helpful to your songwriting.

Many meaningful things can be gleaned from this kind of sleuthing. One thing that might now be apparent is that successful compositions can be built up of a small amount of musical material that is repeated and varied. During our analysis of other songs, you will observe this trait many times. It is a truism that music will likely not be well remembered if it is not repeated. However, it will be boring if it is repeated without variation.

Some Critical Comments about "Amazing Grace"

No one can deny the majesty and shear emotional power this song has accrued over the years, especially in the United States since the attacks of 9/11. So, the absurdity of being so bold as to offer criticism of this gem is not lost on me. Nevertheless, I will offer a few observations about the great hymn with great respect and reverence.

Despite its tremendous popularity and phenomenal longevity, the song does present some features that, I think, do not show great tunesmithing. My criticisms lie mostly with the setting of the lyrical hook, the title, "Amazing Grace," and the setting of other words or syllables to more than one note in the melody.

There are a few methods available to songwriters to emphasize syllables. Important syllables to be accented can be set to music that is also accented, they can be set to longer notes, they can occur at a high point in the melody, at the end of a melodic phrase, or after a dramatic pause. English and some other languages are stress-timed languages, where stresses, pauses, the length of a syllable and the relative pitch used to speak the syllable indicate the prosody in the oral presentation of the language. For the songwriter this means that, absent some special reason, it is always preferable to have the important, and accented syllables of the lyric set in such a manner that they are sung to notes that are similarly stressed. In plain language, the important words need to be placed with the important notes.

The First Issue

The setting of the second syllable, "ma-" in the word, "A-ma-zing."

We do accent the second syllable of "amazing," so setting the second syllable on the accented beat of the measure seems like good thinking. However, this first note of the first full measure of the tune is also a long note, therefore giving added weight to this note and the syllable it accompanies. This seems overdone to me. To draw out the syllable, "ma" momentarily distorts the perceptibility of the word. One could argue that such a "mispronunciation" creates memorability, and perhaps it does.

In Example 47, I present the traditional setting of the lyrics for the opening measures of "Amazing Grace" alongside a new setting. My proposed new setting supports what I believe is a more common pronunciation of the word, "Amazing."

Example 47: Proposed New Setting of Lyrics for "Amazing Grace"

The Second Issue

It takes too long to get to the third syllable, "-zing" in the word, "A-ma-zing."

Even though we normally pronounce the word "Amazing" so that the second syllable is slightly longer than the first and third, singing the lengthened second syllable at the moderately slow tempo in which the hymn is performed, makes it take too long to get to the last syllable. This extra pause causes momentary confusion in the mind of the listener because this is not the way one normally *hears* the word said. The modification of the opening music presented in Example 47 also provides a shorter singing of the second syllable of "Amazing."

The Third issue

The last syllable of the first word is sung over the span of two shorter notes, providing it extra and undue weight.

Stretching out a syllable over two or more melody notes draws attention to the melody and away from the words, thereby obscuring the meaning of the syllable and consequently the word. The two eighth notes that accompany the syllable "-zing" in the word "a-ma-zing" are an example of **melismatic writing**. I am stretching the meaning of the word **melisma** just a bit since the precise definition is a group of notes sung to one syllable of text.

My argument stands: in pop-style songs, singing any syllable to more than one note makes it harder for the listener to clearly understand what words are being sung. My contention is that the listener's attention is drawn to the performer's technique and away from the significance of the lyric. The modification of the opening music presented in Example 47 features a single note singing of the final syllable of the word, "Amazing."

Of course, criticism of almost anything so tremendously popular and phenomenally long-lived places the critic in a precarious position. My criticism is borne of a desire to illustrate how not to set lyrics and to introduce the notion that songs can become popular for many reasons, not only because they adhere to some certain set of guidelines, alas—even mine!

Musical Arrangement and Record Production of Single Period Songs

From a practical standpoint, all Single Period songs present a challenge and an opportunity for musical arrangers and producers. They are so very simple that they are very, very memorable. At the same time, unvaried repetition in music can foster boredom.

Musicians solve the issue of potential boredom by creating musical arrangements that feature subtle changes in harmonization, instrumentation, and key center. The novelty of the new—an added instrument or voice, an added countermelody, a transposition to a new key, the inclusion of an instrumental solo or interlude—can help overcome the built-in challenges of this simple song form.

A quick listen to the classic recordings of "Mack the Knife" by Bobby Darin (or the wonderfully humorous live recording of the song by Ella Fitzgerald), or the hit recording of "Sunny" by its writer, Bobby Hebb (1938-2010), will demonstrate how these simple song forms can be arranged and produced.

Released in 1966, Bobby Hebb's recording of his song "Sunny" became an enormous success, selling millions of copies and being re-recorded by other performers more than one hundred times. Broadcast Music Incorporated (BMI) has included "Sunny" as number twenty-five in its list of *Top 100 Songs of the Century*.

"Sunny" is typical of the sixteen-measure Single Period song, providing all the benefits and all the issues. The composer, arranger and guitarist Joseph Renzetti arranged the music for the 1966 recording. In his classic arrangement, Mr. Renzetti used a band that included electric guitars, electric bass, drum kit, vibraphone, a horn section, and a group of female back-up singers.

Following is a graphic summary of Joseph Renzetti's arrangement for "Sunny." (Example 48) During the first five verses of the original recording, arranger Renzetti introduces subtle and effective changes that present just enough novelty to keep the arrangement fresh and the song interesting. I am quite sure that Mr. Renzetti's great arrangement helped to establish Mr. Hebb's fine song as the classic it has become. Give the record a listen as you follow along.

Single Period Form 69

Example 48: Graphic Analysis of Joseph Renzetti's Arrangement of the Song, "Sunny."

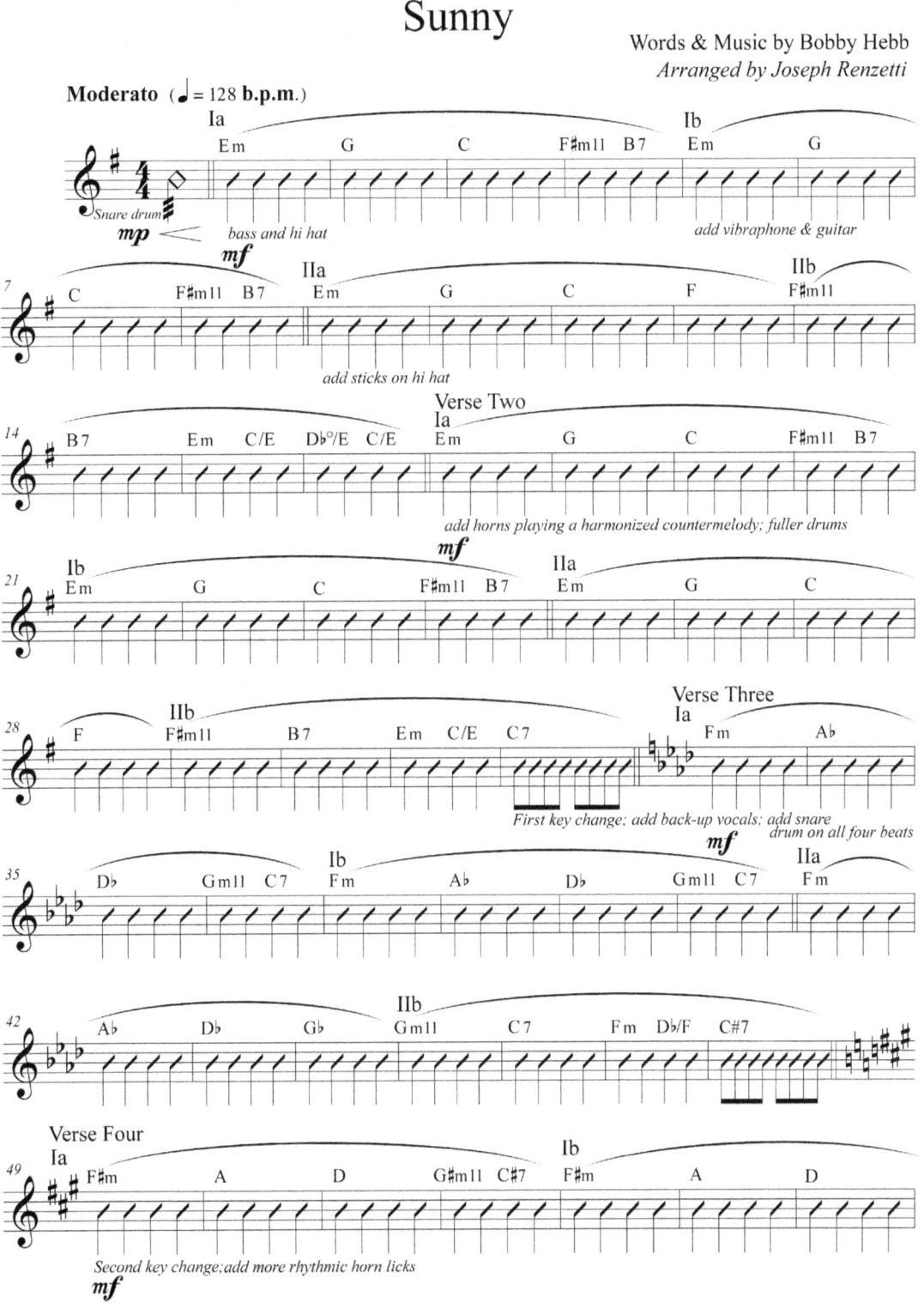

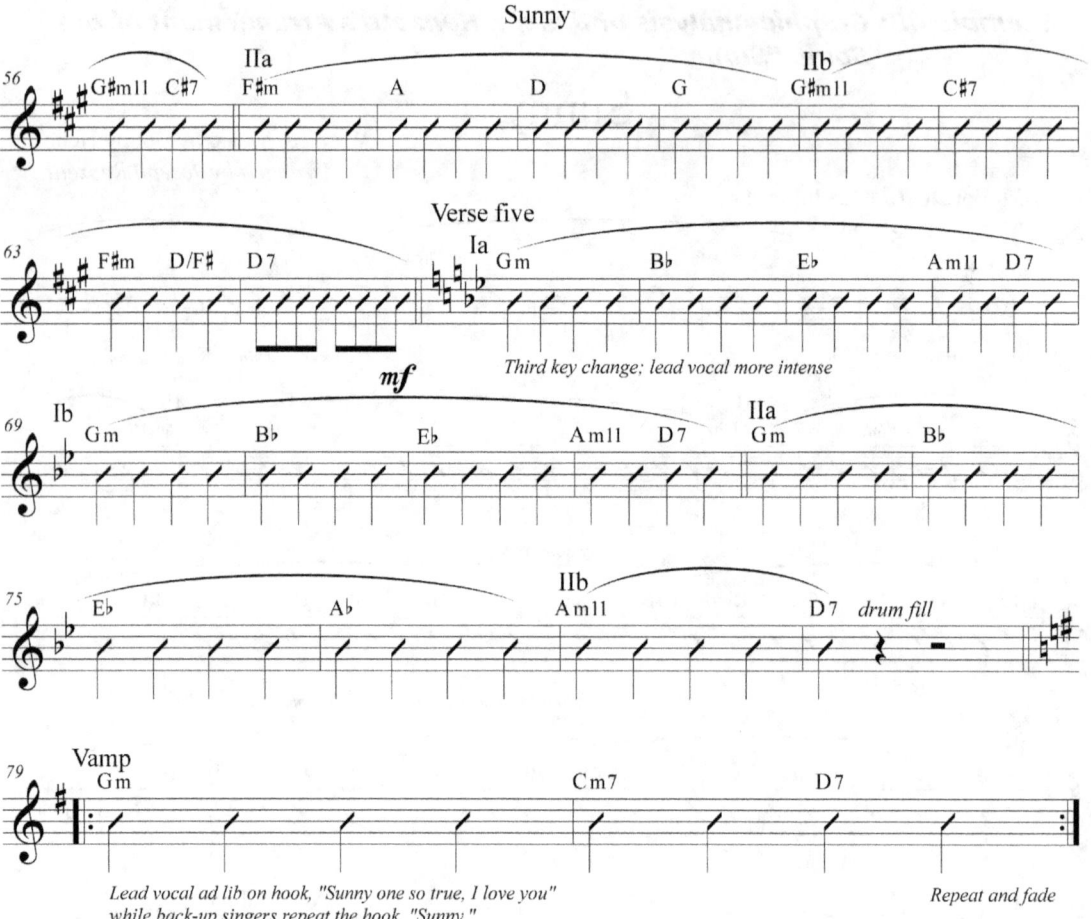

Other Songs in Single Period Form

Many other songs have been created in this form. Here are a few.

- "Mack the Knife," ("The Ballad of Mack the Knife" or "Die Moritat von Mackie Messer") Music by Kurt Weill (1900-1950) and Lyrics by Bertolt Brecht (1898-1956)
- "Old MacDonald Had a Farm," a traditional nursery rhyme (*Roud Folk Song Index*, number 745)
- "By the Time I Get to Phoenix," Music and Lyrics by Jimmy Webb (1946-). This song adds a change to the form in the last verse, but the song is essentially in Single Period Form.
- "The Wreck of the Edmund Fitzgerald," Music and Lyrics by Gordon Lightfoot (1938-). This song is interesting because it incorporates in its single period two five-measure phrases in 6/8 meter followed by two four-measure phrases.
- "I Walk the Line," Music and Lyrics by Johnny Cash (1932-2003). Mr. Cash includes the title hook at the end of each verse and, in performances, followed each sixteen-measure period with a few measures of instrumental interlude.
- "House of the Rising Sun," Music and Lyrics by Huddie William Ledbetter (1888-1949)

Exercises

Exercise #1

A. Compose an eight-measure opening phrase that contains two four-measure sub-phrases. (Have the phrase end on the dominant.) Compose in a key that will make this phrase easy for you to sing. Use "Amazing Grace" as your model.

sub-phrase a

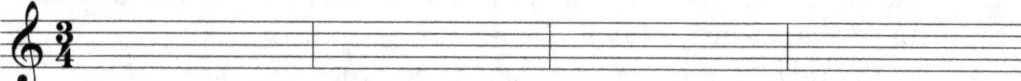

sub-phrase b

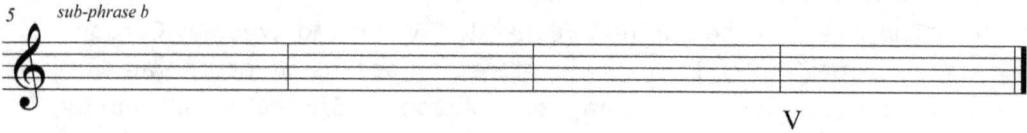

V

B. Begin with a one- or two syllable word that will become your lyrical hook.
C. Next, create a melodic motive that supports and fits your lyric.
D. Finally, create additional lyrics that provide context and elaborate your opening lyrical hook. Then, compose a melody that supports your additional lyrics.

• Since this is to be an opening phrase, be sure to end on the dominant harmony.
• Sing your melody into existence! Compose in a key that fits your vocal range.
• Use "Amazing Grace" as your model.
• Be sure your melody precisely fits the rhythm of your lyrics.

Exercise #2

Using the information I introduced about the way motives are repeated and varied in "Amazing Grace" as a starting point, find other instances where the songwriter has repeated the principal motive in some kind of variation.

Exercise #3

Create a harmonic and phrasal analysis for "Mack the Knife" and "House of the Rising Sun."

Exercise #4

Create additional lyrics for "Mack the Knife" and "House of the Rising Sun" maintaining the same melodic rhythm, form, and rhyme scheme.

Chapter Four

The Blues Form

Songs in Blues Form are mainly composed in a single twelve-measure period. Like "Amazing Grace" and "Mack the Knife" and other Single Period Form songs, blues songs are strophic.

The vernacular term that musicians use for measures is bars. Thus, it is common for musicians to refer to songs in the most common blues form as "twelve-bar blues."

The blues is a product of the American musical melting pot. It was developed in America during the nineteenth century. The blues combines African musical performance styles and the music of the European American Protestant Church.

The blues genre was significantly marked by the experiences of enslaved African Americans and their freed descendants as they struggled for peace and equality in the United States after the Civil War and into the 20th century. That the blues began in the "Deep South" of the United States—South Carolina, Mississippi, Florida (especially the Panhandle and north central Florida), Alabama, Georgia, Louisiana, and East Texas—in the late 19th century is no mere coincidence. These southern states were slow in recognizing the equality of African Americans, an unfortunate remnant of their membership in the Confederate States of America and the philosophy it espoused. Ironically, during this same time, many blacks were also exposed to, and welcomed into, the integrated camp meeting worship services of itinerate preachers.

The blues form exhibits influence from many sources, including simple rhymed ballads, field hollers, work songs, shouts, Protestant hymns, and white and black spirituals.

Spirituals are one of the most important antecedents of the blues. Spirituals include both revival and camp meeting songs and date back to the early part of the 19th century. A major, non-denominational religious movement called the Second Great Awakening swept across the United States during the 1800's after originating in Britain. The camp revival meetings of the Second Great Awakening became an important vehicle for Protestant sects, especially Methodists and Baptists, to bring the unreligious back to God.

Worshipers traveled great distances to camp out in remote locations to hear the teachings of traveling preachers. Camp revival meetings were not only non-denominational, they were also for the most part open to all comers. It was common for African Americans to attend camp meetings with European Americans. The revival meetings of the Second Great Awakening became a true musical melting pot where white European folk and formal music intermingled with black performance style. Indeed, most African American spirituals were created using European American forms.

The folk music traditions of European Americans and African Americans share many elements. For instance, both use melodies based on pentatonic scales. This is not surprising. As we have learned, the pentatonic scale is found in the folk music of people the world over. Many of the pentatonic and major scale melodies of African American spirituals are borrowed from European American and British (especially Scottish and Irish) folk music.

Blues singers, like the folk singers of the Balkans and southern Europe, sometimes sing with a non-tempered scale. In these musical traditions, some pitches are intoned in a variable manner. For instance, blues singing is often typified by singing scale degrees three and seven a bit flat. When these scale degrees are sung this way, they are called blue notes.

The Earliest Blues

The spirituals of black Americans were not only sung in worship, but also as work songs. Eventually, the spiritual genre evolved over time and was adapted to become a vehicle for secular topics. Accompanied by an African American style of performance—adding grace notes, turns, melismas and purposely singing scale steps three and seven "blue" (slightly flat)—spirituals were the beginning point for the blues.

The earliest documented use of the term "blues" is in a composition by W.C. Handy (1873-1958) called, "Memphis Blues," written in 1909. A recording of the piece made in 1914 by the Victor Military Band reveals that, after a four-measure introduction, Mr. Handy employs a varied version of the basic twelve-measure blues chord pattern as his starting point. From there, Composer Handy unfolds a multi-sectional piece in the style of the popular marches of the day. The period from just after the American Civil War through about 1940 was a time when military-style marching music and bands were popular. The "Dallas Blues" by songwriter Hart Wand (1887-1960) was the first copyright registered using the term "blues." This was in 1912.

Call-and-Response

The practice of **call-and-response** is a compositional and performance technique wherein one artist or group of performers presents a musical fragment that is either replicated or responded to by a second artist or group of performers. The call-and-response technique is found in the musical traditions of many peoples. In the classical music of North India, this kind of performing is known as **sawaal-javaab**, literally, question-answer. The call-and-response pattern can also be found in the work songs of Europe. For instance, the anthropologist Alan Lomax, working in southern Italy in the early 1950s, documented the songs of olive pickers. His recordings provide evidence of a leader who sings a line that is followed by a response sung by the workers.

Another common call-and-response practice, begun in the mid-17th century, was the lining out of psalms. In congregations that could not read, a leader would intone or line out the psalm text one line at a time alternating with the congregation's singing of that same line. The lines were sung to familiar melodies often ornamented and varied with passing notes. This was the technique that Reverend John Newton used to introduce "Amazing Grace" to his congregants.

Like these several examples, blues songs and other song forms demonstrate many cases where a phrase of music and a phrase of lyric (the question or call) is answered by a subsequent musical and lyrical phrase (the answer or response). Blues Form songs, and other kinds of songs, often employ the call-and-response pattern like the lining out technique.

Blue Notes

Blue notes are pitches that are purposely performed a little bit flat. The performer determines precisely how flat based on his sense of expressiveness, taste, and the flexibility of the instrument on which he is performing. Singers and instrumentalists who work on wind or string instruments can infinitely vary the pitch as they perform. They can easily play between a semitone and a quartertone flat or sharp at will.

Instruments of fixed pitch are not as supple, so musicians playing a piano or vibraphone, or harp are not able to produce blue notes like singers and saxophonists can. Instead, they must simulate or affect the sense of blue notes by adding flattened versions of certain scale members to the standard major scale. It is usual for blues and jazz musicians to add lowered thirds, fifths, and sevenths to the diatonic collection. In ascending melodic lines, the flatted fifth is represented as a raised fourth. (These two notes are enharmonically equivalent.) Taken together, the diatonic major scale with the addition of the blue notes is called a blues scale or jazz scale. See Example 49.

Something akin to blue notes are found in the music of Asian, Middle Eastern, Mediterranean, Central European, Irish, and English folk musical cultures.

Example 49: The Blues Scale

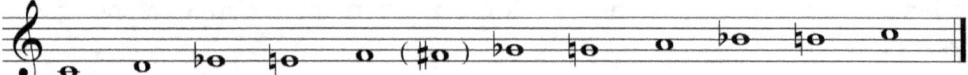

Color Chords in Blues

In traditional European music, the interval of a minor seventh is added to the dominant chord at cadence points to form a V7, for instance at the end of a period when V7 resolves to the tonic. Example 50 shows the chord progression for the standard twelve-bar blues. Note that the interval of the minor seventh is regularly added above the bass of the tonic and subdominant triads to add color. The tonic seven (I7) and the subdominant seven (IV7) are considered non-functional since the sevenths are added strictly as color tones.

The seven-chord built on the dominant (V7 in measure nine) resolves to the subdominant seven chord in the manner of a deceptive cadence. In concert music, a true deceptive cadence moves from V7—vi. Here, vi is a harmonic substitute for IV. The V7 chord in measure twelve allows for the repeat of the song, returning it back to the beginning of the period for another playing with a new lyrical verse.

Example 50: Twelve-Bar Blues Chord Progression in C Major

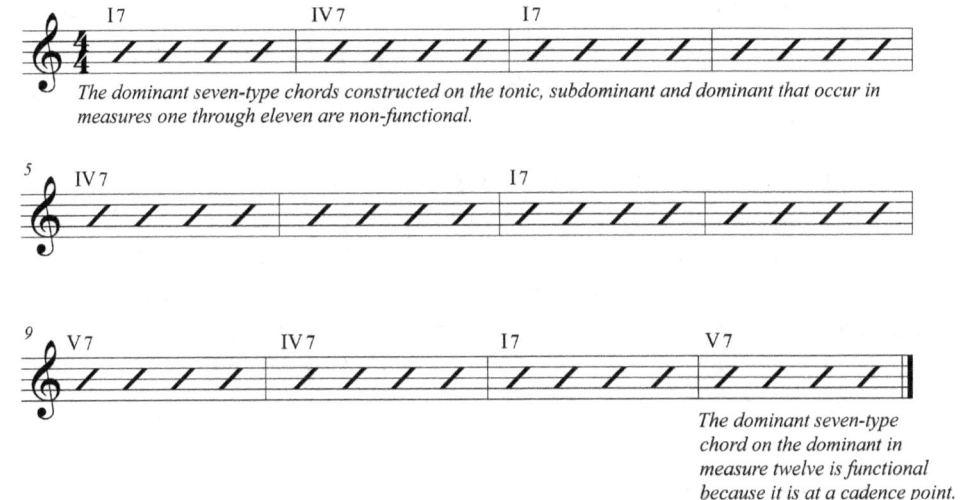

The dominant seven-type chords constructed on the tonic, subdominant and dominant that occur in measures one through eleven are non-functional.

The dominant seven-type chord on the dominant in measure twelve is functional because it is at a cadence point.

Lyrics for Blues Songs

The lyrics of traditional blues songs gave voice to the condition of African Americans after the American Civil War. Blues lyrics often included tales of economic hardship, mistreatment at the hands of the ruling class, crime and punishment, violence, sex, drinking, natural disaster, and travel on the railroads.

Lyrics for twelve-bar blues follow one of two standard patterns. In the first lyric scheme, the singer will use the first four-measure phrase (marked a¹ in Example 51) to present a proposition or convey her general condition, emotional or physical. The singer will repeat that lyric, typically with little variation, in the second four-measure phrase (marked a² in the example). If the lyric is varied, it is to amplify the issues presented in the first phrase.

The lyrics of the last musical phrase (marked b in Example 51), resolves, or at least a sums up, the issues first presented.

Like the other Single Period Form songs we have examined, the lyrics of blues songs are **strophic**. Creative musicians often elaborate, decorate, and otherwise vary their performance from verse to verse in order to create and maintain the listener's (and their) interest as the song evolves.

Twelve-Bar Blues Form

Blues songs are generally created in a 4/4 meter with four beats in each measure and the quarter note receiving the basic pulse. The essential blues form is characterized by a single twelve-measure period that is composed of two unbalanced phrases. The first phrase, A, is eight measures long. The second phrase, B, is four measures. The A-phrase is a phrase group made up of two sub-phrases: a^1 and a^2.

The melodic and lyrical hook are presented in the first sub-phrase (a^1). The melodic hook and its lyric are repeated in the second sub-phrase (a^2). The melody of a^1 is supported by the tonic harmony, often with an added minor seventh, yielding a non-functional dominant seven chord on the tonic (I7). The second sub-phrase (a^2) is harmonized with the subdominant harmony, also with an added minor seventh, yielding a non-functional dominant seven chord on the subdominant (IV7).

Analysis of "Backwater Blues"

It is not clear who created the song, "Backwater Blues." It is credited variously to both Bessie Smith (1894–1937) and Huddie William Ledbetter, also known as "Lead Belly."

The song is an archetypal blues tune. It follows the twelve-measure blues chord progression typical of the blues and the lyrics follow the story development pattern described previously. Like all twelve-bar blues, "Backwater Blues" is strophic (Example 51).

The Blues Form

Example 51: "Backwater Blues"

2.
I woke up this morning, wouldn't even
  get out of my door,
I woke up this morning, wouldn't even
  get out of my door,
Enough trouble to make a poor girl
  wonder where she gonna go.

3.
It thundered and it lightened and the
  winds began to blow,
It thundered and it lightened and the
  winds began to blow,
There was a thousand women didn't
  have no place to go

4.
I went out to the lonesome, high old
  lonesome hill,
I went out to the lonesome, high old
  lonesome hill,
I looked down on the old house where
  I used to live.

Melody and Harmonic Progression

"Backwater Blues" begins with an anacrusis, an "E" that accompanies the word "It" in the opening phrase, "It rained all day and the sky turned dark as night." The pick-up note instigates a sense of forward movement.

The melody in the first two full measures of the first sub-phrase (a¹) incorporates blue notes on both the seventh degree (D♮) and third degree (G♮) of the scale (Example 52). Like most twelve-bar blues, the melody is repeated during the second four-measure sub-phrase (a²). It is supported in the second sub-phrase with the subdominant harmony (IV7).

In this song, the tonic, subdominant and dominant chords are all altered to include the minor seventh above the root to form non-functional dominant seven chords. "Backwater Blues" follows the standard blues chord progression.

The melody of the song flows logically from these chords.

Example 52: Opening Of "Backwater Blues" Showing the Flat Seventh

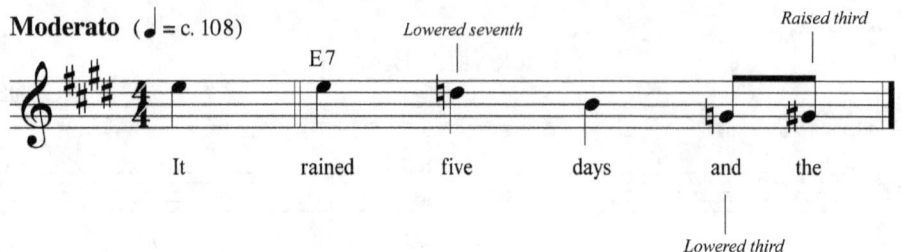

In blues form the first two sub-phrases (a¹) and (a²) can be taken together to form an antecedent phrase group. If the second four-measure sub-phrase were deleted, one would have a simple Single Period song (Example 53).

Example 53: Eight Measures of "Backwater" Without A²

The last sub-phrase (b) delivers a musical and lyrical answer, a consequent phrase group, to the opening phrase group. As in the sixteen-measure Single Period songs (like "Amazing Grace"), the A-phrase (the A-phrase group in the case of blues form) poses a musical question that is answered in the consequent phrase, B.

Lyrics

The lyrics of "Backwater Blues" create an antecedent and consequent arrangement in a manner similar to the arrangement in the lyrics of "Amazing Grace" and other hymns. A basic condition is presented: "It rained all day, and the sky turned dark as night." A rough circumstance that so impressed the storyteller that he or she is obliged to repeat the first telling for emphasis. Then, in the B-phrase the consequence of the awful circumstance announced in the first phrase group is delivered: "There was trouble taking place in the lowland that night."

The pattern of antecedent and consequent, condition and response, is repeated in each subsequent verse. With each new verse, the melody and the basic chord pattern of the accompaniment remains the same.

In his lyrics for "Backwater Blues," (Example 54) Mr. Ledbetter does not consistently use full rhymes as a unifying technique. For instance, he sometimes pairs words that do not rhyme on paper (e.g. Verse 2: "door" and "go"). This kind of *almost rhyme* is an example of assonance and relies on the performer's vernacular pronunciation of the words.

I speculate that Mr. Ledbetter's lyrics were mostly improvised around the core of an idea (in this case a flood) and that it was more important to him to relate the story's message and emotions than to display his mastery of a fancy lyric writing technique.

Example 54: Lyrics for "Backwater Blues"

Backwater Blues, Lyrics by Huddie William Ledbetter

Verse One

It rained all day, and the sky turned dark as night.
It rained all day, and the sky turned dark as night.
There was trouble taking place in the lowland that night.

Verse Two

I woke up this morning, wouldn't even get out of my door.
I woke up this morning, wouldn't even get out of my door.
Enough trouble to make a poor girl wonder where she gonna go.

Verse Three

It thundered and it lightened and the winds began to blow.
It thundered and it lightened and the winds began to blow.
There was a thousand women didn't have no place to go.

Sixteen-Bar Blues Form

The classic chord pattern of the twelve-bar blues has sometimes been modified with very successful results. The hit song, "Watermelon Man," written in 1962 by the pianist/composer, Herbie Hancock (1940-), extends the basic twelve-bar blues pattern at measure eleven by inserting the V—IV progression two additional times. The repetition that Mr. Hancock adds helps to build the drama that then climaxes with a break on beat one of measure fourteen.

Other variations can be found in the literature that expand the basic twelve-bar pattern at other spots. These are valid and valuable. Perhaps the variation that is most common is the Sixteen-Bar Blues Form. Songs in this form include, "I'm Your Hoochie Coochie Man" written by Willie Dixon (1916-1992), and "Let's Dance" written by Jim Lee (1937-). The chord patterns for both songs are included in Example 55.

"Let's Dance," like "Watermelon Man," adds an additional V—IV progression at measure eleven, but then returns to the tonic chord for four measures. As is the case with "Watermelon Man," "Let's Dance" does not add a dominant chord in measure sixteen. There is no preparation for the return to the beginning. It just happens!

"I'm Your Hoochie Coochie Man" is also a one period sixteen-bar blues, but it has some additional features that make it stand out. There is a pick-up measure that leads into the first phrase. The first eight-measure phrase is in a **"stop chorus"** style. In a "stop chorus," the rhythm section plays only the first beat of each measure while someone solos. In "Hoochie Coochie Man," the singer is the soloist. All eight measures of the first phrase are harmonized with a tonic seven chord. The second eight-measure phrase moves to a subdominant seven chord as it follows the chord pattern of the last eight measures of the standard twelve-bar blues.

The Blues Form

Example 55: Variations on the Blues Chord Progression in Sixteen-Bar Blues

This example demonstrates the flexibility of the 12-bar blues. Each songwriter began with the basic 12-bar blues chord pattern and then added four measures to suit his particular needs. Songwriters are always playing with the rules! Often, to great advantage.

Other Songs in Blues Form

Many other songs have been created in this form. Here are just a few.

- "Pine Top Boogie," Music and Lyrics by Pine Top Smith (1904-1929)
- "Dust My Broom," Music and Lyrics by Robert Johnson (1911-1938)
- "Stormy Monday," Music and Lyrics by T-Bone Walker (1910-1975)
- "The Thrill is Gone," Music and Lyrics by Roy Hawkins (1903-1974)
- "Juke," Music and Lyrics by Little Walter (1930-1968)
- "Ice Cream Man," Music and Lyrics by John Brim (1922-2003)
- "Steamroller Blues," Music and Lyrics by James Taylor (1948-)
- "Hideaway," Music by Freddie King (1934-1976) & Sonny Thompson (1916-1989)
- "Red House," Music and Lyrics by Jimi Hendrix (1942-1970)

Exercises

Exercise #1

Using a story from the current news as your lyrical starting point, create a blues tune that clearly presents a predicament in the first phrase group. In your lyrics, have the B-phrase provide a consequence. Explain what happened because of the predicament, for instance.

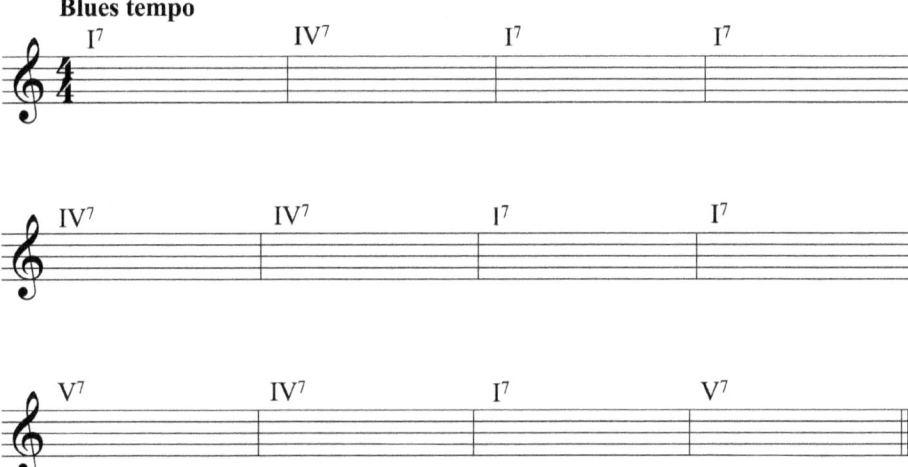

Exercise #2

Compose an opening motive for the first sub-phrase of a new blues tune. Using the concept of repetition with variation, create a second sub-phrase that repeats the motive with variations that take into account the change of harmony (the move to IV^7) required in the blues form.

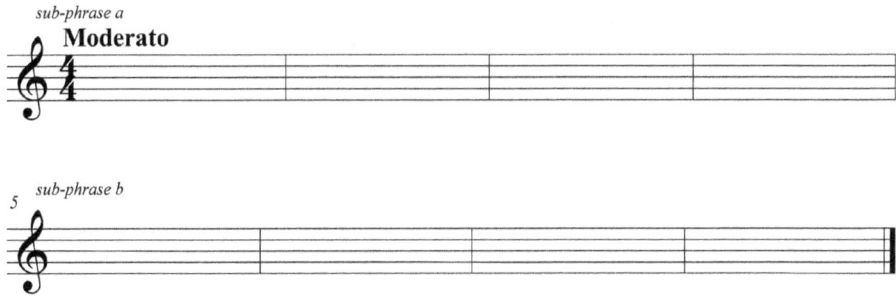

Exercise #3

Create additional verses for "Backwater Blues" or another famous blues song.

Chapter Five

Verse/Chorus Form

The Verse/Chorus form has endured for generations.

The Verse/Chorus form is very flexible and very resilient. Composers over the years have modified it in many ways. In this chapter, along with the straightforward classic Verse/Chorus song form, I will demonstrate the form in a few variations.

Here is a list of successful verse/chorus songs from the mid-1800s through today.

- "Oh! Susanna" and "Old Folks at Home," by Stephen Foster (1826-1864), and "'O sole mio," by Giovanni Capurro (1859-1920) and Eduardo di Capua (1865-1917), in the 19th Century
- "Lucy in the Sky with Diamonds," by John Lennon and Paul McCartney, in the 1960s
- "Superstition," by Stevie Wonder (1950-), in the 1970s
- "Every Breath You Take," by Sting (1951-), in the 1980s
- "Let's Get This Party Started," by Linda Perry (1965-), in the 21st century

Each of these songs contains two periods, a verse, and a chorus.

The Verse in Classic Verse/Chorus Form

The verse period of the Classic Verse/Chorus form is strophic. As we have seen, that means the same (or nearly the same), music is used in the singing of each new stanza of lyric. The lyrics of the verse are expository: they introduce the story of the song and present information about the short drama that is to play out. With each new verse, more details unfold.

Examples of the Classic Verse/Chorus form include: the Black Keys 2019 recording of their song "Go"; Frankie Valli and the Four Seasons' "Walk Like a Man," (Bob Gaudio, 1942-); "I'm a Man" written by Steve Winwood (1948-) and Jimmy Miller (1942-1994), and recorded by The Spencer Davis Group in 1967 and, the band Chicago in 1969; and one of my all-time favorites, "Fire and Rain" by James Taylor (1948-).

Other songwriters use the form in modified versions. In "Deacon Blues," released in 1977 by the band, Steely Dan, songwriters Walter Becker (1950-2017) and Donald Fagan (1948-) modify the Classic Verse/Chorus form by adding an interlude after each chorus. In this case, the interlude is not an element of the arrangement, but an integral section of the song form.

Throughout the twentieth century, through about the 1970's, songwriters wrote in highly standardized forms. This was especially true of songwriters working in "Tin Pan Alley." During this long period, publishers encouraged the writing of songs that could be re-recorded (covered), by as many artists as possible. Songwriters who were also performing musicians, like Carole King, Neil Sedaka, Bob Dylan, John Lennon, and Paul McCartney, changed that trend by writing songs that were much more personal and reflective of their performing style. They took the basic forms—especially the Classic Verse/Chorus form—added or cut measures from the standard eight-measure phrase, incorporated occasional meter changes, and otherwise made the verse/chorus song form their own. This trend of personalization continued into the twenty-first century. Today's songwriters begin with and incorporate the elements of the Classic Verse/Chorus, but weave that form into their record production and musical arrangement to yield a recorded product that is truly unique to them. This is likely why there are fewer and fewer newly released recordings of previously released songs.

In the next section, I dissect some of the many variations I have observed in more recently composed Verse/Chorus songs. I am sure there are more than I here present.

Some characteristics of Verse/Chorus songs remain constant across the many variations. Most are built up of eight-measure phrases, with four-measure sub-phrases. The final words of lyrical phrases ordinarily rhyme, the melody of the verse is typically set at a lower range than the melody of the chorus, and the lyrics of the chorus remain consistent while the lyrics of the verse change with each repetition.

The Verse in The Twenty First Century Verse/Chorus Form

I have observed two trends in how songwriters use the Verse/Chorus song form that emerged beginning around the turn of the twenty-first century. One is what I am calling the "Plain & Fancy Verse" style, the other I am calling the "Rap & Sung Verse" style.

Plain & Fancy Verses

In the Plain & Fancy Verse variation, the first verse is sung in an unornamented manner and in a lower range. Then, the lyric of the second verse is presented at a higher pitch level, often with more ornamentation in the melody. The same chord changes (and similarly arranged accompaniment in the recorded version) are used for both the "plain" lower-pitched, unornamented first verse and second "fancy" higher-pitched, more flowery second verse.

For examples of this Plain & Fancy Verse version of the Verse/Chorus song form, I encourage you to listen to "Because of You," recorded by Kelly Clarkson, "My Hero," released in 1998 by the Foo Fighters, and "Run to the Water" released as a single in 2000 by the band, Live.

In "Because of You," written by Clarkson (1982-), David Hodges (1978-) and Ben Moody (1981-), Clarkson sings the first verse in a lower range, with little ornamentation. She sings the second verse at a higher pitch and with more filigree.

The band, Live, uses the same Plain & Fancy Verse formula in their recording of "Run to the Water" written by Live's lead singer, Ed Kowalczyk (1971-) and bassist Patrick Dahlheimer (1971-).

"My Hero," written by Dave Grohl (1969-), Nate Mendel (1968-), and Pat Smear (1959-), and released by the band, the Foo Fighters in 1998, also uses the Plain & Fancy Verse/Chorus song formula.

Singer/songwriter and pianist, Alicia Keys (1981-), takes the Plain & Fancy Verse variation of the Verse/Chorus song form even further. In the song, "No One" (that Keys wrote with Kerry Brothers, Jr. (1970-), and George Harry (?)), Keys sings four verses, each one is fancier than the next! The verses, and indeed the chorus, too, are all delivered over a constantly repeating chordal accompaniment of I—V—vi—IV.

In "No One," verse two is fancier than verse one, verse three is fancier than verse two, and verse four is even more fancy still!

In her recording, "Raise a Man," singer and songwriter, Alicia Keys weaves four verses over the same background accompaniment, none of which sounds in any way (except that Ms. Keys is singing them), like the other. What I mean is, there is not a clear melody that is easily sung—what Ms. Keys sings *sounds* improvised, like a sung rap. Ms. Keys creates moving, and meaningful verse-like lyrics (they are expository and lead to a chorus) while singing non-repetitive melodies over a strictly repeating four-measure loop. (A loop is a recorded section of music that is edited together to repeat many times.) This improvisation-as-verse goes on for about 40 measures; about 2 minutes and 35 seconds. Next, there is an eight-measure interlude (composed of mostly similar material). Finally, at about 3 minutes and 30 seconds, Ms. Keys gets to the lyrical hook, "Somebody made a man, to show me how to raise a man".

Creative musician, Lauryn Hill (1975-), composes similarly improvised-sounding masterpieces over repeated accompaniments. Listen, for instance, to "Nothing Even Matters," released in 1992. Both the recordings of Ms. Hill and Ms. Keys rely very heavily on the beautiful voice of the singer and her ability to improvise complicated melodies and lyrics.

So, what's going on here? Do the musical creations of Lauryn Hill and Alicia Keys (and Floetry and Erykah Badu and others), represent a sort of pop vocal extension of the free jazz created by Miles Davis in his 1970 album, *Bitches Brew?* All this music borrows elements of pop songs but organizes those elements in uncommon and non-formulaic ways. Whatever is happening, the recordings are masterful and creative, especially in their vocal musicianship and singularity, again attesting to the resilience of the stalwart Verse/Chorus Form.

Rap & Sung Verses

A second popular variation on the traditional Verse/Chorus song form features one or more verses being rapped. A rapped verse might be followed by a sung verse or this order could be reversed with a sung verse starting the record, being then followed by a rapped verse. In either case, the verses are followed by a chorus that is sung.

The song, "Glorious," released by the artist, Macklemore in 2017, is an example of this form. ("Glorious" was written by Macklemore (1983-), Skylar Grey (1986-), Budo (?), Tyler Andrews (1984-) and Tyler Dopps(?)).

The song, "Believer," recorded in 2017 by the American band Imagine Dragons, reverses the form. In "Believer," the first eight-measure verse is sung. In the second eight-measure verse, the band's lead singer, Dan Reynolds, uses a technique that combines rap and chant. He sings the rapid-fire lyrics of the second verse on three **recitation tones**. The band and their producers created the song, "Believer." Imagine Dragons includes, Dan Reynolds (1987-), Wayne Sermon (1984), Ben McKee (1985-), Daniel Platzman (1986-), with producers, Robin Fredriksson, Mattias Larsson. Songwriter Justin Tranter (1980-) also contributed to this hit song.

The Chorus in Verse/Chorus Forms

A **chorus** in popular music refers to a period that recurs, sung each time with the same lyrics. The chorus almost always contains the title of the song. The chorus of a song is repeated many times in most presentations and for this and some other reasons I will describe, is the part that people most often remember.

In popular music, the term verse is used to describe the words and music of the other period of the Verse/Chorus song. The verse period commonly precedes the chorus in recorded performances.

> **Note**
> You might hear persons refer to this period as the refrain, the hook, the hammer, the sing-along, or the channel.

The principal purpose of the music and lyrics of the verse period is to prepare the listener for and lead them to the memorable music and lyrics of the song's chorus.

The verse is where the songwriter introduces the premise of the song, offers context, and otherwise entices the listener to want to hear the chorus. For the most part, all sections of great songs contain melodic, lyrical and accompaniment hooks, but verses tend to have fewer memorable features than choruses.

Verses will usually conclude on a dominant chord of whatever key the chorus is in. Ending on the dominant facilitates an easy harmonic transition to the chorus.

Lyrics of the Chorus

The chorus delivers the consequence for the story or issue presented in the verse. Certain things have transpired in the verse and as a result, the singer/narrator says these other things in the chorus. Songwriters generally include in the chorus a succinct and memorable lyrical hook that sums up the story. The lyrical hook almost always becomes the song's title. A memorable melodic hook always coupled with the lyrical hook. A great song that follows this general lyrical and melodic scheme is Stevie Wonder's classic tune, "I Just Called to Say I Love You." (Example 56)

Lyrical Analysis of "I Just Called to Say I Love You"

Example 56: Lyrics from "I Just Called to Say I Love You"

I Just Called to Say I Love You (Words & Music by Stevie Wonder)

Verse One

No New Year's Day to celebrate
No chocolate covered candy hearts to give away
No first of spring, no song to sing
In fact here's just another ordinary day

Verse Two

No April rain, no flowers bloom
No wedding Saturday within the month of June
But what it is, is something true
Made up of these three words that I must say to you

Chorus

I just called to say I love you
I just called to say how much I care
I just called to say I love you
And I mean it from the bottom of my heart

Stevie Wonder begins verse one by declaring that today is just "another ordinary day." The motivation for his call is not yet stated.

By the time Mr. Wonder leads us through the end of the second verse, we are quite ready to learn what is going on. Why is the narrator bothering to try to convince us that there is nothing important about today? Who cares if there is no rain or that it is not a Saturday in June? And why is he speaking to us in riddles? What are these three words that he feels compelled to utter?

Finally, in the chorus we the listeners learn "what it is." What is special is that the narrator is in love. Further, we discover that he is not speaking to us; we are overhearing a conversation that the storyteller is having with the person on the other end of a phone line. The singular reason for the singer's phone call we discover in the chorus is to express love for the person on the other end of the line. The song's premise is established, the little bit of confusion about precisely what was spoken of in the verses is quelled and, in the chorus, a clear declaration of affection is made to the call's recipient.

This song's lyrics are succinct, sweet, and very successful. "I Just Called to Say I Love You" was one of Stevie Wonder's most commercially successful songs. His recording achieved a number one position on the *Billboard* magazine "Hot 100", "Adult Contemporary" and "R&B" charts, won a Golden Globe and Academy Award for Best Original Song (it was included in the 1984 comedy, *The Woman in Red*) and received three Grammy® nominations.

The simple Verse/Chorus form is profoundly efficient. In just two periods, the songwriter weaves a story and, in one period, repeats a title many times to fix it in the listener's memory. There are many fine examples of this unadulterated Verse/Chorus form, but there are also many more cases of the Verse/Chorus form in slightly modified versions.

Placement of the Title Hook

The lyrical and melodic hook may appear at the beginning, the middle or the end of the chorus (or in more than one place, including in the verses). The chorus period of the song contains the "take away" for the listener. It is the section most listeners will remember, the part of a song that average listeners will sing to you if you ask how a song goes.

In the Stevie Wonder song, the lyrical hook and its melodic hook appear at the beginning of the chorus and then again in the middle of the chorus. This placement is very typical and can be seen in many Verse/Chorus songs.

Of course, there are always successful exceptions to almost every rule about songwriting. For instance, in the song "The Gambler," written by Donald Schlitz (1952-) and made famous by Kenny Rogers in his wonderful 1978 recording, the song's title appears in various places throughout this story song, but not in any of the spots typical of Verse/Chorus songs (Example 57).

Lyrical Analysis of "The Gambler"

Example 57: Lyrics from "The Gambler"

The Gambler (Words & Music by Donald Schlitz)

Verse One

On a warm summer's evenin' on a train bound for nowhere
I met up with the gambler, we were both too tired to sleep
So we took turns a starin' out the window at the darkness
'Til boredom overtook us and he began to speak

Verse Two

He said, "Son, I've made a life, out of readin' people's faces
And knowin' what their cards were by the way they held their eyes
So if you don't mind my sayin', I can see you're out of aces
For a taste of your whiskey I'll give you some advice"

Verse Three

So I handed him my bottle and he drank down my last swallow
Then he bummed a cigarette and asked me for a light
And the night got deathly quiet and his face lost all expression
Said, "If you're gonna play the game, boy, you gotta learn to play it right"

Chorus

You got to know when to hold 'em, know when to fold 'em
Know when to walk away and know when to run
You never count your money when you're sittin' at the table
There'll be time enough for countin' when the dealing's done
Every gambler knows that the secret to survivin'
Is knowin' what to throw away and knowing what to keep
'Cause every hand's a winner and every hand's a loser
And the best that you can hope for is to die in your sleep

The speaker in this song is a storyteller, a narrator. Through the narrator/singer, the songwriter Donald Schlitz weaves a story so compelling and memorable that he has no need to sing the song's title. Another songwriter might have named the philosopher-gambler and sung that name over and again in the chorus, but that would have cheapened the song significantly. Of course, Kenny Rogers' excellent performance and Larry Butler's great production help to keep the listener wanting more.

The combined talents of Schlitz, Rodgers and Butler created a recording so memorable that it flew to the top of the record charts and became a touchstone of country pop. The song, though, with its powerful message and hooky memorable lines is the essential element in the mix of ingredients that made the recording a hit.

Interestingly, it takes one minute and ten seconds for the original recording to get to the chorus. This, too, breaks the record producer's understanding that one must get to the chorus in sixty seconds or less.

"The Gambler" breaks another rule. More often than not, periods of a Verse/Chorus song are balanced, meaning that they are the same length in measures. In "The Gambler," the first verse is one and a half times as long as the chorus.

Most often, the periods of a Verse/Chorus song are eight or sixteen measures long, but lengths can vary. Most popular songs in Verse/Chorus form are written in 4/4 meter, however, songs in 3/4 and 12/8 are not uncommon.

Reverse Ordering of Periods: Chorus First

Some songwriters begin with the chorus. "December 1963 (Oh What a Night)" written by Bob Gaudio (1942-) and a hit for The Four Seasons in 1975, begins with the chorus. So too do "How Sweet It Is," a hit for Marvin Gaye (1939-1984) in 1964 and James Taylor in 1975, and "Come Sail Away" released in 1977 by the band, Styx.

In the original 1964-recorded performance of the song, "How Sweet It Is (To Be Loved By You)" by Marvin Gaye and the James Taylor version of the song from 1975, the chorus period of the song precedes the verse period. The lyrical hook, "How Sweet It Is," is presented at the beginning of the chorus and therefore the beginning of the song. In reality, it is the only lyric of the chorus!

Written by the great songwriting team of Eddie Holland (1939-), Lamont Dozier (1941-) and Brian Holland (1941-), "How Sweet It Is" has some other features worth noting.

The melody of "How Sweet It Is" is composed using the pentatonic collection, as was the case with "Amazing Grace." The composers use a minor pentatonic scale on E for this melody. Many pop song melodies feature pentatonic collections.

Example 58: *"How Sweet It Is" Pentatonic Collection*

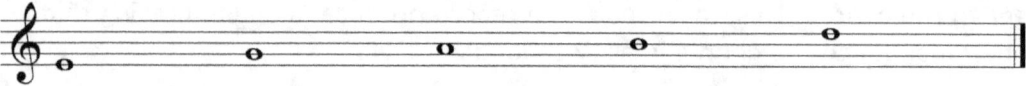

The title of this song is a colloquial expression. The practice of creating a song's title out of a commonly used phrase is noteworthy because it is so very effective and done so often. "You Only Live Once," "For Once in My Life," "Solid as a Rock," "Diamonds Are a Girl's Best Friend," "For All We Know," "Play It Again," "That's How We Roll," "Shake It Off" and of course, "9 to 5" are all illustrations of song titles that evolved from a colloquial expression.

Phrasal Analysis of "How Sweet It Is"

Example 59: *Partial Phrasal Analysis of "How Sweet It Is"*

The harmonic progression of "How Sweet It Is" (Example 59) is also interesting. The song begins on the subdominant (IV∆7), moves to the dominant (V7), and then to the tonic. The entire opening of the song (the Chorus) can be seen as an extended IV—V—I progression.

Verse/Chorus Form

Beginning on the subdominant, or any chord other than the tonic, creates a sense of forward movement because as listeners we want to have the harmony find its way back to the tonic.

Example 60: Melodic Analysis of Phrase IIB of "How Sweet It Is"

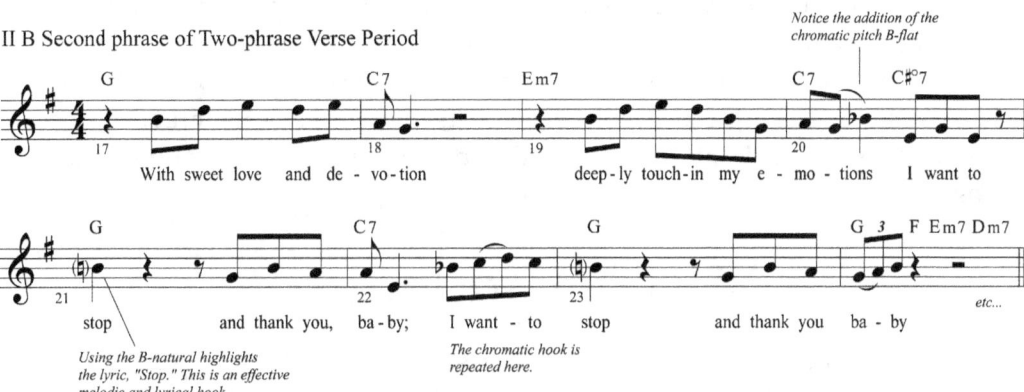

In the second period (Example 60), the harmony progresses from I—V and then, using the blues chord progression as their model, Holland, Dozier and Holland end the first three sub-phrases on the subdominant-seven. The move from V7—IV7 at the end of each of the sub-phrases mimics the deceptive progression found in the standard blues. The chord progression at measure eight of the second phrase of period II facilitates a re-transition to C major allowing a repeat of the Chorus. This is accomplished by reintroducing the F♮ (in the F and Dm chords). The C major harmony in the first measure-and-a-half of the Chorus is the **key of the moment**, a harmony that temporarily functions as the tonic. The sense of C major is quickly defeated when on the third beat of measure two a D7 is introduced, leading the melody, harmony, and the listener back to the home key of G major.

The song, "Come Sail Away," written by Styx lead singer, Dennis DeYoung (1947-), begins (after the six-measure introduction) with what sounds like a chorus since it carries the song's title at its beginning. This eight-measure musical phrase is repeated, but with different lyrics. Wait...*is this a chorus*? Then, there is an eight-measure verse, followed by a foreshortened six-measure section that ends with the lyric, "...to carry on." *Oh no! This is complicated!* In the recording, the band next repeats the introductory material. Then, the beginning eight-measure verses are repeated with new lyrics, followed by that shortened six-measure phrase. Again, the lyric at the end is sung, "...to carry on."

As the band kicks in with a heavier-sounding interlude, the next section begins. That next section is truly a chorus: a repeated "sing-along" section. The sing-along in this case is the song's title, "Come Sail Away." In this example, Dennis DeYoung and Styx created an extended composition using elements of the venerable Verse/Chorus form.

Other creative songwriters, notably Robert Lamm (1944-), and James Pankow (1947-) in their work with the band, Chicago; Billy Joel, in his "Scenes from an Italian Restaurant;" Jimmy Webb in "MacArthur Park;" and of course, John Lennon and Paul McCartney in "Sgt. Pepper's Lonely Hearts Club Band" develop very convincing long form compositions using elements of the Verse/Chorus song interspersed with instrumental interludes, tempo changes, and meter changes.

Further Variation

Let us look now at another successful Verse/Chorus song that includes a new set of idiosyncrasies. First, the writers were able to compose "At the Hop" by stringing together two twelve-bar blues periods. Next, the song's title does not appear in the chorus, but does appear prominently in the verse.

Artie Singer (1919-2008), John Madara (1936-) and David White (1939-) wrote "At the Hop". It was first released on record in 1958 and became a top-selling hit record in a version by Danny and the Juniors. It was covered by the band, Sha Na Na in the 1969 Woodstock Festival and featured in the film, *American Graffiti* in 1973.

"At the Hop" is composed of two twelve-bar blues periods. The first twelve-bar blues period serves as the verse, the second as the song's chorus. Interestingly, both sections include some form of the title, but curiously, the precise title does not appear in the chorus. It is placed squarely in the verse. The chorus includes only a variation of the title, but the title never fully appears in the chorus, proving indeed that all rules are to be broken.

Verse/Chorus Form 99

Phrasal Analysis of "At the Hop"

Example 61: Phrasal Analysis of "At the Hop"

Note that blues form consists of only one phrase and that phrase is also the entirety of the blue form's single period. I have therefore not marked that single phrase, A, just as in the analysis of the blues tune, "Backwater Blues" I did not indicate the single period, I.

In the analysis of "At the Hop" I have indicated the two distinct and interdepentant periods (I and I) and have indicated the sub-phrases, a, a¹ and so on. I have not indicated the blues form's single phrase. It is understood.

I have labeled the first full period as the verse because it is strophic. The second full period has a single lyric and that is invariable. The phrase, "Let's Go to the Hop" recurs in this period many times without change. The songwriting team of Singer, Madera and White chose to call the song, "At the Hop" because of the prominence given to this line in the verses. They could have named it "Let's Go to the Hop" and been similarly successful.

The two most common variants of the Verse/Chorus song form are the Verse/Chorus song with a bridge and the Verse/Chorus song with a pre-chorus.

Often both added sections are found in one song and sometimes other elements might be varied.

Verse/Chorus with a Bridge

Sometimes songwriters add a **bridge** between repetitions of the chorus (Example 62). Doing so creates variety and relief from the monotony that could result from several successive hearings of even a very interesting chorus period. Musical bridges are generally inconsequential phrases that are placed between two more significant sections of music. Bridges usually do not include music that is highly developed or lyrics that add significantly to the plot of the song.

Bridges present stylistic contrast to the verse and chorus periods. For instance, if the melody of the chorus is populated with long notes, then the melody of the bridge might feature notes of short duration yielding a rapid rhythm. On the other hand, if the range of the verse and chorus is large the bridge might have a smaller compass. Often the bridge will start in a key center other than the key of the chorus and verse. If the chorus is in C major, the bridge might be in A minor; if the chorus is in E♭ major, the bridge might be in A♭ major. A change of key center is not mandatory, however, as we shall see in the example below.

Like the harmony of the verses, the harmony of the bridge must lead the listener's ear back to the chorus. Bridges will ordinarily end on a dominant chord of the key of the next chorus.

The great American songwriter, Carole King (1942-) wrote, "You've Got a Friend" in 1971. It was simultaneously released on her album, *Tapestry* and James Taylor's album *Mud Slide Slim*. Both records topped the *Billboard* magazine charts. Mr. Taylor and Ms. King won Grammy® Awards for their individual recordings of the same song, James Taylor for "Best Male Pop Vocal Performance" and Carole King for "Song of the Year."

Verse/Chorus Form

Analysis of "You've Got a Friend"

Example 62: "You've Got a Friend" Verse/Chorus with Bridge

You've Got a Friend

Words and Music by
Carole King

© 1971 COLGEMS-EMI, INC.

"You've Got a Friend" begins in the key of F# minor and resolves in measure seven and eight to A, the relative major. The second eight-measure phrase of the verse period hovers between F# minor and A major, ending on the dominant of A (E) which leads nicely to chorus period.

Verse/Chorus Form

The verse period is balanced as it consists of two eight-measure phrases. The phrases differ though. They are not a simple repeated single phrase.

Example 63: *First Seven Measures of "You've Got a Friend" Chorus Plus Pickup*

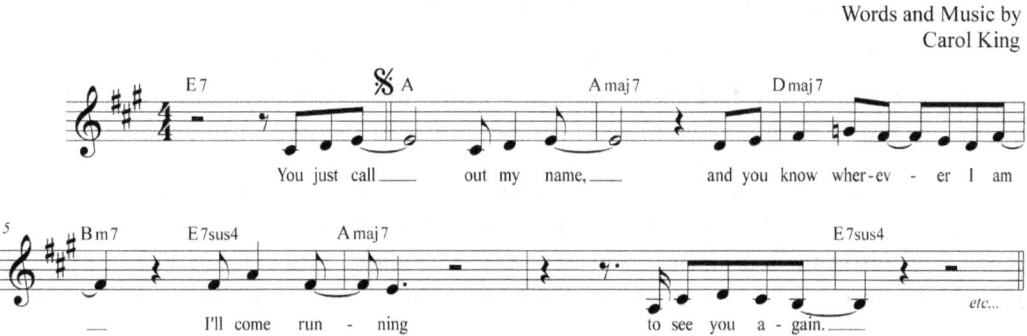

Likewise, the chorus period is composed of two eight-measure phrases (Example 63). The entirety of the chorus is in A major, ending in the first playing of the dominant of F♯ minor the accommodating the return to the key of the verse.

The bridge begins in the temporary key center of D major and flows through a ten-measure single phrase period back to the dominant of A major, the key of the chorus. This allows for an easy return to the chorus at the end of the song.

Ms. King includes a codetta that starts at measure fifty-five. The codetta heightens the sense of drama and supports another singing of the title hook.

Melodically, the bridge of the song encompasses a smaller range, from A3 to A4 than does the verse and chorus. They traverse a range from A3 up to C♯4. The rhythm of the melody in the bridge is also considerably different from that of the chorus. The melodic rhythm of the chorus is a little different, too. In the chorus, the melodic rhythm is somewhat haltering, with much open space created by long rests.

Other Verse/Chorus songs that have a bridge include "Can't Stop" written by Flea (1962-), J.A. Frusciante (1970-), A. Kiedis (1962-) and C. Smith (1961-); and "Fix You" written by members of the band Coldplay.

Verse/Chorus with a Pre-chorus

Many Verse/Chorus songs add a short phrase of new musical and lyrical material that is placed just prior to the chorus. This is a **pre-chorus**. The pre-chorus further prepares the listener to hear the important message of the chorus, heightening the anticipation of its arrival.

Listen to Halestorm's 2017 Grammy winner, "Love Bites (So Do I)" written by lead singer and guitarist, Lzzy Hale (1983-) and songwriter Dave Bassett (?) for a good example of this Verse/Pre-chorus/Chorus variation.

The song "Need You Now" recorded by Lady Antebellum, features an interesting twist on the Verse/Pre-Chorus/Chorus Form. In this song, the first verse is eight measures long, followed by a more intricate (higher pitched) second verse of only six measures. This foreshortened second verse serves as a pre-chorus and leads nicely into the chorus. This pattern of verse followed by verse-as-pre-chorus repeats throughout the recording.

Let's return to "How Sweet It Is" for a look at how the writers prepare the listeners for the chorus.

Holland, Dozier and Holland add a second phrase to the verse that serves as a pre-chorus (Example 64). This phrase, like the phrases of all Holland, Dozier, and Holland songs, contains several melodic and lyrical hooks. At measure twenty, they introduce the first chromatic pitch, a B♭ in the key of the example. Its use is highlighted and made more special in the next measure, when they write a B♮ accompanying the word, "Stop."

The entire eight-measure phrase serves as a pre-chorus and leads the listener into the repeat of the chorus.

Example 64: B-Phrase of Period II as Pre-Chorus

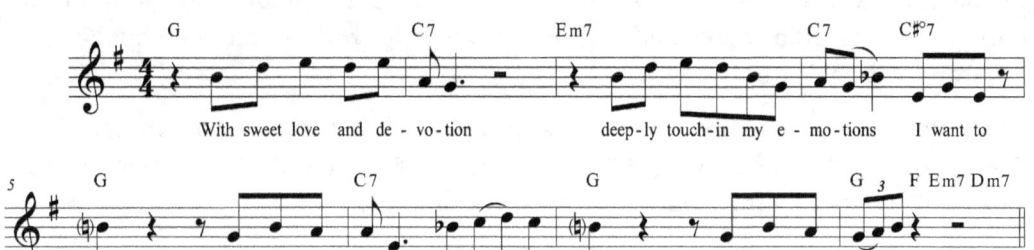

Verse/Chorus songs that include a pre-chorus might also include a bridge. The song, "Roar," (Example 65) made famous in a recording by the singer Katy Perry (1984-), does just that.

Phrasal and Melodic Analysis of "Roar"

Example 65: Overview of "Roar"

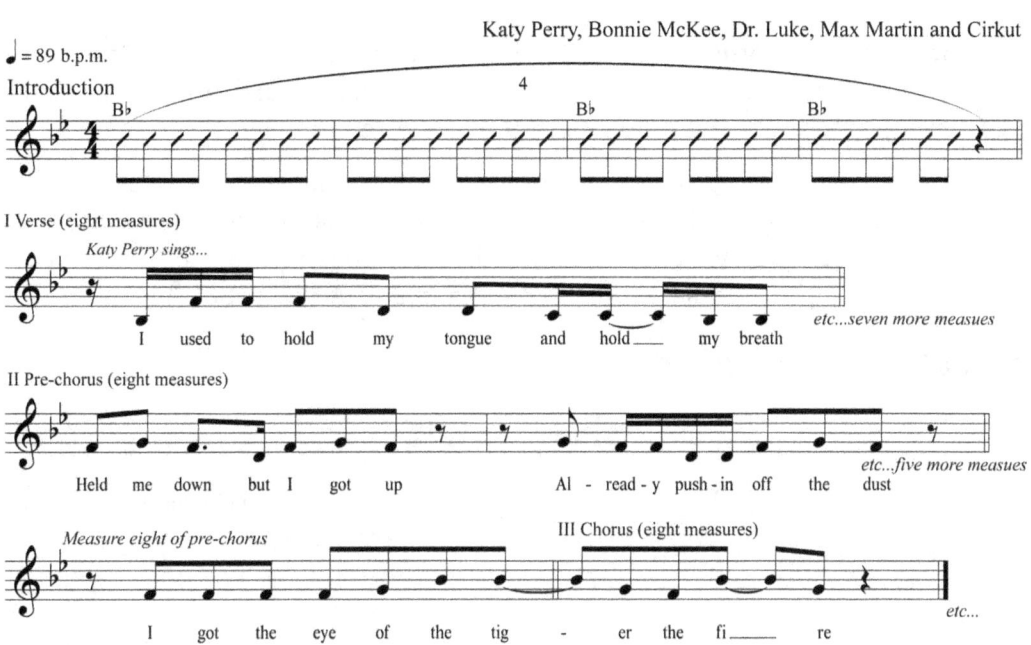

After a four-measure instrumental introduction, there is an eight-measure verse. An eight-measure pre-chorus follows the verse and leads directly to an eight-measure chorus. The chorus of this song is followed by a five-measure extension.

In the repeat, the verse is foreshortened to last just four measures. This is followed by a repeat of the eight-measure pre-chorus, an eight-measure chorus and then, an extension that is lengthened to a full eight measures.

At this point, the writers introduce a bridge of sorts. In the highly personal original recording, Ms. Perry repeats the title "Roar" over a rhythmic ostinato for seven measures before repeating the chorus and its eight-measure extension.

Although a bit unconventional in its inclusion of the extensions after the choruses and the sui generis bridge "Roar" does follow the general plan of the Verse/Chorus song with a pre-chorus. Like "Amazing Grace," the melody of "Roar" is pentatonic. It uses the pitches in Example 66.

Example 66: Major Pentatonic Melody of "Roar"

The melody is composed exclusively of pitches from the pentatonic scale in B-flat

Many other Verse/Chorus songs add emphasis to the chorus by including an extension on some playings of the chorus. The extensions are often only a few measures long, perhaps half the length of the entire chorus.

The song "Shake It Off" (Example 67) written by Bryan Michael Cox (1977-), Jermaine Dupri (1972-), Johntá Austin (1980-) and Mariah Carey (1969-) made famous in a recording by Mariah Carey, adds extensions to the chorus as does the song, "Jeremy" by Eddie Vedder (1964-) and Jeff Ament (1963-).

Example 67: "Shake It Off"

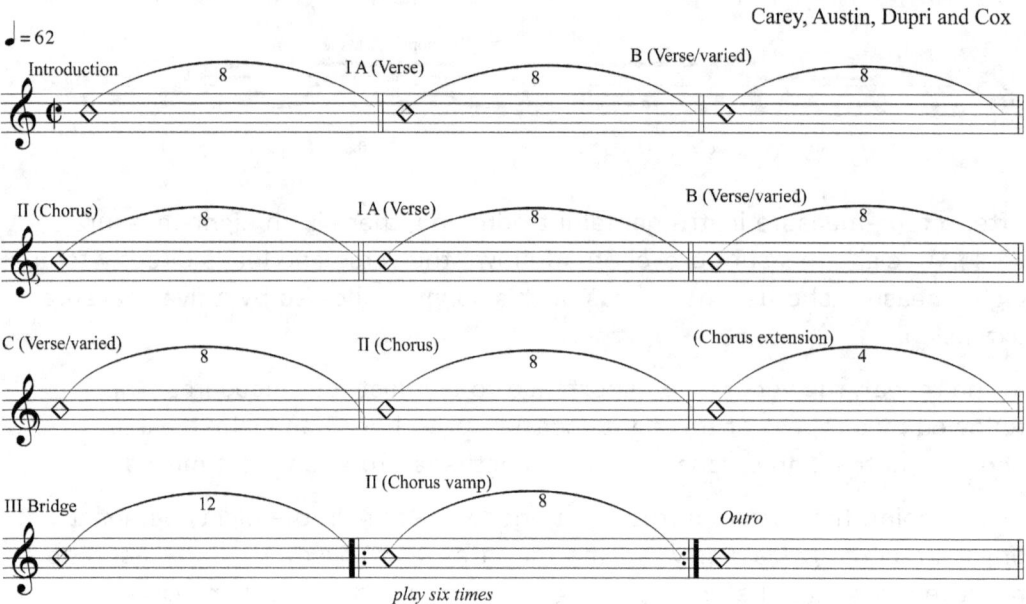

Phrasal Analysis of "Jeremy"

Example 68: *Phrasal Analysis of "Jeremy"*

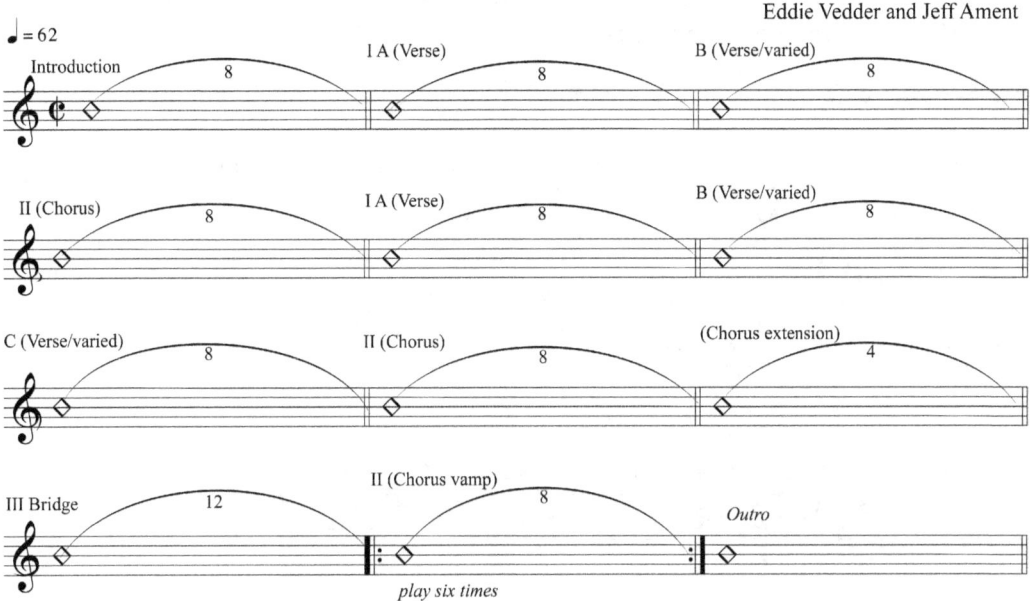

"Jeremy" was released in 1992 by the band, Pearl Jam. In "Jeremy," (Example 68) Eddie Vedder and Jeff Ament create a song that follows what is on the surface a simple Verse/Chorus form. There is an introduction of eight measures followed by a verse of eight measures. Next, Messrs. Vedder and Ament place a second verse that serves as a pre-chorus. It is a varied version of the verse that places Mr. Vedder's voice in a higher **tessitura**.

After the initial playing of the chorus, the verse and the varied verse/pre-chorus recurs to set up the second chorus. The chorus is then repeated and followed by a twelve-measure interlude that serves as a bridge. The interlude/bridge is followed by five playings of the eight-measure chorus period and a **codetta** or **outro** (a short phrase that ends the arrangement).

Many Verse/Chorus songs employ the solo-as-bridge strategy in recording. This is a perfect gambit to use in the production of a song that does not include a bridge. Sometimes, but not in this instance, the arranger creates a key change at the point when the chorus returns.

Exercises

Exercise #1

Analyze the melodic rhythm and lyrics of a verse/chorus song you like. Compose a new melody that uses the same melodic rhythm (and does not plagiarize the song you analyzed).

Exercise #2

Use the chord progression and harmonic rhythm below to compose the melody and lyrics for the Chorus Period of a new pop tune. The title of your song should be prominently featured in your lyrics. Base the title on a colloquial expression.

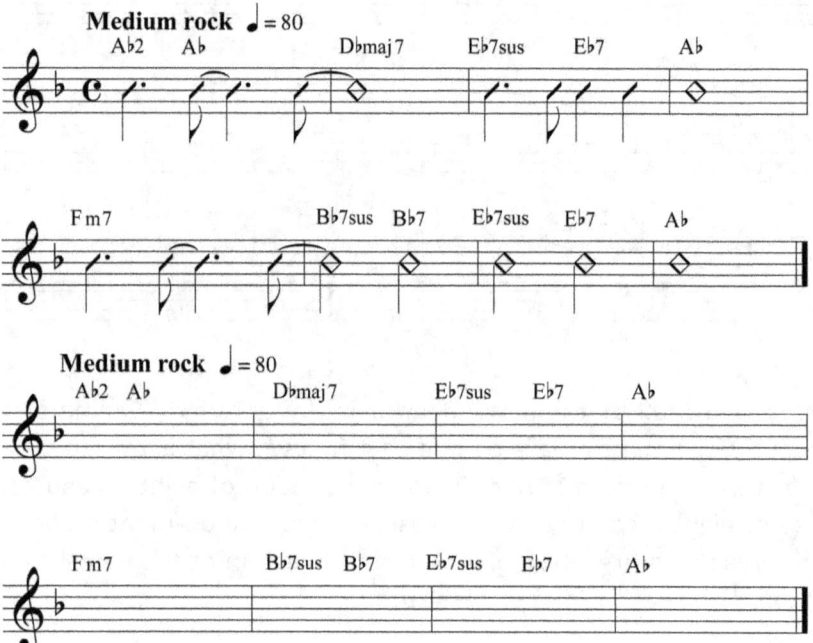

Verse/Chorus Form

Exercise #3

Use the chord progression and harmonic rhythm below to compose the melody and lyrics for the Pre-Chorus of a new pop tune in Verse/Chorus Form.

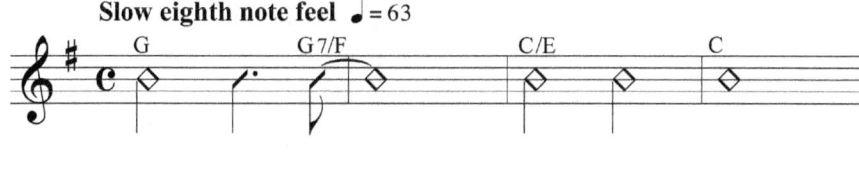

Exercise #4

Listen and analyze the songs "You and I," "Don't Look Back in Anger" and "Royals." Find the writers and their birth/death dates.

Chapter Six

Twentieth-Century Bar Form

The second Double Period form we'll work with is what I call **Twentieth-Century Bar Form**. This is the form used in the writing of many of the songs found in the "Great American Songbook" – the name that singer Tony Bennett coined to describe the most important, most influential, and most often recorded songs of the twentieth century. The "Great American Songbook" is principally made up of songs written for Broadway musical theatre and Hollywood musical films produced from the 1920s through the 1960s.

Songs in Twentieth-Century Bar Form are characterized by their thirty-two-measure length and the distinctive pattern of their phrases (AABA). Each phrase of a Twentieth-Century Bar Form song is eight measures long, and each period contains two phrases.

Period one (labeled "I" in my examples) is composed of two eight-measure phrases that are nearly identical. I label them A^1 and A^2. We will soon see that phrases A^1 and A^2 are essentially the same but end differently. Period two (labeled "II") is composed of two eight-measure phrases labeled B and A^3.

The potency and great success of the Twentieth-Century Bar Form is based on the prominent placement of the title hook at the beginning or end of the A-phrases, and the number of times the A-phrase is heard—a minimum of three times in thirty-two measures. The A-phrase is performed each time with only minor variations that occur at the end of the phrase.

History

Twentieth-Century Bar Form is a variation of an older form called simply, **Bar Form**. The historic Bar Form is a two-section form whose parts follow a formal pattern of AAB.

During the Middle Ages, **Troubadours** created **ballades** in Bar Form. The troubadours were itinerant composers and performers who lived in Occitania (a region that roughly encompasses the southern half of France and parts of Italy and Spain). The troubadour tradition, lifestyle, and music influenced others to create similar movements and art. In northern France, the **trouvéres** and in Germany, the Minnesinger, like the troubadours, composed and performed songs whose lyrics dealt mainly with courtly love. The troubadour, trouvér and Minnesinger traditions declined during the fourteenth century around the time of the Black Death, about 1348.

During the fourteenth century in Germany, the Minnesinger's tradition gave way to the tradition of the Meistersingers. The Meistersingers were members of a guild for lyric poetry, composition, and a cappella art song singing. The journeymen composers and poets of the Meistersinger guilds referred to their particularly artful works as *Bar*, most likely a shortening of *Barat*, a skillful thrusting move in fencing. The pattern of their songs was AAB: two repetitions of one melody or **Stollen** (meaning, stanzas) followed by a different melody, called **Abgesang** (meaning, after song). The Meistersingers used the term *Ton* (close enough to our modern *tune*) to refer to one such complete song in Bar Form

The traditional Bar Form (AAB) can be found still in many Lutheran chorales (a form of hymn). As detailed in Chapter Four, American blues songs are also written with an AAB formal design.

Another Antecedent

Stephen Collins Foster (1826-1864), known to some as the "father of American Popular music," was the country's first successful composer of popular songs. Foster wrote the music and lyrics for more than two hundred songs and enjoyed great success during his lifetime. Foster's songs were regularly performed in recital and in homes and were arranged for the popular brass and percussion bands of the day. Several of Foster's songs are still popular, and often heard. These include "Oh! Susanna," "Camptown Races," "Old Folks at Home," "My Old Kentucky Home," "Jeanie with the Light Brown Hair," "Old Black Joe," and "Beautiful Dreamer."

Both "Beautiful Dreamer" and "Jeannie with the Light Brown Hair" were written using short phrases. The phrases of "Beautiful Dreamer" follow a formal design of ABA. The formal design of the phrases for "Jeannie with the Light Brown Hair" is AABA.

The opening phrase of "Beautiful Dreamer" is eight measures long. Its harmonic progression is circular: it starts and ends on the tonic. This is followed by a B-phrase that is just four measures long. The B-phrase is also circular: it begins and ends on the dominant. Foster returns to the opening melody for a truncated version of the A-phrase. (It is just six measures long.)

The form of "Jeannie with the Light Brown Hair" (Example 69) mimics the formal design of Twentieth-Century Bar Form songs, however, while the phrases of this form are usually eight measures long, the phrases of Mr. Foster's song are shorter. The beginning A-phrases are each just four measures. Stephen Foster varies the second A-phrase to produce a melodic high point at its end. The B-phrase is contrasting in its melodic rhythm, lyrics, and purpose—it is a circular phrase that begins on the dominant harmony and ends on the dominant. Composer Foster repeats the A-phrase at the end of the song. He varies it here again, this time to have it end on a tonic harmony.

I consider both songs as forerunners of the Twentieth-Century Bar Form that I will discuss next.

Example 69: Leadsheet Analysis of "Jeannie with the Light Brown Hair"

Jeannie with the Light Brown Hair

Stephen Foster

While Stephen Foster's song is half the length of typical Twenty-first Century songs in the AABA form, it nevertheless shows the same essential pattern of phrase construction.

In the early part of the twentieth century, American and European songwriters working in popular music began to modify the traditional Bar Form pattern (AAB) in a couple of ways, most importantly by adding a repeat of the A-phrase in the second period (after the B-phrase). These modifications yielded the two-period songs of the Twentieth-Century Bar Form with phrases presented as AABA. Other modifications and variations were made, too.

The formal design of Twentieth-Century Bar Form songs mimics that of the **Rounded Binary Form** found in concert music. The Twentieth-Century Bar Form is the most common form used during the first half of the twentieth century.

The Twentieth-Century Bar Form remains a touchstone amongst professional songwriters. Best-selling songwriters as individual in their styles as Billy Joel ("New York State of Mind"), James Taylor ("Don't Let Me Be Lonely Tonight"), Thelonious Monk (1917-1982), ("Round Midnight"), Carole King and Gerry Goffin (1939-2014), ("Will You Still Love Me Tomorrow"), John Lennon and Paul McCartney ("Yesterday"), Richard Rodgers and Lorenz Hart ("My Funny Valentine"), and Billie Joe Armstrong ("Wake Me Up When September Ends"), have all been successful writing songs in Twentieth-Century Bar Form.

Let's now look in detail of the characteristics of this special form.

The Harmonic Motion of the Periods

The two periods of a Twentieth-Century Bar Form song are balanced and are each sixteen measures long. The A-phrases of a Twentieth-Century Bar Form song are called verses, while the B-phrase is called the bridge.

The verse of a Twentieth-Century Bar Form song is presented twice at the beginning of the song and once again after the bridge. To facilitate the repeat of the verse in the first period the composer will end the first verse on a dominant. To make the transition to the bridge, the composer sounds a dominant in the key of the bridge. Bridges of songs in Twentieth-Century Bar Form are typically composed in a contrasting but complementary key. Bridges for major key songs will most often be in the key of the subdominant or the submediant. In minor key songs, bridges will often be written in the key of the mediant. The bridge ends in such a way as to facilitate an easy transition back to the key of the verse.

The Title is the Hook

Unlike verses in Verse/Chorus songs, verses in Twentieth-Century Bar Form songs always contain the song's lyrical and melodic hook. The lyrical hook of the Twentieth-Century Bar Form song is always the song's title.

The title hook is most often placed at one of two places: either at the beginning of the verse or at the end of the verse. Listen through the Twentieth-Century Bar Form songs I have listed earlier in this chapter. You will find that in the songs, "New York State of Mind," "Don't Let Me Be Lonely," "Will You Still Love Me Tomorrow," and "Wake Me Up When September Ends," the composer places the title hook at the end of the verses. The composers of "Yesterday" and "My Funny Valentine" placed the title hook at the beginning of the verses. A complete sampling of Twentieth-Century Bar Form songs would probably show an equal distribution of title hook placement. Note that lyricists sometimes take liberty with these rules, substituting an exact repetition of the title with a modified version.

A Bridge Provides Contrast

The bridges of all Twentieth-Century Bar Form songs allow contrast in one of two ways: they are in a new key (or will hint at one); and their melodic rhythm will may be different from that of the verses. If the verses feature a melody made up of quick notes the melody of the bridge might have a slower pace and vice versa.

Analysis of "Wake Me Up When September Ends"

Released in 2005 on the band Green Day's album, *American Idiot*, "Wake Me Up When September Ends" (Example 70) is a perfect instance of Twentieth-Century Bar Form. The song, written by lead singer Billie Joe Armstrong and the band, is composed of thirty-two measures that strictly follow the AABA phrase structure.

Twentieth-Century Bar Form

Example 70: Harmonic Motion and Formal Design of "Wake Me Up When September Ends"

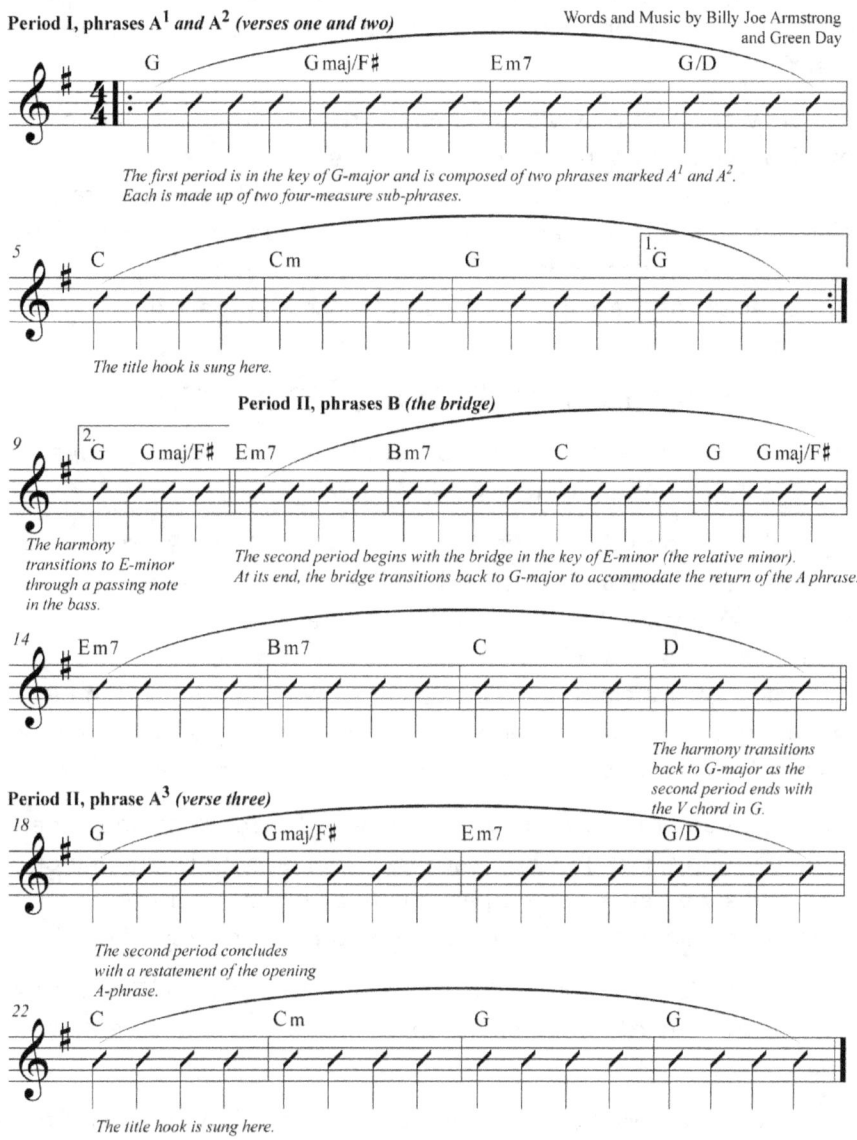

The song begins with an eight-measure A-phrase that is immediately repeated to form the first period of the song. The creators of the song place its title-hook at the end of each iteration of the A-phrase. The second period, like all second periods in Twentieth-Century Bar Form songs, begins with the B-phrase, a bridge of eight measures.

The bridge contrasts with the A-phrase verses. The A-phrases of the original recording are in the key of G major. The bridge begins in the key of E minor, the **relative minor** of G major. The term relative minor or **relative major** is used to describe the relationship between two keys—one major one minor—whose tonics are a major third (or major sixth) apart, where each key shares the same pitch collection.

The bridge of "Wake Me" only visits E minor briefly: it transitions back to the home key of G major almost immediately, in the third measure of the bridge, during the first four-measure sub-phrase. The second four-measure sub-phrase also begins in E minor and transitions back to G major in its third measure. The entire bridge ends on the dominant harmony of G major to facilitate the repeat of the A-phrase to end the second period.

Some Additional Features

Billie Joe Armstrong and his bandmates from Green Day infuse "Wake Me" with two other features common to many pop songs.

First, they make use of a descending bass line. Note that the first beat of the first five measures of the song descends the G scale: G—F♯—E—D—C. The use of a bass line that descends, either diatonically (as is the case in "Wake Me Up When September Ends"), or chromatically (as in our next example) is so often employed in popular music that it can be considered idiomatic. (The British composer, Henry Purcell, employed this bassline technique in, "When I Am Laid in Earth" from his opera *Dido and Aeneas* composed circa 1688.)

The second quite common technique employed by Armstrong and Green Day is to move the harmony from IV (the major subdominant) to iv (the minor subdominant). As we have seen earlier, this is an example of borrowing or modal mixture. In this case, iv (Cm) is borrowed from the key of G minor.

The standard, "My Funny Valentine" (Example 71) from the 1937 Broadway show *Babes in Arms* by Richard Rodgers and Lorenz Hart is also in Twentieth-Century Bar Form.

This song is like "Wake Me Up When September Ends" in that it features a descending bassline and it has a bridge that moves to a relative key. This time, though, the bassline is chromatic and since "My Funny Valentine" is written in minor, its bridge moves to the relative major key.

Twentieth-Century Bar Form

Example 71: Harmonic Motion and Formal Design of "My Funny Valentine"

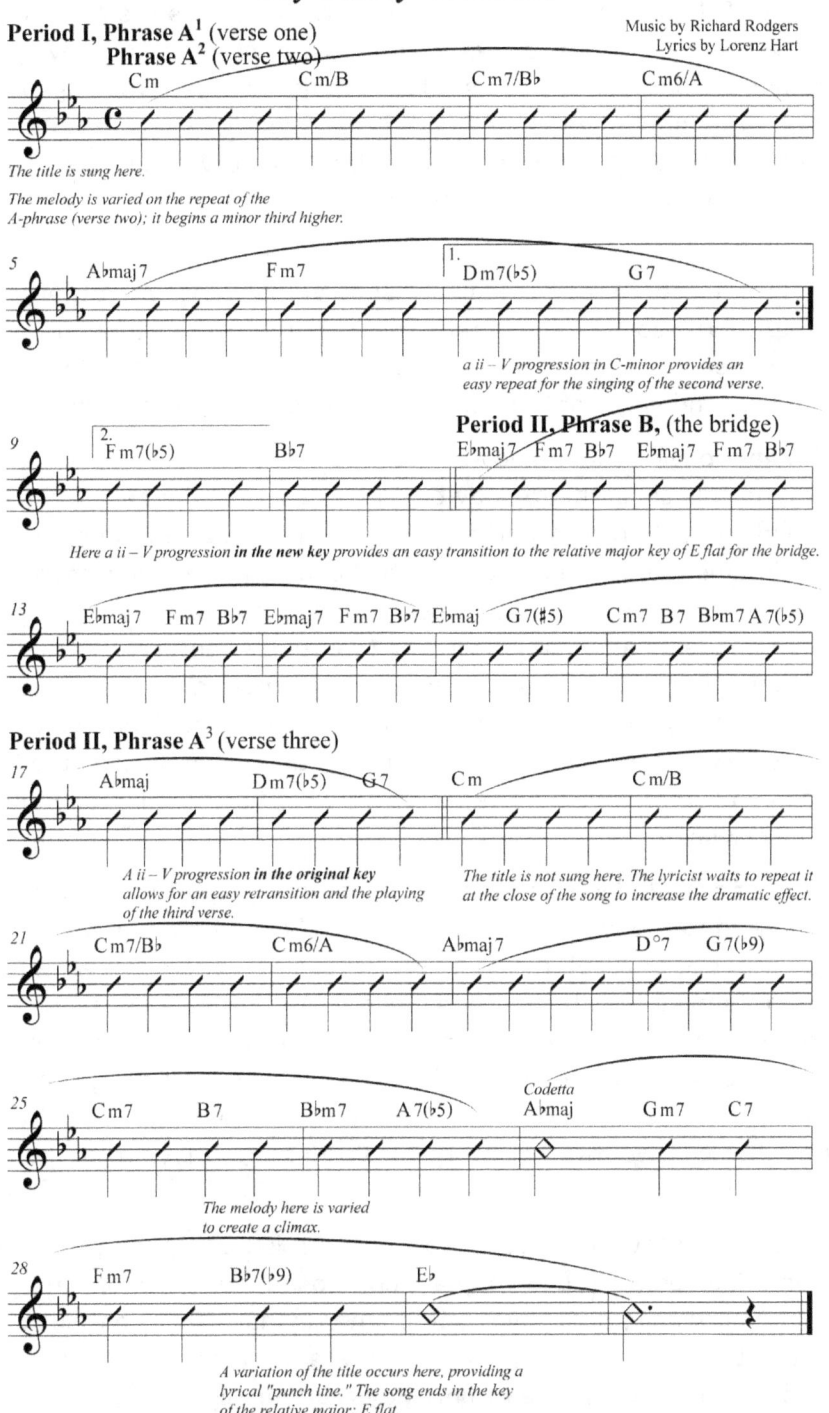

"My Funny Valentine" begins in our example in the key of C minor. The first period is composed of two eight-measure phrases. The first phrase ends on the dominant of C minor, facilitating the repeat. The second A-phrase ends on the dominant of the key of the bridge, E♭ major. E♭ major is the relative major of C minor. As we saw in "Wake Me Up When September Ends," moving harmonically from a minor key to its relative major or vice versa engenders harmonic contrast and a degree of novelty that keeps the listener interested in hearing more of the song. Most listeners will not identify this kind of harmonic change in the same way as will a trained musician, but most do sense that something fresh has happened.

In Chapter Five, I introduced the Plain & Fancy Verse along with other variations of the Verse/Chorus song. You will remember that in these variations the song's second verse is somehow modified. Interestingly, Richard Rodgers modifies the second verse of "My Funny Valentine" in a similar manner.

Richard Rodgers begins the melody of the first verse (Phrase A^1) on the tonic note of key. (In this case, the melody begins on C.) Then, he begins the melody of the second verse (Phrase A^2) on the third of the key, an E♭. Composer Rodgers maintains the listener's comfort by keeping the melodic rhythm mostly the same. Clever. Subtle. Successful. Richard Rodgers, a master musical craftsperson, made small variations in the Twentieth-Century Bar Form to make it his own. In the process, he created songs that have endured for many, many years. To complete the harmonic, melodic and lyrical journey, Rodgers and Hart end "My Funny Valentine" with an uplifting move back to the key of E♭ major. "Each day (with you, my love), is Valentine's Day," (so I'll let you know that in a major way!).

When the composer Rodgers returns us to the home key of C minor in the second and third iterations of the verse, it is likely listeners feel a subconscious sense of relief in having arrived back to where the song began. The feeling of familiarity is further enhanced as Mr. Rodgers begins the melody of verse three (Phrase A^3) on the tonic. The sense of departure, of movement away from the original harmony, and then returning home is a significant feature of the Twentieth-Century Bar Form and often exploited well by songwriters. Not all Twentieth-Century Bar Form songs move to the relative major or minor key.

A song I wrote called "Gentle Heart" (Example 72) is published in a choral arrangement. The verses of this song are composed in the key of A major. The bridge moves, suddenly, to C major. Although they have some pitches in common A, B, D and E), A major and C major are not closely related. This is what music theorists consider a **remote key relationship**.

Twentieth-Century Bar Form
121

Example 72: Moving to Key Other Than Relative Minor for the Bridge

Gentle Heart

Quietly, like a lullaby ♩ = 80
Period I, phrases A¹ and A² (verses one and two)

Words and Music by
Louis Anthony deLise

Gent - le heart, beat - ing quick in - side me(you)
Gent - le hands, that will touch to - mor - row

Verses are in the key of A-major

Grow - ing each day with the Lord's love and Grace.
Car - ing and strong they will share His em - brace.

I have chosen to provide no traditional preparation for the new key coming up in the bridge, C-major.

Period II, phrase B (the bridge)

Lov - ing eyes, full of hope, full of wis - dom

The bridge is in C-major, a key that is considered "distant" from A-major. The distance is softened by my use of the chord progression from the first period transposed to the new key.

The D-minor harmony is common to C-major and A-minor (the parallel minor of A-major). The use of this chord, common in both keys, aids the transition back to the home key.

know - ing the joy His life will bring.

The iv-V⁷ progression allows for the retransition to A-major, the key of the verses. The D-minor 7 chord is "borrowed" from A-minor.

Period II, phrase A³ (verse three)

Gent - le love grow - ing strong in - side me(you)

etc...

I move from the key of the verses to the key of the bridge with no preparation at all, except that in measure eight, the dominant chord, E7, is preceded by the dominant of C major: the G chord. The G chord sounded in the key of A major is quite striking because its root is the flat seven of A major. I will argue that the G chord does resonate with listeners and does, in fact, foreshadow the harmonic move I make to defeat A major and supplant it with the key of C major.

The transition back to the key of A major is convincing and complete as I move in measure seven of the bridge to a minor subdominant (iv) and then the dominant of A major. The minor version of A's subdominant is borrowed from the key of A minor, where one finds a D-minor chord build on the subdominant. I then move (in measure eight) to the dominant of both A major and A minor, E7. Once there, I can easily move the song back to the home key of A major.

Variations

Songwriters do not always strictly follow the rules. We have already seen this in the Rodgers and Hart song "My Funny Valentine," where lyricist Hart does not adhere to the formula I just presented.

Another notable illustration of not following the rules is the song we have discussed before, "Yesterday," by John Lennon and Paul McCartney.

The title "Yesterday" appears at the very start of the song. Just like in "My Funny Valentine," it is the first word of the verse sung over a very powerful but simple melodic motive. The word "yesterday" is also the last word of the first verse.

In the second verse, the melodic motive returns, this time accompanying the word, "suddenly." The word "suddenly" also appears at the end of the second verse. Its appearance at the end is made more poignant as Messrs. Lennon and McCartney make it part of a line using the word, "yesterday."

> "Oh, yesterday came suddenly."

The third verse also begins and ends with the title hook, "Yesterday." The third verse appears, of course, after the bridge. The bridge for "Yesterday" moves harmonically to the relative minor of the home key (the song is in F major; the bridge moves to D minor.)

One might conclude that, while it's a fine idea to learn the rules, judging by the success of "Yesterday" and "My Funny Valentine," it's also a fine idea to break the rules you learn.

The Introductory Verse

Many songs for Broadway shows or movie musicals from the 1920s through the 1950s written in Twentieth-Century Bar Form include an **introductory verse**. An introductory verse is a rambling sixteen- to thirty-two measure period whose lyric sets the stage for the song that is to follow. The introductory verse for "My Funny Valentine" (Example 73) is typical of the periods used to begin many Twentieth-Century Bar Form songs.

Example 73: Introductory Verse of "My Funny Valentine"

Coda and Codetta

The accompaniment of the third verse (A^3) of Twentieth-Century Bar Form songs is usually modified to end the song. Songwriters need to create a verse three that resolves to the tonic harmony on the final chord in the final measure.

Sometimes, though, songwriters will attach a **coda** or **codetta** to strengthen and make more final the end of the piece. Codas in concert music are often long and involved, sometimes including the presentation of new musical material. A codetta is a diminutive version of a coda that can be added to the main part of a song. Its sole purpose is to announce the song's conclusion.

In their original form, "My funny Valentine" and "Yesterday" include a codetta. Following are the codettas for "Yesterday" (Example 74) and "My Funny Valentine" (Example 75).

Example 74: Codetta of "Yesterday"

The codetta ends with the opening rhythmic motive adding continuity to the song.

Example 75: Codetta of "My Funny Valentine"

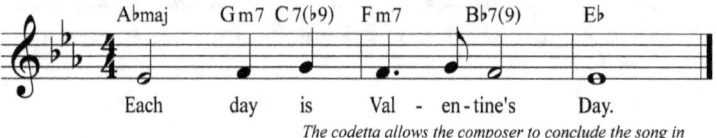

The codetta allows the composer to conclude the song in the relative major key

Other Songs in Twentieth-Century Bar Form

Many other songs have been created in this form. Here are just a few.

- "At Last," Music by Harry Warren and Lyrics by Mack Gordon (1904-1959)
- "Blue Moon," Music by Richard Rodgers and Lyrics by Lorenz Hart
- "Bye Bye Blackbird," Music and Lyrics by Mort Dixon (1892-1956) and Ray Henderson (1896-1970)
- "Five Foot Two, Eyes of Blue," Music and Lyrics by Sam M. Lewis (1885-1959), Joe Young (1889-1939), and Ray Henderson
- "I Get a Kick Out of You," Music and Lyrics by Cole Porter (1891-1964)
- "I Got Rhythm," Music by George Gershwin (1898-1937) and Lyrics by Ira Gershwin (1896-1983)
- "Jingle-Bell Rock," Music and Lyrics by Joe Beal (1900-1967) and Jim Boothe (1917–1976)
- "The Lady is a Tramp," Music by Richard Rodgers and Lyrics by Lorenz Hart

A template of the Twentieth-Century Bar Form is presented in Example 76. On the template, you will find the periods, phrases, and sub-phrases indicated along with the possible locations of the title hook.

Example 76: Twentieth-Century Bar Form Template

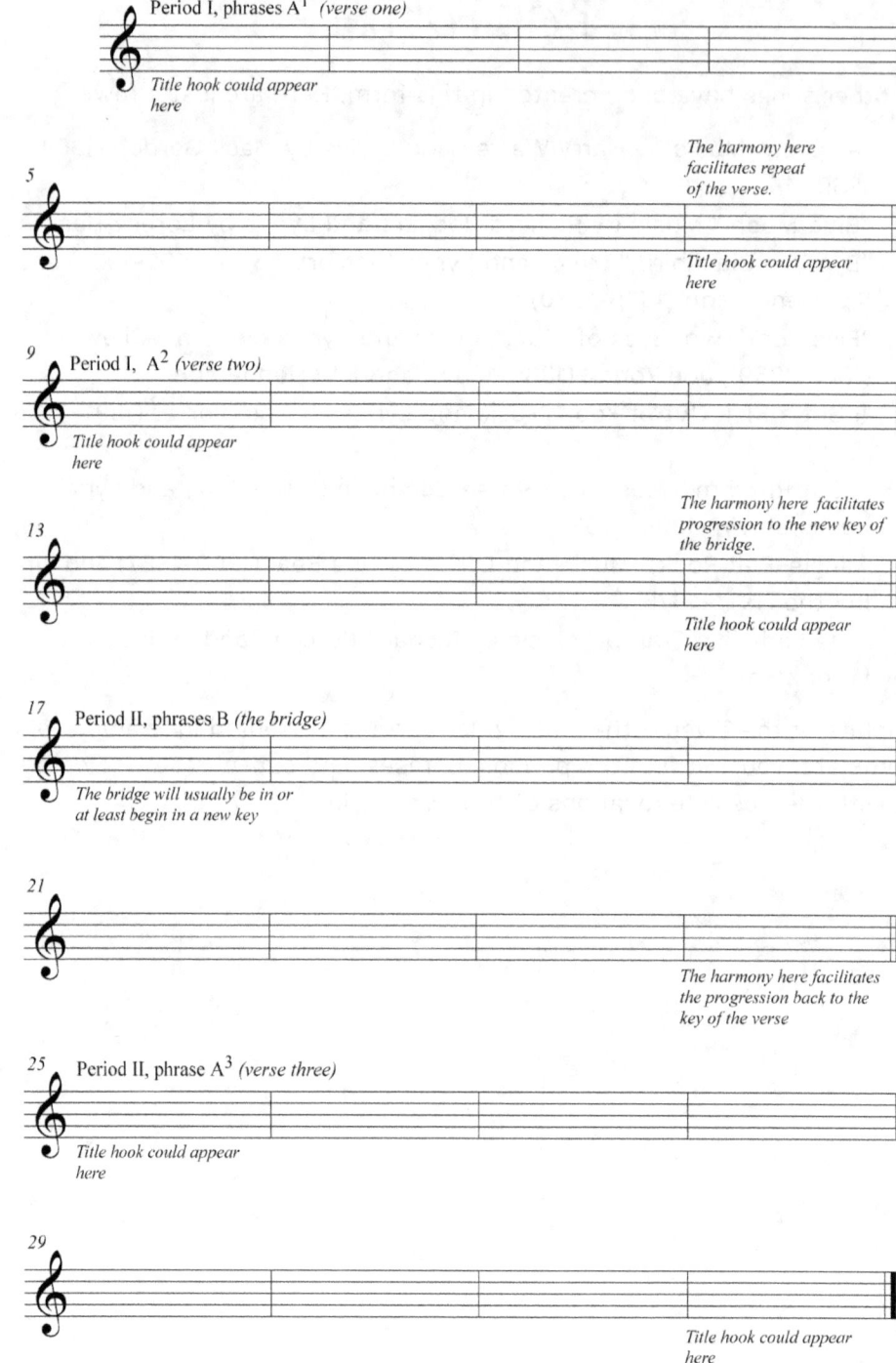

Exercises

In my personal experience coaching aspiring songwriters, I have found that many have difficulties writing songs in Twentieth-Century Bar Form. I suppose this might be because the form is no longer as popular as it once was and is therefore "not in their ears." Many inadvertently compose a Verse/Chorus song instead.

Careful listening and study of the songs mentioned in this chapter will often help with this issue. I heartily encourage you to dissect the songs and listen to classic recordings by singers including Ella Fitzgerald, Frank Sinatra, Tony Bennett, Joe Williams, Nancy Wilson, Mel Tormé, Diana Krall.

Exercise #1

Compose one eight-measure period that can end with either a tonic or a dominant. (It is acceptable to resolve on a tonic and then move to a ii—V cadence.)

Exercise #2

Develop a concise phrase that will become a title hook. Use any of the songs in the supplied list as a model.

Compose only the melodic hook that will accompany this title hook. Compose it in 3/4 meter in a key you are not used to working in. (Guitar players might want to choose a flat key.)

Exercise #3

Using the template in Example 76, compose a hit song in Twentieth-Century Bar Form whose lyrics sing about something other than romantic love. By now, this should be a pretty simple assignment!

Exercise #4

Compose a melody and lyrics to complete this AABA song.

You will need to compose the final eight measures using the material from the first period. Feel free to compose a codetta if you choose.

Chapter Seven

Pop Song Binary Form

Most songs composed in what I call **Pop Song Binary Form** are thirty-two measures long. Like Twentieth-Century Bar Form songs, they are composed of two sixteen-measure periods, however, the layout of the phrases is different. In this chapter I label those periods as "I" and "II."

Each sixteen-measure period consists of two balanced eight-measure phrases. The phrases in the first period are labeled "A" and "B". The phrases for the second period are "A" and "C". See Example 77.

Since the A phrases occur at the beginning of both the first and second periods, this form is said to be a **parallel construction**. This parallel construction yields a phrase structure that lays out as ABAC, where A and B form the first period (I) and A and C form the second period (II).

Example 77: Pop Song Binary Form Template

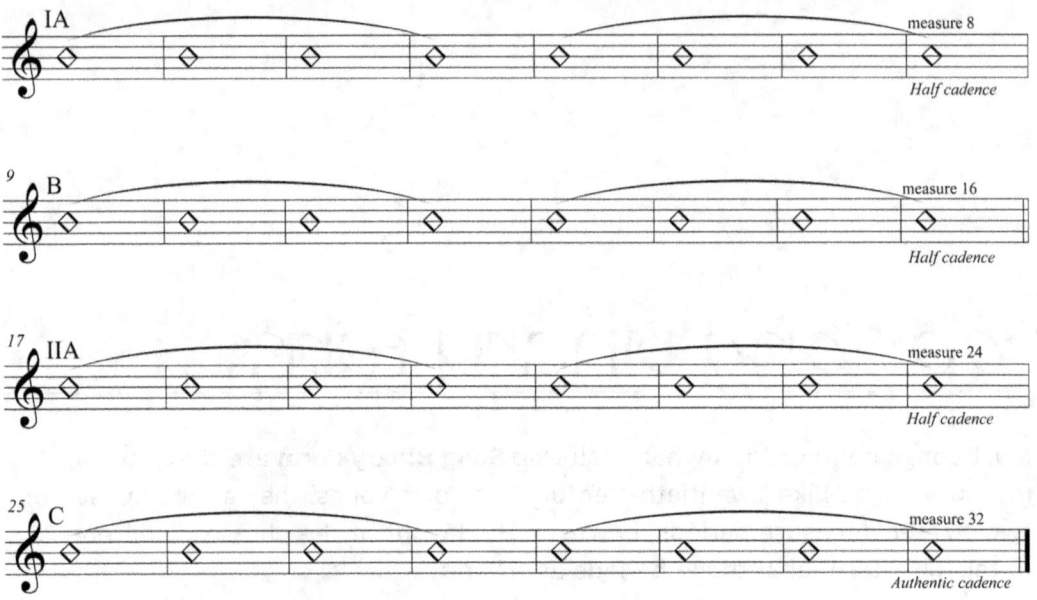

There are four small periods, each eight measures long. They are A, B and C. The small A period is repeated beginning at measure 17.

There are two large periods, each is sixteen measures long. They are marked I and II. Each consists of two smaller (eight measure) periods. Large Period I is measures 1 through 16; Large Period II is measures 17 through 32.

Harmonic Motion and Cadences

The Pop Song Binary Form is all about delaying resolution. The main goal of the composer writing in this form is to avoid a final sounding authentic cadence. An authentic cadence is a harmonic progression moving from the dominant to the tonic. In well-written Pop Binary songs, the authentic cadence is delayed until the very end of the song.

Delayed Lyrical Conclusion

In every Pop Binary Form song there are a few concluding words in the last line that sum up the song's sentiment. This lyrical "punch line" also includes a restatement of the song's title. Let's look at some examples of lyrics for songs in this venerable form. We will begin with "The Days of Wine and Roses," (Example 78) a song written by lyricist Johnny Mercer and composer Henry Mancini.

Example 78: Lyrics "The Days of Wine and Roses"

The Days of Wine and Roses (by lyricist Johnny Mercer and composer Henry Mancini)

IA
> The Days of Wine and Roses
> laugh and run away,
> like a child at play

B
> Through a meadowland toward a closing door,
> A door marked, "never more,"
> That wasn't there before.

IIA
> The lonely night discloses
> Just a passing breeze,
> filled with memories

C
> Of the golden smile that introduced me to,
> The Days of Wine and Roses...

A beautiful love affair has ended. All that is left are the wonderful memories of the "golden smile" that caught the narrator's eye and began this romance with libation and flowers. The very object of the singer's affection, the lover whose smile is golden, is not mentioned until the closing line of the lyric when she sings, "...and you."

By making this song's lyric non-specific, Mercer makes it universal. He could have named names ("The wine I shared with Shirley"?), but he wisely chose not to. Instead, Mercer created a lyric that most adults can understand at a visceral level.

Let us analyze another. "Here's That Rainy Day" (Example 79) is a song written by composer Jimmy Van Heusen (1913-1990), and lyricist Johnny Burke (1908-1964), for the 1953 Broadway show, *Carnival in Flanders*.

This Pop Binary song, like many in this form, is very popular amongst thoughtful creative musicians. We will look at the lyrics for "Rainy Day" and come back to the music for this one and "Wine and Roses" later.

Example 79: Lyrics "Here's That Rainy Day"

Here's That Rainy Day (Lyrics by Johnny Burke)

IA

Maybe I should have saved those leftover dreams,
Funny, but Here's That Rainy Day.

B

Here's that rainy day they told me about,
And I laughed at the thought that it might turn out this way.

IIA

Where is that worn out wish that I threw aside,
After it brought my lover near?

C

Funny, how love becomes a cold, rainy day.
Funny that rainy day is here.

In "Here's That Rainy Day," Johnny Burke weaves another recollection of love gone sour. Using the metaphor of a rainy day to represent love lost, Burke paints a sad tale that matches well Van Heusen's poignant melody and harmony. This is what the narrator was warned about, and he dismissed: if one loves, one can be hurt. Chagrined, the narrator admits in the final line of the lyric that, indeed, that "rainy day is here." This is the not-so-funny punch line, the kicker, of this great standard.

Not all Pop Binary songs have sad lyrics. The song "My Romance" mentioned earlier, is from the Broadway musical and Hollywood film, *Jumbo*. Composer Richard Rodgers and lyricist Lorenz Hart wrote it. In "My Romance" the writers sing about love gone *right*!

In his book *Songcrafters' Coloring Book*, Grammy-winning songwriter and author Bill Pere describes songs with lyrics like those in "My Romance" as **list**

songs. In a list song, the lyricist presents a collection of things, feelings, or thoughts that supports her thesis.

In "My Romance" (Example 80), lyricist Hart beautifully enumerates all the many things that his romance does not need. Then, at the kicker in the last line of the lyric, Mr. Hart writes that his romance "doesn't need a thing but you." The writers create so many beautiful images in this lyric and then dismiss them out of hand as being unnecessary to achieve romantic fulfillment. Thankfully, the only component the singer truly needs is their lover.

Many Pop Binary songs mention the title hook very few times. In "Here's That Rainy Day" and "The Days of Wine and Roses" the lyricists mention the title at only the beginnings and ends of the songs. This is often the case in Pop Binary songs. This is not the case with "My Romance." The title hook lyric appears in almost every phrase of the song.

Example 80: Lyrics "My Romance"

My Romance (Lyrics by Lorenz Hart)

IA

My Romance doesn't have to have a moon in the sky
My Romance doesn't need a blue lagoon standing by

B

No month of May, no twinkling stars.
No hideaway, no soft guitars.

IIA

My Romance doesn't need a castle rising in Spain
Nor a dance to a constantly surprising refrain

C

Wide awake, I can make my most fantastic dreams come true.
My Romance doesn't need a thing but you!

Harmonic and Melodic Analysis of "The Days of Wine and Roses"

In "The Days of Wine and Roses" (Example 81), Mancini begins each phrase with a pick-up note or two. This gives the song a sense of forward movement and is a balance for the many long notes of the great melody. Each eight-measure phrase is divided into two four-measure sub-phrases (note that I have indicated that the phrases begin with the pick-up notes).

Example 81: Harmonic and Phrasal Analysis "The Days of Wine and Roses"

"The Days of Wine and Roses"
Music by Henry Mancini
Lyrics by Johnny Mercer

Like all double binary songs, "The Days of Wine and Roses" is composed of a total of thirty-two measures, arranged in four eight-measure periods. There are half cadences at the end of each eight-measure period, except for the final period (C). It ends with an authentic cadence in the home key.

© 1962 Warner Bros. Inc.

Mr. Mancini's harmony is chock-full of allusions to other key centers and modal mixture, combining in one phrase the harmonies common in more than one mode. For instance, in measure two he writes an E♭9. This is an extremely provocative chord to introduce in the very beginning of a song in F major! Because it is constructed on the flatted seventh degree of the scale, it immediately defeats the sense of F major tonality. "Where is he going, harmonically?" is what a listener's subconscious might ask. The E♭9 proceeds immediately to a D7 chord, causing me to realize that Mancini was thinking of the E♭9 as a tritone substitution for D chord's normal dominant. (Or, my classical theory geek's mind reminds that I could hear this dominant ninth chord as a kind of enharmonically spelled German augmented sixth chord, of course.) Either way, by moving to the D7 chord, Henry Mancini arrives at the dominant 7 of ii, which was his harmonic target all along.

Henry Mancini uses a half cadence to end each phrase, as is common in Pop Binary songs. However, at the end of both A-phrases, the half cadence he writes is in A♭ major, not F major. Then, instead of resolving on A♭ major, he resolves to A minor, the harmony a tritone away.

The tritone abounds in "Wine and Roses." In measures two and eight, and again in measures eighteen and twenty-four, the melody note, A, is written. This pitch is an augmented fourth above the chord root E♭ and demonstrates Mancini's further use of modal mixture, this time borrowing from the Lydian mode.

Like all Pop Binary songs, Mancini and Mercer create a climax in the melody and lyric near the end of the song. In "The Days of Wine and Roses," the melodic and lyrical climax occurs at measures twenty-seven and twenty-eight on the word "to." The melody note E♮ is the leading tone in this key and is the highest note of the song. The composer follows the climax with a gentle winding down of the melody over the next two measures. He gently lands the melody on the tonic to accompany the final word of the song, "you."

Other Songs in Pop Binary Song Form

Many other songs have been created in this form. Here are just a few:

- "A Day in the Life of a Fool," Music by Luiz Bonfá (1922-2001) and Lyrics by Carl Sigman (1909-2000)
- "All of Me," Music by Seymour Simons and Lyrics Gerald Marks (1900-1997)
- "Bill Bailey Won't You Please Come Home?" Music and Lyrics by Hughie Cannon (1877-1912)
- "But Not For Me," Music by George Gershwin and Lyrics by Ira Gershwin
- "I Thought About You," Music by Jimmy Van Heusen and Lyrics by Johnny Mercer
- "Emily," Music by Johnny Mandel (1925-) and Lyrics by Johnny Mercer
- "Someday My Prince Will Come," Music by Frank Churchill (1901-1942) and Lyrics by Larry Morey (1905-1971)
- "There Will Never Be Another You," Music by Harry Warren and Lyrics by Mack Gordon (1904-1959)
- "Yesterdays," Music by Jerome Kern (1885-1945) and Lyrics by Otto Harbach (1873-1963)
- "I'll See You in My Dreams," Music by Isham Jones (1894-1956) and Lyrics by Gus Kahn (1886-1941)
- "Laura," Music by David Raksin (1912-2004) and Lyrics by Johnny Mercer
- "Lullaby of Broadway," Music by Harry Warren and Lyrics by Al Dubin

A careful reader will no doubt notice that none of the songs mentioned in this chapter are newer than the early 1960s. Sad, that! I think that the Pop Song Binary form is wonderfully useful, especially as its lyric leads the listener to the song's end waiting for the punch line. It is admittedly more difficult to work with than the ubiquitous Verse/Chorus form, but if mastered, the results can be magnificent! Perhaps it is time for the Pop Song Binary form to make a comeback...

Pop Song Binary Form

Exercises

There is only one assignment for this chapter.
Use the template below to create several songs in the Pop Song Binary Form.

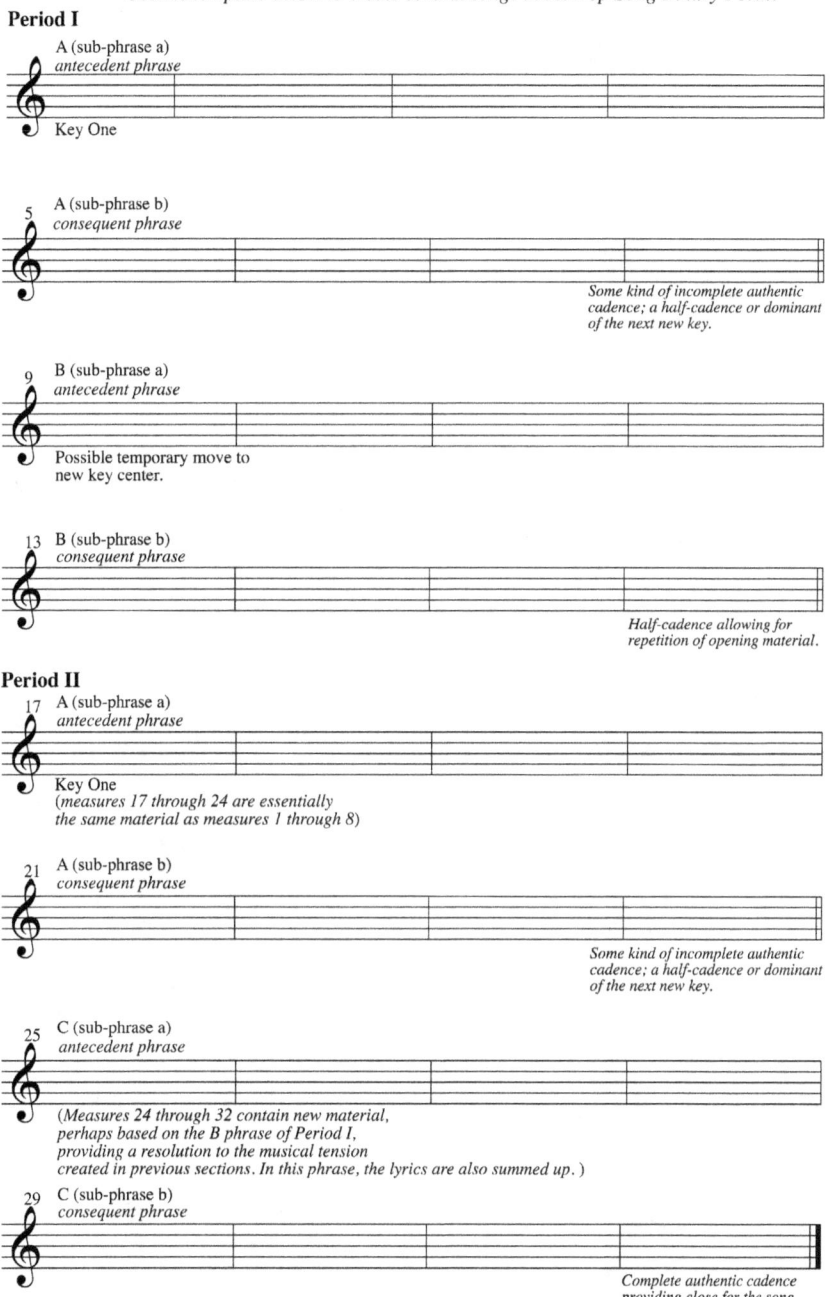

Chapter Eight

Lyrics

A song's lyrics engage the listener, creating a direct connection to the writer's heart (or at least her mind). But good lyrics do not only speak to the listener, they speak *on behalf of* the listener, and provide an opportunity for the listener to identify with the singer. The singer acts as a kind of Everyman who puts into song what we all sometimes feel but very often cannot quite find the right words to express. The most effective and successful songs have lyrics that are supported by music that touches the listener at a core emotional level.

The Most Important Link to the Listener

Melody, harmony, and rhythm work together with lyrics to communicate to listeners emotionally and intellectually. Humans give meaning to music because of many things, including learned interpretations, social context, habit and, according to researcher Elizabeth Tolbert of the Peabody Conservatory, "conditions that are biologically grounded in our evolutionary history." Musical meaning is sensed on a primal level, as is touch and smell. Sound, in this case melody and accompaniment, quite literally moves the listener. But no matter how catchy or memorable, music without words remains abstract in its meaning. A song's lyrics supply something concrete that most listeners immediately understand and remember. The rest (the vocal performance, the accompaniment, and the production) they "get" on some subconscious feeling level.

One Big Thought Said Plainly

Lyrics are best when written in vernacular language. Everyday easily understood language sets the most direct course for the songwriter's message. Songs can be about most anything, but must always express just one emotion—happiness, sadness, love, hate, fear, hope, agitation, or sorrow. Even songs with lots of patter (the term music people use to describe wordy, rapid-fire lyrics) must contain just one message (Example 82).

Billy Joel's song, "We Didn't Start the Fire," is very wordy! The message is simple, though: the world is a mess—we did not make it this way!

Example 82: Lyrics to "We Didn't Start the Fire"

"We Didn't Start the Fire" written by Billy Joel

Verse:
> Harry Truman, Doris Day, Red China, Johnnie Ray,
> South Pacific, Walter Winchell, Joe DiMaggio,
> Joe McCarthy, Richard Nixon, Studebaker, television
> North Korea, South Korea, Marilyn Monroe,
> Rosenbergs, H-bomb, Sugar Ray, Panmunjom
> Brando, "The King and I" and "The Catcher in the Rye"
> Eisenhower, vaccine, England's got a new queen,
> Marciano, Liberace, Santayana goodbye

Chorus:
> We didn't start the fire
> It was always burning
> Since the world's been turning
> We didn't start the fire
> No we didn't light it
> But we tried to fight it

There are many things to notice about this infinitely clever lyric.

Mr. Joel creates a sense of controlled confusion with his list of names and things sung in patter. From the start, we have no real clear idea what is happening. The words are familiar, but why are they juxtaposed as they are? We do not know, and we will not know until the singer gets us to the chorus.

The confusion is made appealing for a few reasons. First, the words chosen are titillating and their juxtaposition, provocative. Next, Billy Joel seasons the list with an occasional internal rhyme:

> (Doris) *Day*, (Johnny) *Ray*, (North) *Korea*, (South) *Korea*; "(The King and) *I*" and "(The Catcher in the) *Rye*;" *vaccine* and *queen*.

Rhymes help anchor a lyric and, along with the melodic rhythm, help the listener hear and remember what is being sung.

The meaning of the words of the verse is made clearer once the title is sung in the chorus, "We Didn't Start the Fire." Somehow, all these other folks and things started the metaphorical fire, not us. The lyrics of the chorus support the proposition put forth in the title: this mess has always been with us and, try as we might to alter the condition of the human experience, it is still pretty much a mess.

The Title in the Hook

Lyrical hooks in successful songs always include the song's title. (Actually, there may be a song whose title does not appear in the lyrics, but I cannot remember it. Ergo the problem with not including the title in the lyrics.)

Lyrical hooks draw listeners in and help them remember a song. Lyrical hooks are typically short phrases of words that are coupled with a melodic motive. A **melodic motive** is a short, rhythmically impressive, and memorable melodic fragment. The lyrical hook of "We Didn't Start the Fire" is its title. As is the case with many Verse/Chorus songs, the title of this song appears at the very beginning of the chorus. The primacy of this placement and its repetition supplies its import.

The lyrics to Billy Joel's "We Didn't Start the Fire" are much more dense than are the lyrics to most popular songs. Lyrics are generally more like the sentiments on a greeting card than they are like a scholarly poem. Pop song lyrics need to be easily grasped and remembered because music is ephemeral: it occurs in the performance and then vanishes into the ether. Poems, even those that are read aloud, are read, pondered for their meaning, and sometimes read again. A reader can return to a line or a stanza without much difficulty. Song lyrics are "once and done" until the next time the song is played.

Lyrics, a Composite of the Writer's Experience

Successful song lyrics are theatrical events staged in the theater of the listener's mind. To express a feeling, describe an event, or memorialize a person. Lyricists will draw from their experiences, including movies and television shows they have viewed, books they have read, events they have been part of, and other songs they have heard.

What about inspiration?

Songwriting can be the product of inspiration but writing only when inspired is not a good career plan. It is much more helpful to have a desire to express something in a novel way coupled with ability and craft (borne of talent and training), coupled with significant effort. Writing is hard and often lonely work. The experience of hearing the product of that work, a performance, or a recording of a song you wrote, is fun. That is probably why we keep at it!

When I was working as a percussionist in a symphony orchestra, I had the pleasure of playing a series of shows with the great lyricist Sammy Cahn. He told the audience he was once asked, "What comes first, the music or the lyrics?" The master wordsmith quickly replied, "Neither! It's the phone call that comes first." What I believe Mr. Cahn meant was, give me a good reason to devote my talent and artistry to this painful exercise. Tell me the goal and provide some parameters. Then, I will put in the sincere and dedicated effort, devote my significant talent, and draw on my experience and expertise to craft a unique product that fulfills the assignment.

The Subject of Your Song

Songs can be about most anything; an idea for a song can come from anywhere. Characters and plot lines can be drawn from life experiences including people-watching, reading or classic scenarios recast in your personal voice.

Whatever the subject matter, lyrics always express one clear message that is best summed up in the song's title. The title and the singular message of the song are supported and amplified in the remainder of the song's lyrics. Any line or word that does not substantively further the essential message of the title does not belong in the song and must be edited out.

Where do ideas come from? Everywhere and anywhere: newspapers, blogs, magazines, television, conversations overheard...and other songs.

Something to Write About

When no one is calling to commission a song, you can create your own commission by setting up parameters of a proposed song. Defining what you propose to write might go something like this, "I want to write a song that has the same kind of gist as some other song." Or, "I want to write a song in G minor that has the feel of an updated version of James Brown's (1933-2006), "On the Good Foot."

By defining the parameters of your proposed song, you will avoid the most frightening aspect of a professional life in a creative occupation: **The Blank Page**.

Many writers, composers and songwriters included, become paralyzed when offered the opportunity to write *anything*. The paralysis is made worse only when one is working on a commission and the client says, "Oh, you know what to do. Just write anything." Rest assured, there is a great possibility that whatever you write will be wrong!

By creating a set of rules for what your proposed song is *not* going to be, you are clearly defining what it *can* be. Other things you might want to define at the beginning of the creative songwriting process include what kind of singer you are writing for, who your audience might be, what genre you are writing in, what the tempo will be, what the instrumentation might be and so on. By placing limits on our creative selves, we speed along a writing process that might otherwise languish.

> **Note**
>
> Many great songs are new versions of existing stories or ideas.

Let's look at a song I co-wrote with Philip Hardin (1957-) as a case study.

Phil came to my studio one afternoon in February or March with some good ideas for a Christmas cha-cha that was also a love song.

I thought these were outstanding concepts and quickly suggested we might model the song's lyric after the story related in the Christmas pop classic, "I Saw Mommy Kissing Santa Claus." I also suggested we write in a major key and in a Twentieth-Century Bar Form (AABA).

We had it all: the form, the feel, the tempo, the lyrical concept, and the kind of singer (it had to be a woman with a cute, but solid pop-mezzo). All we needed now was thirty-two measures of hit melody and accompaniment and a bunch of words that said the same kind of things as "I Saw Mommy Kissing Santa Claus," but in a unique, un-plagiarizing way! In a little more than an hour, Phil and I had created the song "Nick and Me" (Example 83).

In no way does "Nick and Me" resemble its model, except that the narrator expresses affection for this person pretending to be St. Nicholas.

Such modeling is not the exception, it is the usual. As the Italian scholar, Umberto Eco wrote,

> Until then I had thought each book spoke of things, human or divine, that lie outside books. Now I realize that not infrequently books speak of books; it is as if they spoke among themselves.

In the same way, songs speak to other songs; songwriters often model their new creations on those of other songwriters.

Lyrics   145

Example 83: Leadsheet for "Nick and Me"

The Prosody of the Lyrics Must Match the Rhythm of the Melody

A listener's ability to understand a lyric is lessened when a word in that lyric is incorrectly accented. The rhythm of the language, called prosody, must match the melodic rhythm. Lyricists must conform the rhythm and accents of their lyrics to the rhythm and accents in the melody otherwise the words will be misheard and misunderstood by the listener.

For instance, the word *romance* can be pronounced with the strong accent occurring on either the first or second syllable,

ró-mance, or
ro-**mancé**.

Ah, what to do? Two different songwriting teams answered the question.

In the great standard of 1936, "A Fine Romance" (Example 84) by composer Jerome Kern and lyricist, Dorothy Fields (1904-1974), the word is accented on the first syllable. In the Rodgers and Hart song, "My Romance" (Example 85), the word is accented on the second syllable.

Example 84: Opening Line of "A Fine Romance"

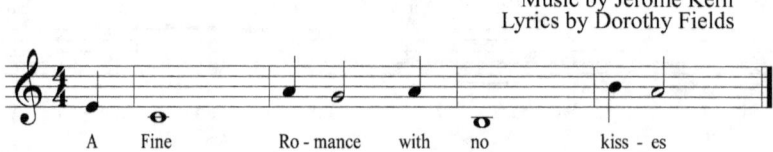

Example 85: Opening Line of "My Romance"

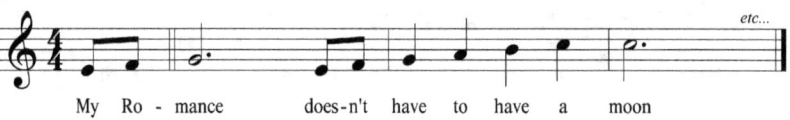

In both songs, the lyricist handles the issue of the lyrical prosody by placing the accented syllable on the **downbeat** of the measure. In Western pop music, the first beat of the measure is given the strongest accent.

Placement of the Title

As we have seen, the title is the most important lyric of the song. It telegraphs to the listener, in a few words, what the song is about and equips the listener with a shorthand method for remembering the song, and how to search for it when they want to hear it and buy it. It is the most important bit of information that songwriters and their publishers want the public to take away.

Song titles are placed in particular positions based on the song form. Table 7 shows title placement in the lyric.

Table 7: Title Placement Based on Form

Form	Title Placement
Single Period Form (AAA)	The title will be placed at the start of the first phrase ("Amazing Grace")
Twelve-Bar Blues Form	The title will be placed at the start of the first phrase ("Backwater Blues")
Verse/Chorus Form (ABAB)	The title will be placed at the beginning or the end of the chorus, or in both places. The lyricist may also choose to place the title at the end of the verse or pre-chorus, just before the chorus ("*We Didn't Start the Fire*").
Twentieth-Century Bar Form (AABA)	The title will be placed at the beginning or the end of the A sections and almost never in the bridge ("*Nick and Me*").
Pop Song Binary Form	The title will be placed at the start of the first period, and often at the start of the second period and at the conclusion of the song ("*My Romance*").

Rhyming and Other Poetic Devices Used in Lyrics

Like most poetry, song lyrics often include rhymes. When words rhyme, listeners notice them. Rhymes echo in the listener's mind and help emphasize certain points and make the language of the song memorable.

Two words, or the final syllables of two words, are said to rhyme if they sound exactly alike. When lyricists place rhymes at the end of a line of text, this is called an **end rhyme** or **terminal rhyme**. When a lyricist rhymes a word in the middle of a line of text with the last word of a line, or if two words in the middle of a line rhyme, it is called an **internal rhyme** or a **middle rhyme**. Full

rhymes, also called **ordinary rhymes**, are two words or the final syllables of two words, that are sung or said exactly alike (Example 86).

Example 86: Some Words That Rhyme

> Bracket/Jacket/Packet
> Ice/Price/Nice/Dice
> Dagger/Swagger/Stagger
> Apprehend/Defend/Attend/Amend
> Mellow/Cello/Fellow/Yellow

Half Rhymes

Songwriters sometimes find themselves in a creative situation where a full rhyme is just not possible. Instead, they fashion a **half rhyme** or **imperfect rhyme**. These word pairs almost rhyme, but really do not. Half rhymes (sometimes also called **slant rhymes**) are word pairs that end with the same consonant, but do not share the same preceding vowel sound. I believe that half rhymes are less good and are to be avoided in crafting your lyrics. The words *moon* and *run* do not rhyme, only their last consonants are the same. They are half rhymes when paired as a couplet, as are the words *bridge* and *grudge*, and *self-assured* and *doors*. This last word pair, *self-assured* and *doors* are from the closing couplet of the John Lennon and Paul McCartney song, "Help!"

> But these days are gone, I'm not so self-assured,
> Now I find I've changed my mind, I've opened up the doors.

It is very hard to argue that the Beatles were at all injured using this half rhyme. But it is the only couplet in the song that is not a full rhyme. Could John Lennon or Paul McCartney come up with a line that rhymes? Considering their vast output and masterworks like "Yesterday" and "Here, There and Everywhere," it is likely they could. But, even in their seminal "Eleanor Rigby" there is a half rhyme:

> ...as he walks from the grave
> no one was saved.

Ah, the lovely lyrics. Where do they all belong? No one is perfect, but I do like the challenge of making words work well. My advice: try to rhyme, unless you have Sir George Martin producing your album and a company like EMI Records underwriting your project.

The words, *day* and *grey* are technically also considered half rhymes (at least in the British spelling of grey), since they are not spelled the same. For the purposes of song lyrics though, where it is the sound of things that matters, they are perfectly acceptable words to pair, as are *pack* and *maniac*, and *pain* and *campaign*.

Polysyllabic Rhymes

In **polysyllabic rhymes**, the last two or three syllables match exactly (See Example 87).

Example 87: Polysyllabic Rhymes

elation/sensation
intersection/affection
feline/beeline/streamline
addiction/benediction/affliction
laborious/victorious
sufficiency/deficiency

A special kind of invented polysyllabic rhyme can be found in the very old song, "I Can't Give You Anything But Love." In the first stanza of this 1928 tune by composer Jimmy McHugh (1894-1969) and lyricist Dorothy Fields, Ms. Fields constructs a polysyllabic rhyme for the word "Happiness" by rhyming it with a half rhyme on the "-i-" of "happiness" (pronounced as a long ē) and a full rhyme on "–ness":

Dream a while...scheme a while
You're sure to find...happiness and I guess...

Such an old song! "Why include it here as an example?" you ask. Because this relic from the roaring twenties was recorded so many times—we should all be so lucky—it deserves scrutiny. Most recently, "I Can't Give You Anything But Love" was included the album *Cheek to Cheek* (released in 2014), in a duet by Tony Bennett and Lady Gaga (1986-). Let's hope that one of your songs is still being recorded eighty-six years after you write it!

Assonance

The literary device known as **assonance** takes place when two words that are in proximity share the same vowel sound but start with different consonant sounds. The repetition of vowel sounds can create internal rhyming within the line, as is the case with the words *reticence* and *penitence*.

The opening line of the song, "Everything Happens to Me," with music by Matt Dennis (1914-2002) and lyrics by Tom Adair (1913-1988), contains three words that create assonance,

"I make a date for golf and you can bet your life it rains."

The words, *make*, *date* and *rains* all have a long ā sound. The assonance in this line helps make it memorable.

Alliteration

Words are said to be **alliterative** if they have the same starting letter or sound and are placed adjacent or near each other. For instance, the quick succession of "b's" in the title hook of the song, "Bye, Bye Blackbird" with music by Ray Henderson (1896-1970) and lyrics by Mort Dixon (1892-1952), are alliterative as are the "L's" in the Bacharach and David song, "The Look of Love."

Rhyme Schemes

As we have seen in our analysis of the various song forms, lyricists most often create lyrics that have a distinct rhyme scheme. We use letters to identify the pattern of the rhymes in lines of lyrics. Many rhyme schemes are possible.

Table 8: Possible Patterns for a Four-Line Lyric

Pattern
ABAB
AABB
AAAA
ABBA
AxAA
AxxA
xAxA

("x" is used here to indicate the absence of a rhyme)

Exercises

Exercise #1

Create a syllable-by-syllable analysis of the lyrics for one of your favorite pop tunes by transcribing the lyrics onto a new sheet of paper. Place a hyphen between each polysyllabic word. For instance, "Philadelphia" would become "Phil-a-del-phi-a."

Using your syllabic analysis as a guide, create a new lyric with the same syllable count. For instance, "Philadelphia" has five syllables. It could be replaced by another five-syllable word or by a phrase like, "You and I are one."

Exercise #2

Use the lyric you created in Exercise #1 as the basis for a new song. I suggest you build your new song in a very different style, key, and tempo as the original song you analyzed.

Exercise #3

Begin a list of potential original song titles that incorporate alliteration as a key element, as does "Philadelphia Freedom," "Sexy Sadie," "Cuckoo Cocoon" and "Jumpin' Jack Flash."

Exercise #4

Begin a list of potential original song titles that use colloquial expressions, like "Nine to Five," "I Got It Bad (And That Ain't Good)," and "One in a Million."

Exercise #5

Compose a story song.

Go somewhere public where you can observe people: a park, a train station, a museum, or a diner (I prefer "greasy spoons" for this exercise. Don't order more than coffee in consideration of your health, though). Sit. Watch. Listen. Learn.

Then, choose a person about whom to write. Next, write in prose about an imagined episode from your main character's life–past, present, or future.

The next step is to reduce your story to a single thought that can become your title. See, at this point, if your prose story and title can inspire you to create a lyric and a tune or part of a lyric and tune.

Chapter Nine

Reasons to Write, Methods to Monetize

The American composer, Ned Rorem, was once asked the question, "Why do you compose the way you do?" His reply was, "Why do I compose?" Then he added:

> Less from self-expression than because I want to be an audience to something that will satisfy me. The act dispels the smokescreen between my ego and reality. However my gifts may seem a luxury to others, I compose for my own necessity, because no one else makes quite the sound I wish to hear.

A Reason to Write

Perhaps most of us who compose do so to fill a need we perceive. We want to hear certain music at a certain time, so we sing it into existence. The experience of singing music into existence often happens first in families. Parents and other adults sing songs to the children in their care to make mundane, everyday tasks feel special, to mark occasions like marriages, births, and funerals, and to create and maintain traditions. Some of the songs that adults sing to kids are classic family songs, like the "Guten Abend, Gute Nacht" ("Cradle Song" or "Lullaby" by Johannes Brahms) or "Row, Row, Row Your Boat," but moms and dads also spontaneously make up the songs they sing to the children in their lives.

Caretakers often partner routine events like going to sleep with newly created tunes. Apparently, children learn this creative impulse quickly, as toddlers can readily be observed imitating their parents as they make up songs in play with their friends.

Researcher Dr. Lori A. Custodero, of Teachers College at Columbia University in New York, believes that parents across all cultures make expressive, nonverbal vocalizations to their children. Dr. Custodero observed that children respond in kind to singing, thus they complete a circuit that she says is often one of the first ways human beings relate to one another. She postulates that parents from all civilizations sing lullabies and other songs to their children and that children from all civilizations spontaneously make up songs as they play. It's easy to imagine that this song-creating urge began with our early ancestors thousands of years ago.

Songs That Fill a Void

Songs are composed for many purposes and are used in many ways. Certainly, at its core, the need for humans to make music with their mouths probably has to do with our urge to tell people how we feel. Most of the songs we compose have lyrics that explain our feelings about something, be it a lover, a car, a political ideology, or a can of tuna fish.

For some, composing is a spiritual activity, or a pursuit borne out of a spiritual experience. Whatever one's personal spiritual bent, it seems that music does communicate on a deeper, subconscious, and mostly unexplainable level. Music can be transformational, coming from a place of deep emotional reflection and experienced by listeners at their essential core.

Fame and Fortune

An obvious byproduct of composing a song that becomes hugely popular is the twin likelihood that the writer will become famous and make a lot of money. These lofty goals may very well be reasonable to some, but if this is the "why" behind your urge to make music, forget it. Consider seriously a career in hedge funds or speculative real estate development.

The truth is I have never met a hit-writing songwriter whose primary goal was to become rich and famous. Hit writers with whom I have worked, Eric Bazilian (1953-), William DeVaughn, Lzzy Hale, Robert Hazard (1948-2008), Bobby Eli (1946-) and Patti LaBelle (1944-), wrote songs because they liked to, were great at it and felt they had something to say in a unique way.

I do not mean to imply that financial gain and notoriety are not desirable or that these very successful tunesmiths did not desire financial solvency. It is only that I believe success is measured in many ways. Becoming rich and famous are but two.

Studying music, becoming proficient as a composer, performer, arranger, or producer—or all of these—is a reward in itself. Learn about the business of music, too, and you might find that you can make a significant part of, or all of, a good income from your art. Pursuing any artistic expression for the cause of becoming wealthy is a fool's game that will yield massive frustration and likely result in your working in some other field anyway.

But financial success can happen.

You can write a song that becomes popular and that can lead to financial rewards. However, the surest way to succeed is to honor yourself and the art of music by becoming better than most at musical self-expression. Anything less is a get-rich-quick scheme.

End of sermon! Let's look at some of the ways people use songs.

Common and Novel Ways People Use Songs

Ask any ten folks on the street to define accomplishment in music and you will likely find that seven or eight of them will mention having a hit record as *the* measure of success. Popular culture, television, and film do little to dissuade people of this notion. Left out of films and television shows are stories of all the great musicians who work behind the scenes to help craft and polish aspiring writers' and artist's products. Similarly, the stories of the thousands of creative musicians who compose songs for other reasons than making a hit record are also not generally told. But the truth is that there are many excellent musicians who craft music that does not hit, and a lot of music that does hit is just plain awful.

In the early chapters of this book, I wrote about the how-to aspects of the craft of songwriting. For the remainder of this book, I will write about my strategies for entering, staying in, and succeeding in the songwriting business. I will enumerate my suggestions for actions you can take to advance your career including my thoughts about how you can work to create opportunity and become a part of a hit record project.

Now, go back and reread the last two sentences. The key words in those two sentences are *songwriting business*, *opportunity*, and *record project*.

Songwriting as a Business

Writing music just for the heck of it is a swell thing to do. I sometimes write songs for no direct business reason other than for practice, learning or for my own amusement. Sometimes the music that comes from these self-indulgences finds its way into a commissioned project, sometimes not.

But here's the thing—unless you treat your composing as a business you will remain a hobbyist, and that is OK. Composing songs for fun is a very cool hobby to have, and it's a whole lot safer hobby than, say, jousting.

If you want to be in the music business, and specifically in the songwriting business, you must create a business model that includes regular times when you compose, do filing, record keeping, accounting, maintaining social media accounts and website, keeping your performing rights organization accounts current, and other business things—especially marketing of your primary products: your songs, recordings, and you! To be sure, to achieve success in this overpopulated, fiercely competitive profession, one needs to know about both the art and the commerce, the craft, and the business of songwriting. A professional songwriter can reasonably expect to spend as much time and energy promoting her or his product as was expended in creating it.

Writing every day is difficult. You will probably discover many reasons why you should do something else: your shoes need polishing, your dishes need washing, or your significant other desires your undivided attention. You get the idea.

The truth is, exercising your creative skills is like exercising your body's muscles. The more you do it, the stronger and more limber you become.

You are probably thinking that what I am suggesting is an impossible thing, because you are not inspired every day. So what? You were probably not very inspired to do your algebra homework either. You did it, though. Songwriters who write only when inspired are uninspiring songwriters.

I have worked for a few of these wannabe songwriters over my years in the music production business. If you are the kind of person who can only write when some major life event happens, fine. But that is like practicing your instrument only when you feel moved to do so. That is an OK attitude for a hobbyist, but not a very good or realistic business model for the aspiring professional. The model I am suggesting does not require that you lead a miserable life or an upbeat one, either. I only suggest that you spend a regular part of each day of the life you lead devoted to the exercise of creating new songs.

Not All Well-Written Songs Are Hits. Not All Hits Are Well-Written Songs.

It is likely you already know these music industry truisms. You have written some songs you know are great or you know persons who have. Yet, these creations have somehow not won the acclaim you think they should. Similarly, you have heard recordings of poorly constructed songs that have become commercially successful.

In their book, *Music Business Handbook*, Dr. David Baskerville and his son, Tim, write:

> A hit song is one that gets significant radio airplay, streaming, and downloads. *Good* song is harder to define, but, at a minimum, it must be well crafted musically and, if it's not an instrumental, lyrically as well.

They go on to say that good songs share these characteristics:

- They are *memorable*. They stick in the mind. This is accomplished by use of a *hook*, a catchy phrase or refrain that repeats several times in the song.
- The song has immediate appeal.
- The lyrics contain one overall theme and the writers use vivid phrases or imagery to relate it.
- The song is well crafted and exhibits an arc: it has a discernible beginning, middle, and end.

It takes more than great musical and lyrical artistry to cause a song to top the trade magazine charts.

Hit Songs Are the Products of the Music Industry

Hit songs are the product of the music industry and are the result of a successful collaborative effort of songwriters, record producers, recording engineers, musicians, singers, mastering engineers, record label executives, promotions persons, art directors, advertising professionals, and broadcast professionals—and is immensely dependent upon luck.

Sometimes songs become successful because the highly competent persons who run the well-oiled music business machine use a technique called **push marketing**. A poorly written, poorly produced song can sometimes be made into a wildly successful product. The same is true of mediocre performers.

While frustrating for the journeyman tunesmith, these occasional equivalents to the successful late-night cable television product are a fact of music business life.

Well-crafted songs have a good chance of commercial success if they have an appealing first performance (especially if by a well-known performer), the record company invests its money and personnel in promotion, the song and the recording suit the tastes of the current music buying public, and the record is distributed effectively. Absent any one of these important elements even a great song can become a miss rather than a hit.

Your Work Recorded and Published

Once we have completed our creation, and we are convinced we have tweaked and polished our diminutive masterwork beyond all second-guessing, what do we do with it?

If you are a member of a band, you bring your new song to your next band rehearsal and try to convince the rest of the band that this is the tune that will win you the record business lottery.

If you are a choir director at a house of worship, or a music therapist, you bring your tune in to the next rehearsal or meeting and teach it to your constituents.

There are options beyond the personal connections or needs you might have in your music-related work. These are publishing and recording. These are two distinct music business endeavors that are more than ever very closely intertwined.

What is Music Publishing?

The chief business activities of **music publishers** are two: first, to exploit the **intellectual property** they own by seeking to have it performed, recorded and otherwise used by as many musicians as possible; and second, to collect fees for the use of their intellectual property and then to administer the distribution of those fees to the creators of the music and lyrics.

Music publishers make a very little bit of money for each piece of print music they sell; for each recording made and distributed on disc, stream, or download; and for each time one of their copyrights is used in a film or broadcast, or when one of their compositions is performed in a venue. Publishers work with **performing rights organizations** (PROs) and others to collect payments, called **royalties**, which they then split with composers and lyricists. So, if it pays only pennies at a time, why bother? Because publishers (and smart writers) know that *if* a song hits, they have the equivalent of a **musical annuity**!

Music Publishing and the Recording Industry

Beginning in 1501 when Ottaviano Petrucci (1466-1539) of Venice published the **Harmonice musices odhecaton**, the first collection printed entirely from movable type, and lasting through about the mid-1990s, the business of publishing music was limited to firms that were substantially capitalized.

Music publishing and printing was a very expensive proposition. Publishers needed to purchase and maintain the music typesetting machines and large printing presses. They needed to hire the expert tradespersons and musicians who could edit, arrange, and typeset music and run the complicated gear. Moreover, in later centuries, music publishers needed to employ a sizable staff of administrators, graphic designers, and marketing experts.

The print music publishing business began to change in the 1960s when the Xerox Corporation of Rochester, New York, introduced the first dry paper copiers, making it a bit less costly for start-up music publishers to enter the market.

Publishing Joins Recording

Up until the invention of the gramophone by Thomas Edison in 1877, music publishers were almost exclusively concerned with creating and marketing music in print (although, from the late nineteenth century through the mid-1920s, a small part of publisher's revenues came from the production of rolls for player pianos). As the popularity of record players increased and the popularity of the parlor piano and the sheet music to play on it waned, music publishers' goals shifted from music printing towards records. Having their titles recorded became an important and increasingly profitable pursuit.

Records Advertise Publishers' Songs

The early part of the twentieth century was also a time when broadcast radio gained in reliability and popularity. Publishers quickly grasped the vast potential causing recordings of their songs to be produced. Radio could now advertise their songs. Publishers who had once relied on song pluggers to demonstrate their songs in department stores now heard their products introduced to the public at little or no cost to them.

Realizing that recordings could not exist without the intellectual property they controlled, publishers were soon able to convince their collaborators in the burgeoning record industry to pay for the privilege of recording their songs.

Publishers and Writers Earn Royalties

Perhaps the most important collaborator a songwriter can have is a great publisher. A music publisher will provide the songwriter with the business wherewithal to get the songwriter's songs out to the public and will ensure that the songwriter receives as much compensation as he can for his work. A great publisher is a songwriter's essential partner.

What Is Being Sold? How is a Songwriter Paid?

The product of an artistic endeavor is called intellectual property under the copyright laws of the United States as contained in *Title 17 of the United States Code*. In the music business, songs and recordings are construed as intellectual property.

Like other kinds of property, intellectual property can be owned, sold, rented, stolen, or given away.

Erik Sabo, Esq., is the Music Industry Professor at Saint Joseph's University in Philadelphia. He offers advice on how to protect and make money from your music:

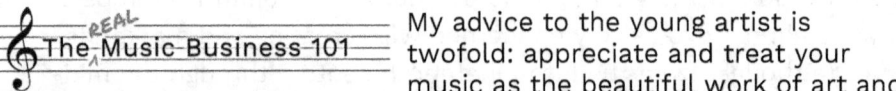

The real Music Business 101

My advice to the young artist is twofold: appreciate and treat your music as the beautiful work of art and property it is, needing love, respect, and guidance; and look for opportunities to place and license your music in areas that have now become commonplace or might be naturally overlooked.

Pursue synchronization deals with video game companies, anime cartoon outlets, music supervisors, film theaters, and Fortune 500 corporations. Take ownership of the fact that your song is a piece of property, a piece of intellectual property (entirely more fun to own and as lucrative as real property), so treat it with the care and respect you do your instrument, work with the property as you do your band mates and the music, guide the property so that you may monetize your efforts and make a living from your craft and love of music.

Making money with your property gives you the freedom and independence you want as an artist, therefore understanding your copyright and trademark interests is critical. Artists must become as fluent in their property rights, copyright, and trademark, as they are in speaking the language of music.

Licenses and Royalties

Whenever music professionals want to record or perform a piece of musical property, if an arranger wants to make a new arrangement of a composition, or when a production company wants to include a composition or recording in a score for a new film, television program, or commercial announcement a **license** must be obtained from the owner of the musical property (the licensor) and a **royalty** must be paid by the licensee.

There are several kinds of licenses and royalties. These include **mechanical** and **performance licenses,** and **mechanical** and **performance royalties**. **Synchronization** agreements cover the use of compositions and recordings in films or broadcast productions. Music performed as part of theatrical productions, including dance, are paid based on an agreement covering what are called **grand rights**. (All the other licenses and royalties are sometimes called **small rights**.)

Mechanical License and Mechanical Royalty

When a record producer or recording artist wants to record a piece of music owned by a publisher, he or she must obtain a **mechanical license**. The term mechanical license dates to the dawn of the last century when music publishers made their compositions available on **piano rolls**. (A piano roll is made of paper with special perforations that triggers a mechanism in the piano that causes it to play.)

There are presently two companies that facilitate the issuance of mechanical licenses to those who make commercial recordings. The Harry Fox Agency (*www.harryfox.com*) and Music Reports (*www.musicreports.com*) also collect and distribute mechanical royalties to copyright owners.

The **Mechanical Licensing Collective** (MLC) is a great new tool that American songwriters will have beginning on 1 January 2021. It will provide a streamlined method for songwriters and publishers (including self-published songwriters) to issue and track mechanical licenses to streaming companies.

The MLC will have two primary responsibilities: it will identify and pay songwriters and music publishers when their compositions are streamed; and it will research and pay out any earned but unclaimed money (commonly known as "black box money").

The MLC was created through the enactment in 2018 of the Music Modernization Act (MMA) (*www.copyright.gov/music-modernization*). The inauguration of the MLC will coincide with a 50% raise in the royalty amount songwriters and publishers will receive from streaming services. (At this writing, the royalty payment increase is the subject of litigation with Spotify and Pandora and others suing to prevent the pay increase. Notably, iTunes and Apple Music have accepted the new terms without reservation or protestation.)

The **Music Licensing Collective** (also "MLC") (www.supportthemlc.com) will act as the official entity tasked with licensing and administering rights under the new Music Modernization Act (MMA).

Performance Royalties

Publishers and their composers developed entities called **performing rights organizations** (PROs) to collect and distribute fees called **performance royalties** for the performance of their songs.

Publishers, composers, and lyricists share performance royalties that are collected and distributed by PROs. In the United States, there are presently five PROs:

- The American Society of Composers, Authors and Publishers (ASCAP);
- Broadcast Music Incorporated (BMI);
- SESAC (formerly, the Society of European Stage Authors and Composers);
- Global Music Rights (GMO);
- Pro Music Rights (PMR).

PROs are not all created equally. For instance, *ASCAP* and *BMI* are not-for-profit and non-profit corporations, respectively, while *SESAC*, *GMO*, and *PMR* are for-profit companies.

ASCAP was founded in 1914, SESAC in 1930 and BMI in 1939. Music business veteran, Irving Azoff founded GMO in 2017 as "an alternative to the traditional performance rights model." (The most notable difference is that mere mortals need not apply for membership. One must be *invited* to join.) The fifth-ever performing rights organization to be formed in the United States, Pro Music Rights, is a for-profit company. PMR was founded in January of 2018 and has grown quickly. At this writing it controls a market share of about 7.5% in the USA and represents about 2 million works.

Collective Rights Organization (CMO): SoundExchange

SoundExchange is a non-profit organization established in the early twenty-first century by the Copyright Royalty Board to collect and distribute digital audio transmissions royalties on behalf of *featured recording artists* and *owners of master rights* such as record labels, and independent artists who own their masters. SoundExchange is the sole entity in the US to collect and distribute digital audio transmission royalties for thousands of non-interactive Internet radio outlets (including Pandora); cable TV audio music channels (like MusicChoice); webcasters (including original programmers and retransmission of FCC-licensed radio stations); and satellite services such as Sirius XM Radio.

SoundExchange does not collect for interactive performances of sound recordings in on-demand services (like Spotify), where the listeners select the tracks they want to listen to and in what order they want to hear them.

As record companies grew more and more important, the symbiotic relationship between publishers and record companies also grew. The allegiances between music publishers and record companies survive to this day, the near monopoly once held by large publishing houses and large record companies has been somewhat shattered by technological developments that began in the late twentieth century and the Do-It-Yourself (DIY) Music Industry.

Music Publishing and the Film Industry

Beginning in 1927 with the release by Warner Brothers of the sound film, *The Jazz Singer*, filmmakers have included music as a necessary part of their productions. Today, film companies including Walt Disney Studios, 20th Century Fox, Warner Brothers and Sony Pictures Entertainment, each have music publishing subsidiaries with whom their producers closely work.

Producers use songs as an adjunct to the instrumental musical underscore that accompanies the action of theatrical, educational, and documentary films. Songs may appear as the theme song for the film, as part of the underscore, or as a **diegetic** sound element, as source music. Source music is the music you hear in a film that appears to be coming from a radio or from a band playing on-camera. Having one of your songs included as part of a film's soundtrack is one of a songwriter's most lucrative and major accomplishments. It is certainly well worth the effort, but how does it happen? How does a songwriter have her song even considered for inclusion in a film?

I spoke with film composer Joseph Renzetti about how an aspiring songwriter might get a song into a film. Renzetti, who earned an Academy Award in 1973 for his score for *The Buddy Holly Story*, said this:

The very best way to have a song become part of a theatrical film is to somehow be known to the music supervisor or, better yet, the director. Being there and being known to the decision makers is the best method.

The next best thing is to be a known commodity when the production team becomes stuck. A song might have been written for the film project, but at the last minute, perhaps during the mix session, the director decides it's just not quite right. Someone in the team knows you to be a person who can quickly deliver and, voilà! All of a sudden, your song is part of a major film soundtrack!

Having a great reputation as a songwriter who can quickly and successfully create a song that well fits the needs of the film's producers might come as the result of networking and you having had even moderate success in an allied field, like having had a hit record, or having written for television or a high-profile music library.

Finally, getting your songs to filmmakers is one of the jobs of a good music publisher; maybe it's their most important job, because having a song in a film can lead to notoriety and income in so many other parts of the music industry.

Most large publishers, especially those directly connected with film studios, market their songwriters' songs to filmmakers. Some publishing companies specialize in securing synchronization (synch) licenses for their writers. I list a few of the important ones in "Working Independently" below.

Developing Your Practice

Surely polishing your chops as a songwriter is of utmost importance, but just as important is refining your skills in the music business. These include cultivating a good reputation as a music professional, good work habits, building a network of suppliers and clients, and refining your general business skills. Let's begin with burnishing your reputation.

Becoming Known as a Songwriter

As an aspiring music businessperson, you need to become known to others in the professional music business community. You will likely be surprised at how helpful others in the community will be; musicians are a very caring gaggle of folks, especially if you are talented and have a good attitude.

You can meet other like-minded musicians in lots of ways. For instance, you can make use of social networks like MeetUp, Facebook, and LinkedIn to join groups of musicians, songwriters and others interested in having a career in the music business.

When you qualify for membership, you can join The National Academy of Recording Arts and Sciences (The Recording Academy).

The members of the Recording Academy are the top-notch recording industry professionals who are making hit records. The Recording Academy regularly schedules business/social events where you can meet members and other aspiring artists. They also sponsor educational workshops where you can learn new skills from experienced professionals at the peak of their powers.

ASCAP, SESAC and BMI, as well as groups like the Nashville Songwriters Association, also present educational workshops, and open songwriter sessions where fellow aspirants and professional songwriters and can listen to your new songs and offer suggestions.

In your hometown, you may also find it helpful to attend the meetings of groups like the Lions Club, the Rotary Club, and the Chambers of Commerce. While much more of a long shot in terms of obtaining a direct assignment or even a direct connection, being known as a songwriter by members of these organizations could aid you in meeting others who share your passion and interest, or better yet, need your services. Being around and being known are necessary ingredients for opportunity, our next subject.

Opportunity

It is quite impossible to have success in anything without first having opportunity. You can't win if you are not permitted to play.

To me, opportunity, means both being permitted to participate and being equipped to contend. Success is about opportunity, and opportunity is something you make by staying observant, being around the action and being prepared.

Preparation comes from learning, researching, studying, and practicing your craft. (Hey, you bought this book—that is a very good start!). But there are other things.

There are other ways to learn and other things in music to study. Work with a great songwriting coach, take a class to study music theory with an inspiring and learned teacher, learn from a motivated educator how to play an instrument and how to sing—these are all terrific pursuits that yield powerful skills that can help propel you towards your goal of achieving success in the songwriting business.

Instrumentalists, please notice that I am suggesting that you learn how to sing in addition to learning to play your instrument. You don't have a great voice? No problem. Having a great voice is not a prerequisite. Having a good understanding of how singers make music, how ridiculously perilous it is to count on your voice as a tool, how remarkably easy it is to sing just a little flat or sharp—these are all things every musician, and especially every songwriter, should know at a visceral level.

Finding opportunities means staying observant. One is not helped by wearing blinders, by looking in only one direction to find places and persons who will want to make good use of your songwriting abilities. Opportunity often comes looking for you in the most common of places and for the most ordinary of reasons.

Your path to writing a hit song for the world's next big recording personality might just be through writing a song for a local stage production, even if you know nothing about theatre and were frightened by an actress as a small child. Your road to the Songwriter's Hall of Fame might first find you writing a fight song for a political candidate for whom you would never vote. Alternatively, your trail to triumph might include a detour to the land of radio spot advertising where you will write one of the world's best pieces of advertising music, even though you hate jingles and advertising, and are a devout Socialist.

I am not for a minute suggesting that you "sell out." How could I? I know not what this phrase means! What I am suggesting is that in my mind, to write is to write is to write. You do it because you are good at it, you need the practice, you want to work, you believe you compose with a unique voice and you want to see what new opportunities will come from taking advantage of the door that was opened for you.

All the writing opportunities I have just described can be considered practice for the larger opportunity that may or may not come along. In the meantime, you are plying your craft and honing it while you do. But wait...did I just say that your big chance might or might not happen? Well, yes. Yes, I did.

The unfortunate truth is that sometimes no matter how talented, methodical, well-trained, persistent, kind, obedient, cheerful, thrifty, brave, clean, and reverent—the top-tier chance for tremendous triumph takes a backseat to luck. Sometimes there is that, but mostly luck is opportunity of a different name.

David Ivory is a successful record producer, songwriter, and college professor. In addition to having earned a Grammy nomination for his work with The Roots, Mr. Ivory discovered the Grammy-winning band, Halestorm. He writes here about *his* first brush with fame at age twenty-five:

When I was about twenty-five (besides owning my own professional studio), I was playing guitar and working with a successful touring band. Two of my bandmates and I wrote a song that our New York publisher, Hit and Run Publishing (owned by Phil Collins and Peter Gabriel), was able to get to the great rock band, Molly Hatchet.

This was a very big deal for us. Molly Hatchet wanted to cover one of our songs! They were signed to Capitol Records and at this point Hatchet had had several platinum albums. The only sticking point for us was that to get the deal done, we'd have to give up some of the writing credits and a piece of the publishing.

We struggled for a long time with what to do. We were really bummed because we wrote the song and, in our minds, they did "nothing." Now they wanted what seemed like a large cut.

In the end, we decided that having one of our songs recorded by a famous band on a major label was worth it. We agreed to the terms and the song was released. In the end, having this credit really helped me establish my career. It truly opened up many other writing and producing opportunities and helped set me up for a life-long career.

Of course, Molly Hatchet did do something: they worked hard and smart and used their resources to become famous! Now, they were choosing to share some of that fame with Mr. Ivory and his writing partners. The band, Molly Hatchet, was providing for them a shortcut to success on a major label.

Projects

Music making is often a team sport. The obvious examples are bands, choirs, and orchestras. There is also collaborative songwriting. Writing with another creative person can be an exhilarating and rewarding experience. It can just as often be a tedious and tantrum-filled exercise in frustration. I am confident that these will be self-limiting. All the activities I have listed I see as projects.

Work-for-Hire

Sometimes songwriters are offer employment on a **work-for-hire** basis. In a work-for-hire arrangement, the songwriter gives up all future rights to additional income in consideration of a one-time payment upfront. Work-for-hire deals are most commonly the province of the beginner and are often a source of regret later in that writer's life.

Any of the business opportunities listed in the next section can be presented as a work-for-hire job. The talented aspiring songwriting professional needs to exercise tremendous patience and self-control when offered a work-for-hire opportunity since signing away all future rights and income based on your present efforts might be a choice you will regret later and for a very long time.

Top Uses for Songs

What is it to be in the songwriting business? In its simplest incarnation, it is an exchange of goods for services where one person pays another to create an original song. Most of us want to be the writer of a song that becomes a classic for which we become well known and wealthy. There are other ways that songwriters can be paid for their creative efforts.

Songs are created for use as recorded entertainment, film and television themes and underscoring. They are written and recorded to motivate people (as in national anthems, corporate anthems, and commercial jingles). They are used for education (songs that teach, like "Baa, Baa, Black Sheep," "Fifty, Nifty United States" or hymn tunes used to teach the verses of the Bible). Songs are written for stage performance (like operas or Broadway-style shows) and for religious and secular print publishing (the music written especially for use by school and community choirs).

Here are some common ways songwriters ply their trade as well as some that may surprise you.

Major Label Releases

Having a song released on a commercially distributed record **album** is one of the pinnacles of success in the songwriting business. It is even more thrilling if your song is chosen as a single, but either way, being part of a major label album release is a big deal opportunity. How does it pay? The present rate of payment in the United States (legislated by Congress) for songs on albums, is 9.1¢ per song for each album distributed. This is the mechanical royalty. The mechanical royalties ("the mechanicals") are split equally between the publisher and the writers. That means that the publisher and writers each receive half of $91.00, or $45.50 for every one-hundred albums sold.

In addition to the mechanicals, songwriters (and their publishers) whose songs hit and receive radio, television and internet play will earn performance royalties. Performance royalties are collected and distributed by one of the five PROs with which the publisher and writer are a member. Writers whose songs are included in a major release album, but are not the hit single, will likely see little or no performance royalties. This is still lucrative and a big deal, since the savvy songwriter will promote the heck out of being on a hit album. They can leverage their connection to a hit album and a hit artist into other professional opportunities in music. This is opportunity knocking hard on your door. Listen and open the door.

Dance School Albums

Smart songwriters often look for less obvious opportunities to practice their trade. Most of the less obvious opportunities can be found in businesses that need music, but that market to a smaller segment of the population than does the commercial record industry.

These may not be the hit record opportunity that you pine for, but they are real opportunities to have your music performed and recorded and for you to be paid. They will provide you practice, income, experience, and exposure.

Albums of music specially tailored for the needs of dance schools and dance instructors represent a very small portion of the total sales of record albums. There are hundreds of dance schools around the country. All use music to teach ballet, jazz, hip-hop and ballroom dances. Many dance schools use albums that are specifically produced to fulfill the educational needs of dance instructors.

Songwriters will derive income from mechanical royalties at the same payment rate as paid for commercially released mass-market albums. However, since per-album sales are limited, composers often push for significant upfront payments. Songwriters who write for dance school albums might receive performance royalties, since many dance schools are signatories to an agreement with a performing rights organization.

Performance royalties from anything other than the repeated broadcast of a hit record will be small or non-existent, but diligent songwriting professionals can report use of their compositions to their PRO. Albums from small labels, like

The Ballet Dance Company, populate the music-for-dance-class market. For more information about music created especially for dance classes, go to *DanceClassMusic.com*. There you can find the names of labels you can contact about having them record your songs for their albums.

Production Music Libraries

Production music library companies create tracks that are licensed exclusively for use as background music in broadcast commercials, television programs, educational, motivational, and corporate films. They are not licensed for entertainment like commercially released recordings.

Production music library companies are always in need of new material, but most of what they need is instrumental music and they will want their acquisitions to be in the form of a master-quality recording. This means that unless you are an experienced producer and arranger, you will need to hire someone to arrange your music and make your recording.

Production music library companies generally function as small record labels, but rather than market their wares to the general population, they market exclusively and directly to radio stations, television stations, networks, audio, video, and film producers.

Because music library compositions are licensed strictly for use as soundtracks for other audio and visual productions, you should not expect a hit record-like income from any piece you license to these companies, but you will be paid. Here is how.

Production music library companies function on a few different levels and are structured using a few different business models. The largest companies are often part of a large jingle production company. These businesses, like FirstCom Music and Killer Tracks, will employ a staff of composers, arrangers, and producers to create their new albums. Staff composers are salaried. They will often not receive a share of synchronization or mechanical royalties, but may receive performance royalties through their PRO.

Synchronization royalties are paid when a piece of music is synchronized with the moving image of a film. Synchronization (or synch) fees vary greatly from production to production. The larger production music library companies issue commercial, television and film producers and others with synchronization licenses for the use of their productions and compositions in their work. The synch fee is dependent on the type of use and may range from around $100 for the use of a composition in a locally played radio commercial, to several thousand dollars for the synch of a piece in a feature film.

Some larger music library companies, including NonStop Music (owned by Warner/Chappel Publishing) and Hens Teeth Music of Australia pay songwriters and producers a split of derived income from synchronization.

Other smaller production music library companies like AirCraft Music Library and Prolific Arts Music use a **buyout music library** model. In this scenario, all end users pay the same amount to purchase the rights to use a track in any way they would like, for as long as they like.

Buyout music library companies are often owned and operated by composers and producers who also create the majority of the library's tracks. However, because libraries need so many tracks to fill their catalogs and their clients' needs, many libraries contract with independent producers and composers from whom they acquire tracks.

A songwriter desirous of working with this kind of music library company will need to compose instrumental pieces and cause them to be fully produced, either undertaking the production herself or contracting it out to a professional producer.

A songwriter with a fully produced instrumental track of her song can expect to receive an advance against royalties of $200 to $1,000 from a music library publisher. This could yield additional royalties or be a work-for-hire agreement that will pay nothing additional.

Broadcast Commercials

Another great place where songwriters can work and get paid well is in the music for advertising business. Today, the field of music for advertising also includes composing new music for websites and for advertising on the internet. It can also occasionally include composing a special advertising song for an in-store kiosk or other display.

Jingle production houses are often associated with production music library companies and exist on a few levels. There are companies that produce locally played or regionally played jingles, and those that produce jingles that accompany television and radio advertising that plays nationally. Many medium-sized cities have at least one jingle company that produces local jingles and the occasional regional spot. The nationally aired commercials are mostly produced in New York, Los Angeles, Chicago, Nashville, and Dallas.

The larger jingle production companies, for instance Tuesday Productions and Jam Creative Productions, Inc., employ staffs of songwriters, composers, producers, and arrangers who crank out radio and television jingles daily. These salaried employees retain no ownership in their creations, working on a work-for-hire basis. Songwriters in this field can receive performance royalties for their broadcast jingles, but these are normally quite inconsequential or nonexistent.

In addition to producing radio jingles, a jingle producer may also produce **radio station IDs**. These are the very short **shotgun** announcements and **sweepers** that one hears on pop radio. They sing the name of the station, the station's motto and perhaps a DJ's name. They will often be created in the style of the music the station plays. Songwriters who create these products are part of the company's salaried staff and will receive no additional payments, including performance royalties.

Many jingles are produced by one-person shops and are made on a buyout basis with no additional payments ever made to the songwriter. Songwriters who work in these smallest of the small jingle shops are often well-qualified audio producers, instrumentalists and singers, or partners with some other music-type who is. Folks who produce in this business model can expect to create local jingles and receive from $1,000 to $5,000 for each jingle production. From this, they will need to pay for studio, musicians, and singers. Generally, this kind of buyout business arrangement yields no performance royalty on the backend.

Anthems

Corporations and sports teams sometimes hire songwriters to create a song for the launch of a product or campaign. This kind of **anthem** is similar in spirit to a national anthem but will usually be in a contemporary style. Lee Greenwood's "Proud to be an American" is the model here.

Corporate and sports team anthems are more often than not produced by jingle production companies as an adjunct to their other work, since they are in fact long form jingles.

Children's Albums for Education & Entertainment

Recording icons from Johnny Cash to Def Leppard have written and recorded songs made especially for children. But, many lesser-known performers have developed very successful careers working as specialists in the music-for-children market.

There are two sub-genres that live under the larger umbrella category of children's music. Children's *educational* albums teach in an entertaining way about specific subject matter, like conservation, the environment, historical figures or events, math techniques, science facts, language skills, and more. Children's *entertainment* albums are mostly just for fun. The artists who inhabit this world sing about dragons, clouds, silly dances, and games. While the music and messages are directed at children, these albums are *musically* very far from childish. In the capable hands of the serious artists who dedicate themselves to making great music for children, these albums feature the same kinds of musical sensibilities and production techniques as are found in recordings in other genres, even as they educate and entertain.

Kindie Rock is the name given to children's music made by independent artists, both for entertainment and education, that successfully melds contemporary musical styles into recordings with messages especially tailored for children. (Don't let the 'rock' part of the handle fool you. Children's music, Kindie or otherwise, incorporates creative musicians who are expert practitioners in everything from Baroque to hip hop.)

Genre-blending children's music specialists include,

- Dave Kinnoin (Pop/Rock);
- Greg & Steve (Pop/Rock);
- Johnette Downing (New Orleans Roots-Pop);
- Jonathan Sprout (Americana);
- Miss Amy (Pop);
- Lucy Kalantari and the Jazz Cats (Jazz age inspired music for kids and families);
- They Might Be Giants (Alternative Rock);
- The Okee Dokee Brothers (American Bluegrass);
- Two of a Kind (Pop);
- Secret Agent 23 Skidoo (Hip Hop).

These artists are active professionals who have successfully established specialized record labels and publishing companies that support their artistic endeavors as writers and performers.

I spoke with the Grammy-nominated children's music artist, Jonathan Sprout, about the realities of a career in children's music regarding fame, fortune, and grown-ups' expectations:

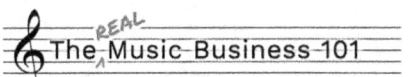

The *REAL* Music Business 101

Most of us in educational children's music fly under the media radar. For security reasons, our shows are often not open to public or press. On top of that, teachers and administrators want to know that our music and performances are going to supplement and amplify what the kids are learning in the classroom. Often, there are competing demands that make life challenging. I know though, without a doubt, that I have changed and uplifted thousands of openhearted lives. That sure knowledge certainly makes all the effort worthwhile.

Several large companies also specialize in creating recordings for children. Companies including, Kidz Bop, The Disney Company and Sesame Workshop operate as specialized record labels and publishers. They employ a staff of songwriters and producers to make recordings especially tailored to fill the needs of young children (and their parents).

Remember, these are important jobs that are filled by professional songwriters who were once just starting out and unemployed. Interested? Check the large company websites. They just might be hiring!

Musical Theater

Like the music business in general, most "civilians" (those who are not involved in the trenches of the music business) have a very narrow view of musical theater. In the minds of most, musical theater exists exclusively in Manhattan and London. It does not! **Musicals** are performed all over the world, all the time. What is more, they are regularly created and performed by writers and performers who are not at all famous.

Like hit records and getting a song in a movie soundtrack, being part of a Broadway show is about as good as it gets. And at any given time, there are perhaps twenty songwriters whose songs are being belted out in America's **The Great White Way**. So, for the rest of us, there are options. These include writing shows especially for performances in high schools, middle schools, and community theater.

Successful composers on Broadway negotiate individual agreements with producers that allow the producers to use the music in their shows. Once a show has had a successful run on Broadway, the producers will allow it to be mounted in other cities, in smaller theaters and for shorter runs. In return, the producers will be paid a fee by the local theater impresario. These fees are termed **grand rights**. Grand rights royalties are split between the show's original producers, the songwriters and perhaps some others involved in the creation of the show. The precise royalty and the proportions of the split are negotiable. Once agreed to, the amounts are memorialized in the composer's commissioning agreement.

If a cast album of the music is produced or other well-known artists produce new recordings of the songs from the show, the show's music publisher and the writers divide the mechanical and performance royalties in a standard 50/50 split. If a film version of the show is created, the publishers and writers divide the synchronization royalties equally.

It is an expensive matter to pay the grand rights to produce a famous musical. Often these fees are considered too costly for a school or community theater to pay. These amateur theater groups may opt instead to mount productions of shows that are not at all well known. These shows are written by little known songwriters and published by companies including: Pioneer Drama Service, Musicline School Musicals, and ArtReach Children's Theater Plays. Publishers like these generally charge the presenters a performance royalty for each performance they present. The performance fees, about $45 to $75 per show, are divided in some proportion between the publisher and the writers based on the songwriter's negotiating skills and stature.

Choir Music

There are many publishers of music for choirs. **Choir music** publishers like Alfred Music, Hal Leonard, Shawnee Press and Carl Fischer Music publish both secular and sacred music. Other publishers, like Augsburg Fortress, GIA and Morningstar Music Publishers specialize in music for the church.

Publishers of choral music release their publications in print and in demonstration recordings. Choral publishers are always looking for newly created songs, however they must be arranged in standard choir configurations for two, three or four voice parts (female and male; soprano I, soprano II and alto; or soprano, alto, tenor, bass; etc.). Songwriters who are skilled with this kind of part writing can expect to earn about 10% of the retail price for each printed copy sold. They can also collect royalties for performances through their PRO.

Background Environmental Music

Have you ever had the experience of walking into a clothing store or through a shopping mall where every step you take is accompanied by a great sounding recording you never heard?

The background music you are hearing as you shop is called **environmental music**. It is written and recorded by independent songwriters and producers and licensed for use in businesses by companies like Mood Media (which now includes one of the originators of the genre, Muzak), PlayNetwork Inc, TouchTunes Music Corporation, Almotech Ltd., Imagesound Ltd., Easy on Hold, Soundnet Ltd. (Soundjack), Xenox Music & Media B.V., Express Melody, OpenEar Music, and SiriusXM Music for Business. These companies also supply background music-on-hold, scent, and other marketing services to a variety of businesses in the healthcare, retail, and hospitality industries.

Mood Media and other companies in the background music business acquire master-quality recordings for their catalog from independent songwriters and producers. Interestingly, the music that environmental music companies license can be in almost any musical style: from dance to polka; folk-rock to classical; instrumental and vocal.

These kinds of companies function as publishers paying writers and other copyright owners a mechanical and performance royalty based on the number of installations that play the writer's track and the number of times it is played. Like many opportunities in the songwriting and recording business, producing music for use in business as background is a numbers game because each use pays very little per play. One needs many songs being used in many locations to derive reasonable revenue.

Agreements with environmental music suppliers like Mood Media are commonly non-exclusive. A songwriter can therefore license her music to another publisher for any other kind of use.

Chapter Ten

A New Paradigm

Through most all the 20th century, producing great-sounding radio-ready recordings was a luxury few could afford. Professional multi-track recording studios were very expensive to rent and even more expensive to own and maintain. Add to that the fees for expert professional studio musicians, arrangers, copyists, conductors, and producers and you have a process only a large corporation or the occasional well-heeled patron could undertake.

And if you wanted to sell your record to recoup your investment you would need to add the cost of manufacturing long-playing records (LPs), 45 rpm records (45s) and cassette tapes. These delicate pieces of plastic (readily prone to spoilage with just a bit of heat) needed to be warehoused. Then, they needed to be distributed to retail stores, promoted to radio stations, and otherwise advertised to the public.

Record production, manufacture, distribution, and promotion was the province of the large companies. The twentieth century paradigm also dictated that record companies were responsible for the costs related to artist development. Artist development costs could include fees for grooming and the creation of an image, and fees for vocal coaches, speech coaches, academic tutors, and a wardrobe. This was the era of the large record label, akin to the studio system of film companies in Hollywood.

Small record labels were generally too undercapitalized to be more than marginally successful. Because they were constrained by limited budgets, they could frequently only manage to manufacture and market recordings in a single region of the country. Sometimes very successful regional hits were taken over by large labels that were then able to release those same recordings nationally.

Independent producers who discovered talented artists with great songs were likewise often able to produce an independent master recording that was then licensed to a major label for manufacture, distribution, and promotion.

The business model of the music publishing industry and record industry was forever changed during the late 1980s and 1990s when scientists developed the personal computer. Computer music sequencing, digital audio recording and the Internet all arrived shortly thereafter. These technological developments were the harbingers of what I call the democratization of the music industry. No longer would great recordings be produced only in the music capitals of New York, Los Angeles, and Nashville. Now, almost anyone anywhere could make a recording whose audio fidelity rivaled that achieved in the most elaborate professional studios anywhere in the world. Moreover, distribution and promotion, the twin obstacles to success in the record industry for smaller independent producers, were demolished with the founding of CDNow, N2K, Music Boulevard and their successors TuneCore, The Orchard, CD Baby, Spotify, TIDAL, Apple Music and Amazon Music for distribution and Facebook, YouTube, and Vimeo for promotion.

The *good news* is that the cost of admission has been lowered; anyone can produce and market a recording. The *bad news* is that the cost of admission has been lowered; anyone can produce and market a recording.

This means good things for serious-minded and seriously talented musical artists. It also means that there is a whole lot of ear pollution on the Internet caused by not-so-hot records.

The basics remain: one needs a great song recorded in a great performance to make a hit record. In addition, one needs a better than average understanding of marketing and business to achieve record business success, especially trying to do it yourself.

The ease of access to the dream of music business stardom also makes available a large pool of candidates for thieves and swindlers who would take advantage of all those starry-eyed folks. More than ever, those desiring a career in the music business are best served by collaborating with an expert who has many times navigated the waters of record production, pressing, distribution and promotion. To avoid the clutches of those dastardly miscreants who would take advantage of you at the first opportunity, consult with a qualified and respected record business professional about your music business goals.

If you were building a house, you would hire a credentialed architect and a licensed builder. Your music business career is no less important. Finding that well-qualified expert who will treat your aspirations with care can be difficult. Ask others in your community who are in the music business, visit regional music conferences and attend the workshops and educational outreach programs presented by ASCAP, BMI, SESAC and The Recording Academy. Speak with the presenters at these events and ask them to recommend professionals in your region who can make great recordings and leave you with all five fingers when you shake hands.

The Cast of Characters

Success in the songwriting business requires that you interact with many music business folks. Surrounding yourself with a team of likeminded, goal-oriented people will help ensure that you have a better than average chance to present your music to the public and have it yield a return on your investment of time and money.

Building Your Team

Making a commercially viable recording requires a team of highly skilled music professionals. At the least, this will include a lead singer (assuming this is not an instrumental record you're making), an instrumentalist (to supply the accompaniment), an engineer (to accurately capture the sound performances, and to mix and edit the recording), and, of course, a songwriter. More elaborate projects will probably require that you employ additional instrumentalists, an arranger, a producer, back-up singers, and perhaps a copyist, a musical contractor, and a conductor. You may even be lucky enough to find one highly skilled and experienced professional who can perform many or all these roles singlehandedly.

Furthering your songwriting career will also require that you assemble a team of professionals who are expert in the business of music. This will probably include a music business lawyer, an accountant and perhaps a social media consultant, a website designer, a marketing specialist, a radio promotion professional, and a driver (Just kidding about the driver. Wait for that until you have your first or second hit record.).

The important message here is that success in the music business occurs for the individual when he or she is working in league with other creative, entrepreneurial persons, has prepared by learning at the feet of master practitioners, has tremendous tenacity, resilience and personal determination and seizes each new opportunity as if it is the opportunity of a lifetime.

Professional Manager

A professional manager is a salaried employee of a music publishing company. The professional manager is also sometimes called by the older title of "song plugger" or the title borrowed from the record business, the A&R person (Artist & Repertoire).

This employee has two major functions: first, the professional manager is responsible for acquiring new songs for the publisher's catalog; second, he or she is responsible for causing those songs to be recorded by major recording artists.

To find new songs, the professional manager will review demonstration recordings, listen to performers at clubs and in-concert and generally stay aware of new folks making good music. In his role as a song plugger, the professional manager will send well-made demonstration recordings to all the artists he has on his personal contact list who he believes are good candidates for the tune. A great professional manager always has an ear open listening for new potential hit songs and remains aware of artist's recording schedules and tastes.

The professional manager can be your key contact person at a publishing company and is the person to whom you need to send your new songs.

Musical Arranger

An arranger is a highly skilled creative musician who is expert in taking an existing piece of music (often written by another person) and recasting it into a new and unique musical form. Arrangers are experts in the skill of orchestration and are necessarily conversant in many musical styles. Great arrangers can create a work in the style of Johann Sebastian Bach as easily as they can one in the style of Henry Mancini, Nelson Riddle, or the Black Crows.

Song Doctor

A **song doctor** is a musical professional who helps songwriters craft better songs. Song doctors are part editor, part coach, and part cheerleader. A good song doctor will know what makes classic songs tick and will keep abreast of current trends in popular music, too. Record producers often work as song doctors for the artists they record. A great song doctor will be conversant with the styles of many historical songwriters and will keep up to date on what is current in the recording and songwriting business.

Studio Singer

Studio singers are highly skilled professionals who can blend well with other singers, generously take direction from conductors and producers, read music, sing in-tune and in time, learn very quickly and adapt to quickly changing expectations from the production team.

Studio singers come in two versions: one, the singer who can easily give over her individual vocal personality in favor of blending with a group; two, singers with "character voices." These are persons with vast musical gifts whom, but for ambition, luck or looks, could easily be the voice on a hit record.

Studio Musician

Recording studio musicians are highly skilled professionals who can work well with other musicians, generously take direction from conductors and producers, read music very, very well, and play in many different musical styles. Some studio musicians are equally comfortable working as soloists as well as in ensembles.

Studio players are paid well for their services and generally work within the terms of the American Federation of Musicians of United States and Canada's (The AFofM) recording studio wage agreements.

The AFofM is the musician's union. It was founded in 1896 to protect the rights and dignity of the highly skilled musical experts who perform at the industry's very highest standards. Although weakened significantly in recent years, the AFofM remains an important player in the work of the most accomplished musicians in the country.

Music Copyist

A music copyist is a professional who is highly skilled in the preparation of sheet music parts for recording ensembles, orchestras, chamber ensembles, choirs, or bands. Copyists need to be good musicians and editors since they are required to catch the few errors that arrangers make. Copyists are aware of historically correct practices in musical notation and are expert practitioners of the most current music publishing software. Great old school copyists can quickly and accurately copy out parts by hand from a score, transposing if needed, using a special calligraphy pen and special India ink just in case the computer dies, or something needs to be fixed on the spot.

Conductor

A music conductor is a very highly skilled, creative musician who directs an ensemble of musicians in a performance. Most conductors have superlative music reading skills, highly acute hearing (they can hear minor imperfections in professional musicians' tuning and timing) and have a very refined understanding of various musical styles. Conductors use their highly refined musical understanding and excellent communication skills to work with musicians to create outstanding musical performances.

Music Contractor

A music contractor is a person who makes hiring decisions regarding the personnel for recording sessions, film and television soundtrack recordings, orchestral performances, and stage show productions.

Contractors are professional musicians who are aware of the very best performing musicians in the area and who know the work rules of the AFofM for each work situation.

Record Producer

A record producer wears many hats during the production of a song. The record producer is the key person who is ultimately responsible for the outcome of the efforts of the entire production team.

The most important responsibility of a record producer is to envision a sound for the song that he is producing. No matter what is the sound of the raw version of the song, the producer must imagine the entire collection of sonic elements that will make up the final production. The sonic elements of the final production will include its musical style, instrumentation, tempo, groove (or feel), voice type and so on.

Several things will influence a producer's imaginings about how she will produce a song. These will include: budget (can she hire thirty musicians or three?); the image of the featured artist (is this a famous artist who has his own "sound"?); and finally, the desires of the other stakeholders (how would the record company executive or executive producer like the recording to sound?).

To bring her ideas to life, the record producer will next have to assemble the team. She will need to determine from her vast experience just which arranger is the right one, what musicians can best play in the style she is imagining, what studio and engineer will get the best sound for the project, and what mastering engineer can best polish the recording she has produced without compromising her production. Because a record producer is also the fiduciary responsible for working within a budget, she will make all personnel decisions with one eye on the costs. The producer is responsible for making sure the budget is not squandered. (The Christopher Guest character in *This is Spinal Tap* comes to mind.)

After the producer has firmly formed her vision for the production, once all the musical artists are hired and the crew is working in the studio, the producer's job becomes one of quality control agent. Because the producer is always the person ultimately responsible for the sound of the recording, he or she must have the final word about how the music is recorded and performed.

The producer is often a cheerleader or psychologist to the performers, musical conductor, song doctor and quality control agent—all rolled into one. The producer must be able to hear the most minor of musical blemishes and clearly instruct the performer about how to remedy the problem, all without ruffling any sensitive artist's feathers.

The record producer sits alongside the mix engineer and the mastering engineer and guides each through the final stages of the recording process, always making certain that his or her vision of the recording comes to fruition.

Once the recording has been mixed and then mastered, the producer's job may be done. But depending on the status of the producer and the business arrangement he has developed with the artist and other stakeholders, the producer might be involved in licensing the master recording and overseeing its manufacturing and distribution.

… 184 …

Attorneys

While it is quite true that all lawyers are not created equal, it is even more true and much more important as a songwriter to recognize that not just any attorney can navigate the sometimes-perilous waters of the entertainment business. As the songwriting business shares essential characteristics with other businesses (e.g., there are contracts, rights, property, negotiations, and so on), the vernacular language and common practices of entertainment business law are quite particular, if not peculiar, to that field alone. It is therefore generally wise for songwriters to work with an attorney who is well acquainted with the special requirements of working with musical intellectual property ownership, personal management contracts, record master lease agreements, copyrights, publishing, and the general care and feeding of the creative musical artist.

It is great to be connected with a lawyer who is regularly involved in negotiating agreements with major players in the music business. Often, that lawyer will be able to recommend talent to a publisher or label or be made aware of potential opportunities that might be ideal for a client. This is perhaps the most important thing an entertainment attorney brings to the artist/attorney relationship.

Of course, the major rub is this: young songwriters oftentimes know little about music business contracts and law and rarely have funds to hire an attorney. Short of having a veteran music business lawyer recognize your earnings potential and take you under his or her wing, there is little a new songwriter can do to protect himself.

Lori Landew, an entertainment law specialist who works in New York and Philadelphia, shared these thoughts when I asked her to comment on the dilemma of the impoverished artist who needs to consult with an experienced attorney:

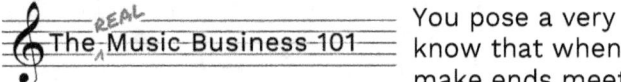
The REAL Music Business 101

You pose a very difficult question. I know that when artists are trying to make ends meet, scraping together money to pay for a lawyer is not going to be high on their list of priorities. It's probably a notch or two below buying instruments or paying insurance for gear. However, it's hard to ignore how important good legal advice from an experienced entertainment lawyer can be, particularly where an artist's rights are concerned.

One affordable resource that exists in many major cities is collectives of attorneys who will work with artists on a pro bono basis. In Philadelphia, for example, there is PVLA, Philadelphia

> Volunteer Lawyers for the Arts. PVLA works with some of the best attorneys in town who are eager to help developing artists who would not otherwise be able to afford their services.
>
> Another approach is to see if you can work out an alternative billing arrangement with an attorney such as a payment plan or some kind of hybrid between an hourly fee for services and a back-end participation in the proceeds from any deal that the attorney negotiates.
>
> And while I would never advocate foregoing legal advice entirely, if an artist cannot find a way to involve an attorney in his/her business, I would recommend consulting with more experienced artists. They may be able to offer some insight into how deals should work and what to watch out for so that the artist can take those insights into the contract discussions. The artist should always have the party offering the deal explain (line-by-line, if necessary) what their agreement says and why each term is there.
>
> Finally, NEVER sign anything before you've read it, understood what it means, and assessed the pros and cons of signing.

Landew mentions the Volunteer Lawyers for the Arts (*www.vlany.org*) in her response. This non-profit organization, established in 1969, provides legal aid and educational programs about the legal and business issues that affect musical artists at any stage in their career. The VLA has branches throughout the country, especially in larger urban areas. A quick Internet search will likely help you find a nearby VLA office and an experienced entertainment attorney who is willing to help you at little or no cost to you.

In the best case, you should at the very least, have a credible music business lawyer read any publishing or production agreement that is presented to you for your signature. One should never sign anything without having someone more knowledgeable and experienced in the entertainment business read it through.

Being aided by a lawyer or not, if signed to an esteemed music firm or running your own Do-It-Yourself publishing and record companies—you will need to undertake all the same activities as any owner of a small business. These include marketing, sales, negotiations, record keeping, filing, correspondence, personnel management, hiring, firing, banking, and accounting. This is a lot of stuff to know and do! You may want to consider taking classes in being an entrepreneur and managing a small business on-line or at a college. Schools in many communities offer classes in entrepreneurship as well as classes in all the specific disciplines I have listed.

Above all, I encourage you to remain keenly aware of what you and others are doing with your intellectual property. Music and lyrics take a long time, lots of energy, and loads of learning to compose. If you're doing it well, there will be lots of *you* in your songs. Well-crafted songs have wonderful intrinsic value and oftentimes great potential financial worth. Treat them with respect and care and others will, too.

Recipes for Success

In this text, I have thus far presented you with the basic materials of music by discussing lyric writing and song forms. I also presented an overview, with some detail of the music publishing and recording industries.

Let's look now at two paths you may pursue as a songwriter: one is for you to obtain representation with a prominent publishing house, and the other is to work independently.

Working Independently

If you are not immediately able to convince a major publishing company and record company that you are their next hit machine, and you believe in yourself enough to treat your career like a business, and if you have the time and financial wherewithal to make the investments, you may choose to form your own publishing company. In today's marketplace, that really means that you will organize yourself as a publishing company *and* a record label. Now, more than ever, easy access to the distribution and promotion platforms offered on the Internet allow all dedicated music business aspirants to establish themselves as independent music content providers.

Sign a Split Agreement

Whenever you have worked with another musician to write a song, you need to have signed a document called a **split agreement**. Split agreements say in plain language who wrote what percentage of each of the music and the lyrics of the song. (See sample split agreement in Example 88.)

Example 88: Sample Split Agreement

SAMPLE SPLIT AGREEMENT FOR SONGWRITERS

Single Song Writer's Split Agreement

Today's Date: _____

To Whom It May Concern:

This is to confirm that we are the sole writers of the musical composition (the "Composition" or "Song") listed below. We agree amongst ourselves to the following writers' and publishers' shares, subject to any other written agreements between or among us, based on our respective contributions to the Composition:

Song Title: (working title) "_____"

Writers' names, writer of & splits:
WRITER ONE: (Name) _____

    Writer of: _____ ____%

WRITER TWO: (Name) _____

    Writer of: _____ ____%

                                                                Total: _100%_

If any samples are contained in the Composition for which the sampled writer(s) / publisher(s) are to receive a copyright interest in and to the Composition, then we agree that our own shares in the copyright and/or monies attributable to the Composition shall be reduced proportionately.

Each party shall control his respective share of copyright administration for publishing the Composition. This song is presently unpublished.

Your signature below will indicate your agreement to the above.

READ, AGREED and ACCEPTED: (Signatures and date signed)

(Writer One) _____(Date)_____

(Writer Two) _____(Date)_____

Produce a Radio-Ready Recording of Your Song

To have a radio-ready recording means to have a potential hit song that is represented in a recorded performance that compares well with anything one might hear on a radio station that plays music in the style of the recording. This means that you must have a singer with a hit record voice, a killer musical arrangement, and great performances by fantastic musicians. Oh, and it needs to be a great recording, too!

Unless you are an experienced record producer, you will seriously need to consider hiring someone who has substantial record production skills. If you live in one of the major recording capitals like New York, Los Angeles, London, Berlin, or Rome, it will likely be an easy matter to ask around and find an experienced producer who you can hire. If you live in the USA, you may choose to contact the Recording Academy chapter in one of the top twelve cities near you for a few recommendations (*www.grammypro.com*).

Hiring an experienced record producer will ensure that you will have top-notch musicians and singers on your session and that your song will be recorded at a fine studio with a great recordist.

Form Your Own Record Label and Publishing Company

Once you have a recording that is well-produced and sounds like it could be played on the radio, you may want to speak with the program directors or music directors of stations in your hometown to see if they might air it. Having a record played on terrestrial radio stations remains an important goal for recording artists and songwriters for a few reasons. Securing airplay helps to build your brand and burnish your credibility. Radio airplay is essentially free advertising that helps educate listeners about your product and might induce them to buy it. Having your record broadcast over the air and on Internet radio stations may also generate performance royalties through ASCAP, BMI, SESAC, GMO, or PMR.

To generate the maximum revenue for your airplay, create a publishing company and become a publisher member of one of the PROs in addition to being a writer member. By being both a publisher member and a writer member of a PRO, you can receive all the royalties generated from performances and other licensing. As a publisher you will also have some new responsibilities. Namely, you will be responsible for keeping track of the income generated by your song and you will need to disperse royalties to any co-writers who you have signed to your publishing company.

Writers will become affiliated with your publishing company by signing a publishing agreement. Sample publishing agreements can be found online at many sites. Probably the fairest agreement is the one found at the website for the Songwriters Guild of America (*www.songwritersguild.com*).

> **Note**
>
> It is always advisable to speak with the elders of your music community, to an attorney and possibly an accountant to learn how best to set up your new venture.

Establishing yourself as a publisher is a fairly simple process. First, come up with three names and research them on the Internet to see if anyone else is already using any of them. Next, make application as a publishing company with your PRO (they will ask you for at least three possible names). Once your PRO has approved one of your names, you will need to check with the proper state office to learn how to register the fictitious name of your new publishing company.

Lastly, open an account with SoundExchange to register yourself as the featured artist, and your publishing company as the record label associated with the recordings you are going to release.

Register your publishing company with either The Harry Fox Agency (HFA) or Music Reports to make possible the collection of mechanical royalties that may accrue from air and Internet play.

Please note that these are general guidelines for creating your business in the United States. I urge you to research the details of registering your business in your own state of residence or operation.

Register Your Claim in Copyright

Once your master-quality recording is complete, you will want to register a claim in copyright. In the United States you can register your claim in copyright by going to *www.copyright.gov*. There you will have the option to file for two copyrights at once: one is for the *composition embodied in the recording* (that's your hit song); the other copyright is for *the recorded performance*.

Check with the proper department of the federal government in the country where you want to register your claim.

For instance, in Belgium, go to *www.belgium.be/en/economy/intellectual_property* for more information about registering your copyright.

Many countries are signatories to the Berne Convention for the Protection of Literary and Artistic Works. If you are registering in a country that is a signatory to the Berne Convention, your copyright will be honored in all signatory countries.

Be careful! Here, as in many music business-related situations, there are crooks out to get the unsuspecting! For instance, there are many official looking websites that are not at all official. In general, these are for-profit companies that may or may not deliver the service you want (obtaining a copyright). They generally charge much more than the actual cost of filing to register a copyright claim with the official government office.

Once you have copyrighted your song, you are entitled by law to place a **copyright notice** on all versions of the song: printed, recorded, online, and in whatever form may come into being at some future date. The copyright for the song will look like this,

© 2019 YourSongs, LLC

You will also have the opportunity to place a copyright notice on all versions of the recorded performance. These will include all physical copies in whatever media (CD, LP, 45, cassette or anything yet to be developed). You will also be wise to place the recording copyright notice in the metadata stored in high-resolution audio formats, in the data on CDs, and on Internet platforms like SoundCloud or Spotify. The copyright notice for a recording will look like this,

℗ 2019 YourLabel Records

While copyrighting a song or a recording does not guarantee that some dastardly dudette will not be able to steal your intellectual property, it will aid you significantly should you ever have to prosecute an infringement case.

Under the present law in the United States, copyright protection begins as soon as the composer and lyricist fix their creation in some tangible form of expression (as soon as they write it down on paper or make a simple recording of the tune), and remains in force for the lifetime of the creators, plus seventy years after the last surviving author dies.

When you register your claim with the Library of Congress, you are simply putting the rest of the world on notice that this is, indeed, your creation. This is an incredibly important thing to do.

Release Your Master Recording

Release your master recording to online music stores and streaming services worldwide by contracting with a digital content aggregator like CD Baby or TuneCore. Doing this will place your recording for sale across the world via digital stores and streaming platforms including Apple Music, Amazon Music,

YouTube Music, Spotify, SoundCloud and Pandora. Make sure that your music cannot be downloaded for free.

Platforms like CD Baby, BandCamp, and ReverbNation may also be helpful for acquiring fans and tracking their interest in your work.

I encourage you to have your recordings mastered by a professional mastering engineer who is conversant with the technical requirements for digital distribution on the various platforms.

Place a Video of Your Recording on YouTube, Vimeo, or Instagram

Your video can be as elaborate or homespun as you like. The important thing is to have a copy of a recorded version of your song on the Internet. Be sure to include a method for viewers to purchase your recording. Build a "call to action" into your video that will redirect prospects to one of the online stores. Having your music played on YouTube or Vimeo will generate a little royalty income and help you to stimulate sales of your song and bolster your brand.

Get Your Metadata in Order

Metadata is a term to describe other data. In the recording and publishing industry, metadata is used to mean detailed information that is encoded in compact discs and digital audio files describing details about the recording. Metadata can include title, subtitle, contributing artists, album, year, record label catalog number, genre, recording dates and ownership, songwriter(s), and the ISRC and ISWC.

ISRC is the International Standard Recording Code, a unique number assigned to each released recording. One can obtain an ISRC by going to *www.usisrc.org* or through the services of companies like DiscMakers, CD Baby, or NationWide Disc.

The ISWC is the International Standard Musical Work Code, which is a unique number assigned for each individual composition when registered through your PRO.

Promote Your Recording to Radio Stations

As you can imagine, getting a top-tier radio station to play your record is like getting a date with a movie star. It might happen, but it is more likely to occur if you meet certain special criteria. For the major broadcasters in any size city, the principal criterion is that your song is recorded and released through a major record label and then brought to their attention by a radio station record promoter they already know on a first name basis.

According to the Federal Communications Commission, as of 2016 there were 15,491 licensed full power radio stations in the United States. Of these, the biggest stations in any town, the ones whose formats include Adult Contemporary (AC), Hot Adult Contemporary (Hot AC), Contemporary Hit Radio (CHR), Active Rock, Pop and Urban are generally only accessible to the machinery of the major record labels. The promotion teams of the major labels have well-established relationships with the big radio stations.

Even with strong relationships, records may be promoted and auditioned, but not added to the station's playlist. Since most large city top-tier stations have an average of only three "adds" per week, competition is more than tough. It's essentially impossible, especially for an independent artist, to break through.

According to Ms. Stephanie Seiple, Vice President of Business Development for Crank Media Intelligence, having a record played regularly on terrestrial radio is still *the* most important thing to have, but getting a record on radio remains one of the most challenging parts of the business.

Working to get a record played on radio is not for the weak! In fact, it is likely an aspiring recording artist will get nowhere without first creating a 'buzz' about their music.

In the end, getting a record on radio is not always about how good the record is, it's about relationships and such. Of course, it helps if you have a great song that is produced well, but in my professional experience, trying to begin with radio airplay is putting the cart before the horse. Radio programmers want to see that you have fans. Therefore, you need to do all you can to create some hype around you and your tunes.

The ideal situation is to hire a professional public relations (PR) person first, but short of that the artist can write press releases and send them to local publications, large and small. Do this while you are making a sustained **guerrilla marketing** effort on the Internet. Use social media and e-mail to stay in touch with your fans. Post to social media. Build a list of contacts by having a *sign-up sheet* at all your gigs. A fledgling recording artist needs to first build up a fan base and *then* talk to radio, or ideally when ready, hire a radio promotion team, or get lucky enough to get signed to a label where a radio promotion team is part of the deal.

Essentially, you need to get a lot of people to know who you are, then radio programmers will want to play your recordings. And, remember, indie acts who are successful in getting songs to radio—finding out who still does some local programming or specialty shows, as well as having a robust social media presence, and high streaming numbers on Digital Streaming Platform (DSPs)—have a better chance of getting signed to a label. Bottom line, you have to be ready to put the hard work in!

The stations that are available to independent artists and independent record labels include those with the Adult Album Alternative (AAA) format and college radio stations. Airplay on these stations can yield record sales and performance royalties and, with a little extra work, you might be able to arrange for performances at venues near the stations and colleges. Include SiriusXM in your solicitation planning. Find the SiriusXM station where your music might fit, find the name of the music programmer for that station, and write to them. (Ask permission to send your CD. At the time of this writing, SiriusXM only accepted replicated CDs.)

Begin by assembling a list of stations that are likely to be responsive to your request for airplay, including as many Internet-only stations as you can find. Next, determine the correct person with whom you should speak. Your contact person will likely have the title, program director or music director. At very small stations, you will do well to make direct contact with a friendly-sounding DJ.

If you succeed in cultivating airplay on the more accessible stations and you create a "buzz" about your recording as a result of your other marketing efforts, you might be able to convince someone at a large station to audition and play your recordings, but not if they are corporate-run stations headquartered in a faraway city.

Corporate-run stations carefully control their playlists from corporate headquarters and are usually not allowed to play recordings by local artists. This is an unfortunate byproduct of the deregulation of the broadcasting industry in the US. If you do decide to solicit a record company or publishing company to distribute and promote your music, you can use evidence of the success you've had garnering airplay as why they'd want to sign you up.

Other Opportunities

Local radio and television stations, especially those that broadcast on the Internet only, sometimes have programs that feature interviews and performances by regional artists. The coverage may not be widespread, and the technique of the interviewer may not be at the level of Terry Gross, but that's OK. Do these interview and entertainment programs anyway. Small stations with few viewers or listeners are a good place to practice your craft. If you do a local interview or performance program, try to obtain a copy of your appearance, and get permission to use at your website or on your YouTube channel. Right—you should have one of those, too!

Submit Your Record to a Synchronization Publishing Specialist

Submit the master recording of your song to publishers who specialize in the business of obtaining synchronization licensing for Sound Recording Copyright Owners (SRCOs) for placements with film and television producers. If you have established your own publishing company, the companies that specialize in synch publishing will become your sub-publisher and will have you sign a licensing agreement for their use of your copyright.

Contracts with synch-only sub-publishers are frequently non-exclusive. That means you can contract with several synch-only publishers and other sub-publishers who specialize in other sectors of the music publishing business, like those who handle record releases or print publishing. However, there is a big downside to being represented by more than one synch-only publisher. The possibility exists that two companies could pitch one of your songs for the same project. This occurrence will likely disqualify you for that opportunity, and perhaps others with those producers.

Companies that specialize in synchronization-only publishing include Crucial Music, Music Dealers, and Jingle Punks. Synch-only publishing companies divide equally with the SRCO the synchronization fees that they garner.

Some synch-only sub-publishers subscribe to a practice called "re-titling."

Let's say that the master recording and song you publish with a non-exclusive synch-only publisher is originally entitled "Sweet Thelma Sue." Each synch-only publisher with whom you contract will add a slightly different twist to your song title. The new name one company uses might be something like "Sweet Thelma 4498" while a second company might call your song, "Thelma Sue002". The synch-only publishers rename songs in their catalog so they can be assured of receiving their share of any performance royalties that accrue from a placement they obtain. This is good, because theoretically, they will not receive payments for any recordings of your song that play on the radio or for placements they did not get.

Some find this entire process distasteful and eschew it. Other writers and SRCOs accept the synch-only business's peculiarities because they understand that by working with non-exclusive synch-only publishers they have been able to access the ears of film, television and broadcast commercial producers who would otherwise never hear their songs. Remember, if you do choose to pursue this kind of publishing or sub-publishing, it will be best to place a recording with only one company at a time to avoid confusion and ill feelings.

Like many career decisions, choosing to work with or not work with a non-exclusive synch-only publisher will truly depend on where you are in your career. One must begin somewhere. The kind of exposure that one can earn from a placement in a feature film, hit television show or network commercial is career altering and is certainly much better than performing free at the local coffee shop or being punched in the chest by an irritated harpist.

An organization you might want to join is NARIP, the National Association of Recording Industry Professionals. NARIP sponsors networking events and paid pitching sessions where you can demonstrate or "pitch" your well recorded songs to industry leading music directors, and television and film producers.

In the June 10th, 2018 edition of *Music Business Worldwide*, Mr. Bill Patrizio, President and CEO of Rhapsody International/Napster, said that Napster ingests about 24,000 new tracks on its service *every 24 hours*...adding to a total catalogue of more than 50 million titles.

Here is what NARIP President, Ms. Tess Taylor, had to say about the intense competition in the fields of songwriting and recording:

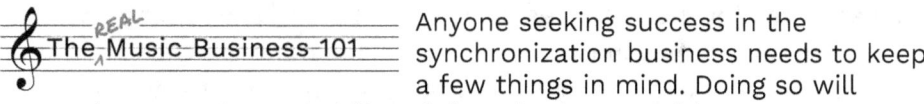

Anyone seeking success in the synchronization business needs to keep a few things in mind. Doing so will increase the probability of them having a positive outcome.

> Because the barriers to entry are now so low that literally everyone is getting in, there is a tremendous over-abundance of music available for music supervisors and other decision makers to choose from. Good music is not good enough, the music you pitch must be great to have a real shot at being discovered, licensed, and placed.
>
> The process of working to get your music placed in a film, television, a video game, or a trailer is not rocket science, but it does require focus and attention to detail to succeed. Great research and building relationships are immensely important, too. These take time; there are no shortcuts here.

These facts of synch life will deter some. Let them strengthen your resolve and focus your purpose.

Be strategic. Saying you want to 'get a synch deal' is too vague to be useful. You need to be clear about what you want and even more aware about what sets your music apart and makes it special. Where would your music be most appropriate? You need to match your music with the buyer and his needs. You will do well to focus at first on only one of the main areas that use licensed music: film, television, trailers, promotional or advertising (this area overlaps sometimes with trailers) and video games. Each of these areas has its own musical needs. If you understand the idiosyncrasies of your chosen area, you will be in much better shape. (By the way—those who do well in synch typically focus on one of these areas first and conquer it before seeking success in other sectors.)

One of the most important things is to understand your rights in ownership of the masters and compositions that you pitch. Moreover, you need to have your metadata in absolutely perfect order. Major music buyers will quickly sniff out and tend not to work with someone who presents as an amateur—even if your music is stupendous! They just won't take the chance of being sued. Period. And, don't expect the music buyer to take his time to explain. In the fast-paced world of production, time is money so pausing to explain these things to someone is unlikely to occur.

Also investigate working with Terrorbird Media, Lip Sync Music, or Music Alternatives. These companies are also in the business of pitching master recordings of great songs to television producers and filmmakers, but they do not take any ownership of your copyrights. Instead, they act as publishers' agents and earn a fee for their services of between twenty and twenty-five percent of your revenues. As you can imagine, it is much more difficult to make the cut with companies like these, but it is well worth the effort since you retain all publishing rights, earn publisher's royalties and writer's royalties.

Sell Music at Your Gigs

Sell your recordings at your engagements. The Do-It-Yourself business model I am presenting in this scenario allows for the likelihood that, in addition to writing great songs, you are a reasonably convincing performer. If you are, and if you are successfully booking performances, you will be well served to have physical copies of your recordings available to sell when you perform. Like other aspects of the recording business, preparing physical copies of your master recording, including compact discs and vinyl LPs, has become democratized. Before the personal computer and the Internet, only large companies and a few significantly solvent individuals could afford to purchase the large minimum orders required by pressing plants.

Today, master files can be transmitted to pressing plants on the other side of the world via the Internet, cover art can quickly be designed, approved, and printed on-line and finished products can be delivered in a day or two. Best of all, the manufacturing can be completed at a cost that is manageable by many. There are many compact disc replicators, such as DiscMakers, Oasis Disc Manufacturing, EasyDisc, and NationWide Disc, who do good work. Many also offer for sale other promotional items.

Another method for selling your musical wares at your performances is to sell download cards. Download cards are credit card-sized vouchers that supply an access code that customers can use to download your recordings from a special Internet site.

The Professional Songwriter's Publishing/Record Release Checklist

Project Type: ☐ Album ☐ Single ☐ Publishing

Title: _____

Copyright Owner(s): _____

Release Date: _____

Artist(s): _____

Writer(s): _____

Producers(s): _____

- ☐ Sign a Split Agreement.
- ☐ Produce radio-ready track.
- ☐ Form and register your own record company and publishing company.
- ☐ Become affiliated with a PRO, a mechanical rights organization (like Harry Fox Agency), register with the Music Licensing Collective (MLC), and with SoundExchange.
- ☐ Register claim in copyright. Label your song and record with correct copyright notices.
- ☐ Contract with aggregator to digitally release and distribute record.
- ☐ Place at least a simple video on YouTube and Vimeo, at your website and wherever else is appropriate.
- ☐ Replicate discs (be sure to obtain ISRCs for your album and single cuts).
- ☐ Solicit radio stations yourself or employ an independent record promoter.
- ☐ Employ the services of a public relations company.
- ☐ Solicit interviews and performing opportunities in all media.
- ☐ Open account with SoundCloud. (Do not allow free downloads.)
- ☐ Solicit publishers who pursue synchronization deals.
- ☐ Sell your discs and download cards at performances.

Copy this form and check off each step as you work through your release.

Signing with a Major Publisher or Label

To convince a major publisher that you are worthy of their investment of time and money, you will need two things in addition to your talent and great songs. It will be very helpful to be represented by a music business attorney and to have a track record of music business success.

This is all very tricky. It is difficult to have a track record if you are just starting out and it is almost impossible to have an entertainment lawyer put time into representing you to large publishers unless you have already made a bit of a splash in the business.

One way to prove yourself is to follow the plan for self-publishing I outlined in "Working Independently," above.

According to renowned entertainment lawyer, Bernard Max Resnick:

The REAL Music Business 101

Getting 'signed' by a worthwhile publisher is not an easy task for an aspiring songwriter, especially if that writer's songs are not already being played on the radio, contained on a hit album, being performed in personal appearances, or generating thousands of downloads and streams on the Internet. You see, publishers are going to make a substantial investment if they sign you to a contract with their company. They want to know *ahead of time* that you are a moneymaker! If they not only believe you are, but see that you are they will invest, groom, and push you to be even more successful.

Do not despair if you do not have a hotshot lawyer on your team. You can contact the company yourself.

Scoring an Audition

Let's assume you don't have representation and you're trying to get yourself signed. Following is a list of things you can do to get an audition with a publishing company.

The first step in having your music signed to a major publisher is to clearly understand what it is you have; what it is you have written. This takes real introspection and reflection. Ask yourself, "What famous artist would sing my song?"

Next, look at chart listings in *Billboard* magazine to find a recording by the artist who you would want to sing your song. Each song listed in the magazine's charts includes the names of the writers, the publisher, and their PRO affiliation.

Next, find the contact information for the publishing company, either on the internet or calling the PRO affiliate. (PROs are generally very helpful in this regard and will readily tell you the address of their publisher members.)

Next, you will need to write to the publishing company to ask permission to send to them a demonstration recording of your song. This is because music publishers will not listen to, or even open packages from, writers who are unknown to them. (This is where having a lawyer with great contacts in the music business really can help speed up the process. An attorney who has negotiated publishing agreements with major publishers will likely be able to pick up the telephone and pitch you and your songs to the publisher.)

Call the publishing company and ask the person who answers the phone for the name and title of their professional manager, talent scout or A&R person and their preferred contact information. Compose a short, well-written business letter to ask permission to send your songs for their review (Example 89). Address the letter to the contact person whose name you were provided at the publishing company office.

> **Note**
> Business letters are just that – business and should strike a tone of pleasant regard for the recipient and her time.

Your business letter should be correct in its form, spelling, and grammar. Do not write as you might speak to a band mate or buddy at the gym. Remember, you are writing to accomplished businesspersons who will be dissuaded from doing business with you if you come off like a goof at the local rock joint. They will be much more impressed and willing to listen to your demos if you conduct yourself with standard business decorum and blow their socks off with your utterly outrageous music.

If you can honestly include in your letter positive reactions to your songs, do so. "My Aunt Martha loves it," is not helpful. However, telling the professional manager that your songs are presently being played on thus-and-such radio stations, and that you have a bazillion "likes" on FaceBook, and have sold thousands of downloads will probably help pique their interest.

Example 89: Solicitation Letter (sent via USPS or e-mail)

> Mr. Robert Smith
> Smith Music Publishing, Inc.
> 777 Outta Dasky Street
> New York, NY 00001
>
> May 11, 2019
>
> Dear Mr. Smith:
>
> I am writing you this afternoon to ask permission to send to you some of my original songs for your review for publishing.
>
> I have experienced very good reaction to these new songs whenever they are performed. Two of my songs are presently in regular rotation and receiving airplay on WXXX, WYYY and WAAA.
>
> For your convenience, I am including the enclosed self-addressed, postage paid post card. Please just indicate if you will review my songs and return the card to me at your earliest opportunity.
>
> Thank you,
>
> *Samuel Songsmith*
>
> Samuel Songsmith
> 333 Chord Change Boulevard
> Bluesville Park, Pennsylvania 77777

If you are sending your request to send a demo in the US mail, you will need to include a self-addressed, postage paid, reply postcard. Include on the card a simple question with a spot where the big mahoff can simply check, "Yes" or "No" to whether they are going give you a shot at fame and fortune! Example 90 illustrates a template for such a Permission Request Postcard.

Mention in your letter that the postcard is already addressed and that there is postage on it. The card could look like the one shown in Example 90.

Example 90: Permission Request Postcard

```
Ms. Jane Smith
Big Music Publishing Company
44 Hit Song Street
Big City, USA
                                    January 15, 2010

Dear Ms. Smith:

I would like to send you some of my songs for you to
consider for publication by your company. May I?

Just check:

         _____ Yes      _____ No

I have already put postage on this card and addressed it
to myself. I would appreciate it very much if you would
mail it back to me.

Thank you,

Sonja Songwriter
Sonja Songwriter
(304) 345-6789
```

```
Ms. Sonya Songwriter
32 Lyric Way
Oh Gosh Golly Holler, WV
                    26222
```

So, why use the old-fashioned US Mail? Well, doing so might just accrue a little notice. You might just be the one person that week or month who does so. That might get you enough notice to have them consider you a "serious contender" and therefore worth auditioning.

If you choose to use e-mail, keep it short and to the point. Always keep your correspondence, whether e-mail or written letter, business friendly, and definitely *not* personal. For instance, *do not* refer to the publishing company executive by their first name until they tell you it is ok to do so. This little bit of formality might help you differentiate yourself from the flock of other aspiring songwriters (Example 91). In an e-mail, request a reply by adding, "Please reply Yes or No."

Example 91: Permission Request E-mail

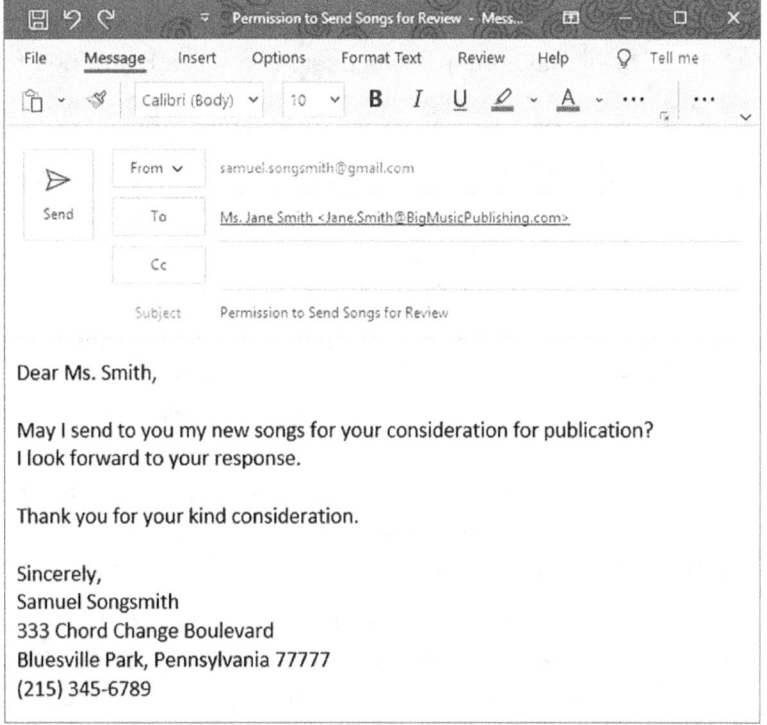

You will need to have a good quality, but not necessarily radio-ready recording to send to the potential publisher. (Here's a hint borne from my personal experience: make it sound *great*. Many of the first listeners at the publishing company will be low-level folks with sock ears. They may not get what you're doing unless you really get their attention.)

Don't Fall for Ads, They Almost Never Work

The REAL Music Business 101

Sometimes songwriters are signed to major publishing deals because of the great success they have achieved with an independent record release. Sometimes you must make your own opportunities. This was the case for my good friend, singer and songwriter, William DeVaughn. Mr. DeVaughn wrote what is arguably a true classic R&B/pop song. But the story of how his record became famous is as unique as his song. He not only created the first song he recorded; he also financed the recording. Here's how and why.

I always advise aspiring music-types to avoid any kind of advertised "opportunity." Most of us have seen advertisements with headlines that read, "Singers Needed!" or "Talented Songwriters Wanted by Major Record Company!" or "Song Poems Needed!" Surely, the companies behind these kinds of ads are scams. They are to be avoided at all cost because in doing business with them, you'll likely lose money, possibly your copyright, and more than that—your spirit and heart for the business of music.

> **Note**
> The image that comes to mind is of a wolf sizing up his prey. There are many music business wolves lurking around every recording studio and publishing company just waiting to devour the next inexperienced writer.

William DeVaughn was a civil engineer technician who worked for the water department in the city of Washington, D.C. where he had grown up. Mr. DeVaughn, a deeply religious man, writes songs from a deep place of love and respect for his fellow humans. William thought that his song, "Be Thankful for What You Got," expressed well his desire for humanity to do better and he thought he would do well if he could reach a wider audience.

William saw a small advertisement in the back of *Billboard* magazine. (The kind I tell everyone to avoid.) "Songs Needed!" it shouted. William seized what he thought was a golden opportunity. He made an appointment and then boarded a train to travel the short distance north to Philadelphia where he would meet the man behind the ad.

When he arrived at the record company office, Mr. DeVaughn learned that company would be happy to record his song, but he would have to finance the venture. It would cost $900 to have his song recorded. William, a young man with an old man's soul, thought long and seriously about his chances in the music business. He didn't know much about how the record business worked. Maybe this was how it's done, he thought. (It isn't.)

Fortunately for Mr. DeVaughn, the principals of the little rip-off record label hired a very talented musician named John Davis to produce and arrange William's song. Mr. Davis in turn hired the great MFSB session musicians,

Norman Harris, Bobby Eli, Ronny Baker, Vince Montana, Earl Young, and Larry Washington to play on the date at the famed Sigma Sound Studios.

"Be Thankful for What You Got" sold over two million records and finished at number one on the R&B charts and number four on the pop charts. Follow-up records never faired quite so well, but William did have a top twenty record in the 1980s with another great song he wrote called, "Figures Can't Calculate".

Sometime later, the District Attorney of Philadelphia brought charges against the record company and its principals. The owners signed a consent decree. That is where a company says, "we didn't do anything wrong, but we will never do it again." After receiving no payments for his later work, Mr. DeVaughn returned to his career with the D.C. water department and has essentially retired from music.

Some Final Thoughts

In this chapter, I have offered my ideas about why people compose songs, ways in which they can develop an income from their writing and some traditional and non-traditional paths to success. I have also included the job titles and job descriptions of the persons involved in a songwriter's successful career. These are very important business practitioners you will want to have on your team as you journey towards songwriting profitability.

Chapter Eleven

Coda

In this text I have shared with you many of the tools you need to compose your own songs. I have shown how scales and chords can be coupled together in rhythm to yield melodies and harmonic accompaniment.

I have shown how lyrics must be single-minded and how they need to precisely fit the rhythm and accent pattern of the melody. Finally, I have passed on the essential information you will need to work in the songwriting business and to bring your music to the world.

Your assignment—have fun with what you now know. Play through the song fragments included in this text. Sing the melodies. I know—you do not play so well and your singing leaves a lot to the imagination, right? Wrong. It does not matter at what level you perform right now. What matters is that you understand the general concepts I have presented and that you nurture your musician's heart. Sing your songs into existence. Let it happen for you.

Try linking together some of the chord progressions I have introduced. See what comes up. Perhaps as you play through your new chord progression, a melody will reveal itself. Sometimes it happens like that.

As a teenager, I learned a lot about songwriting by playing through songs from anthologies like *The Real Book*. These were very helpful as they incorporated good chord charts that showed how to form the chords used in their collections. I've supplied such charts in the Appendix. Any time you can spend playing through songs that are well written or listening to great recordings of those songs is time well spent. In doing so, you are truly learning from masters. If you apply some of the analysis techniques I have shared with you in this text, you will learn even more.

Appendix

In Sections *Scales*, *Scales in Comparison* and *Common Chord Symbols* I present the scales and chords commonly found in pop songs.

In Sections *Common Chord Progressions in Minor* and *Common Chord Progressions in Major*, I present several common chord progressions. Mine is by no means a complete or even thorough compendium of harmonic motion. These are truly just *some* of the many, many ways chords can progress one to another.

The chord progressions I present can serve as "song starters." I suggest you play around with them. Have fun combining them and otherwise varying them. See what you can come up with. There just might be a hit song awaiting your discovery, hiding amongst the appendices!

Scales

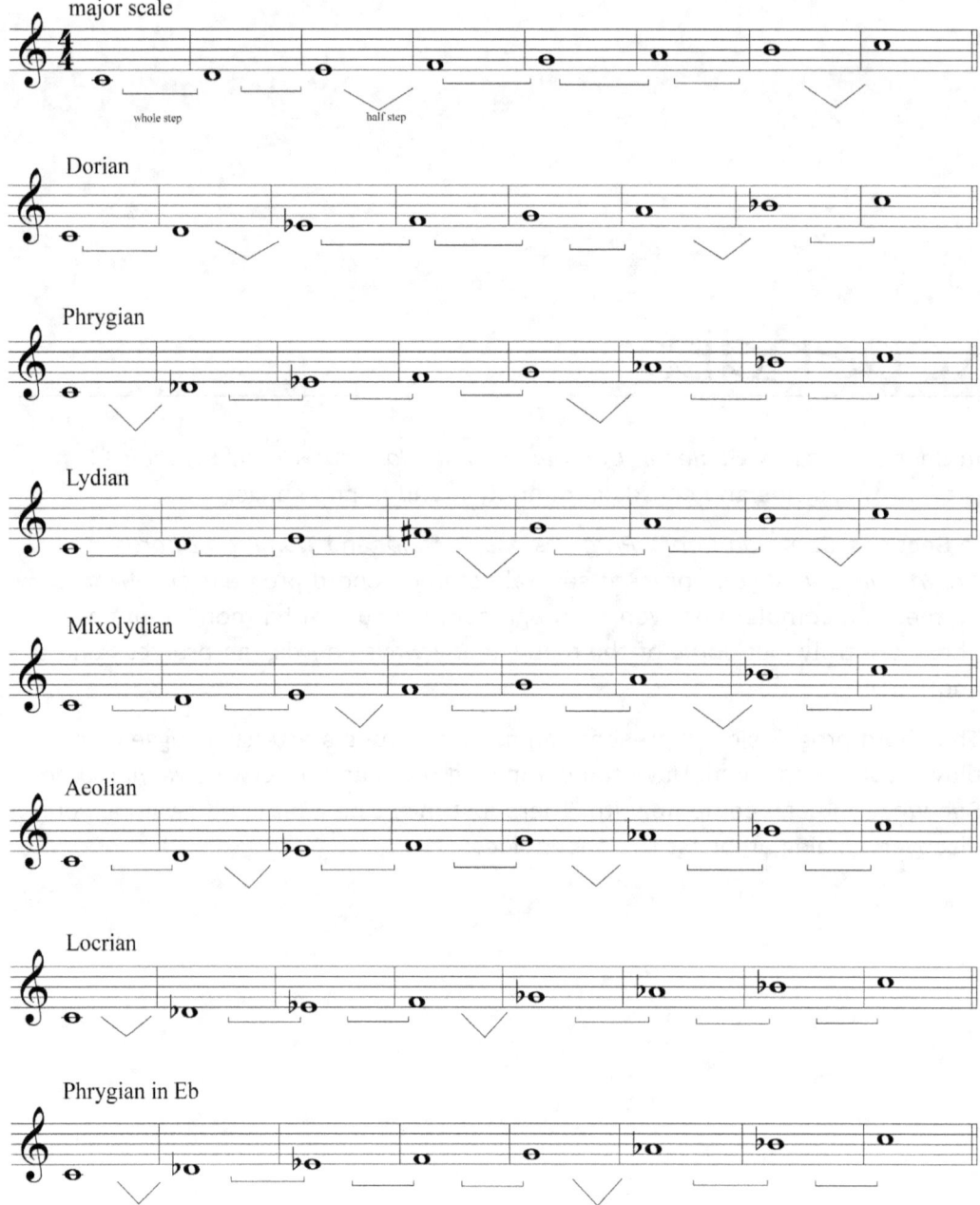

Appendix

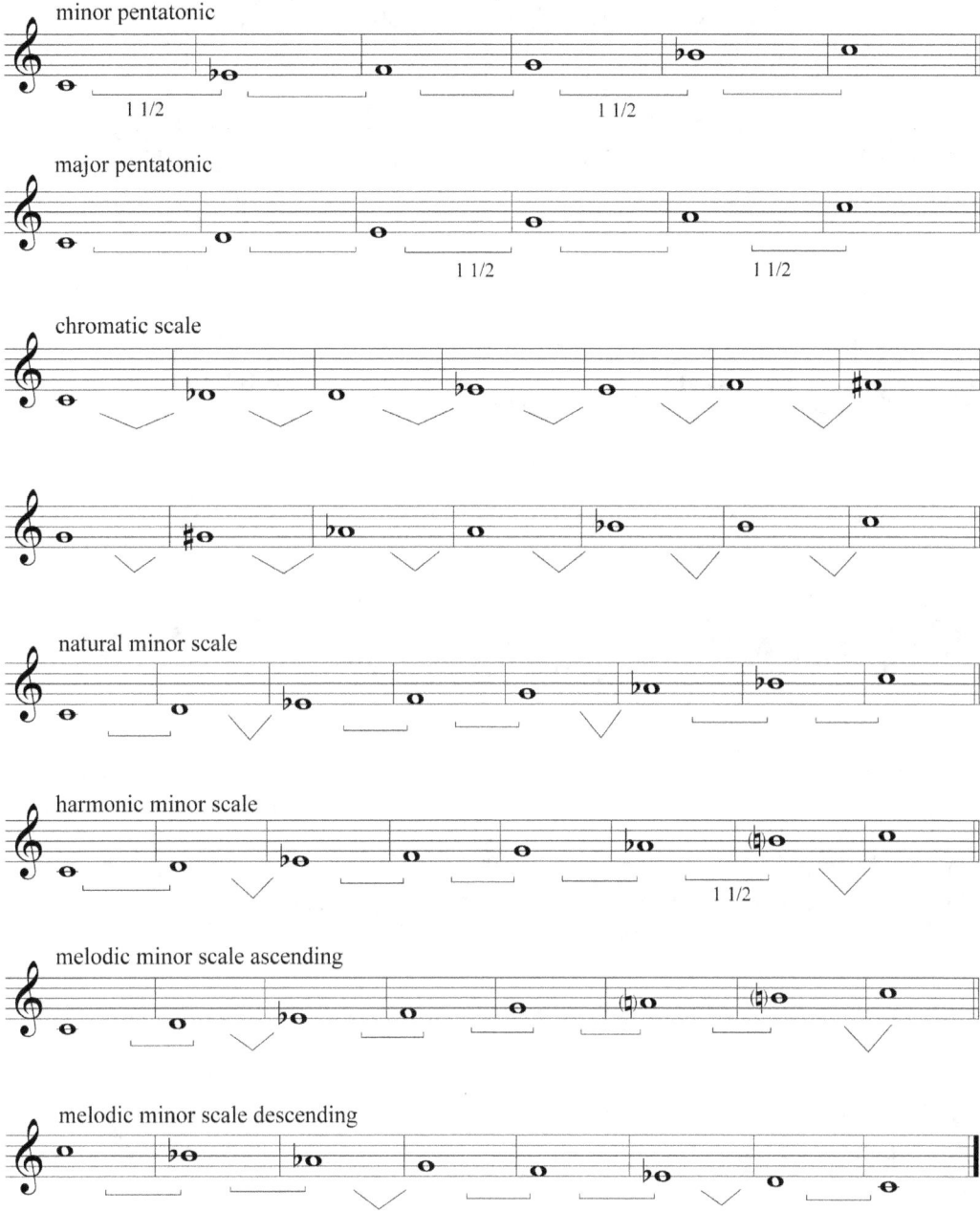

Scales in Comparison

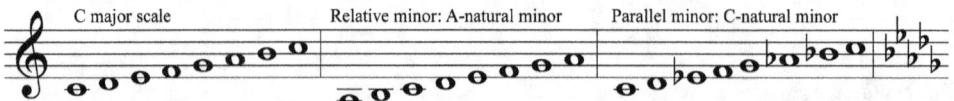

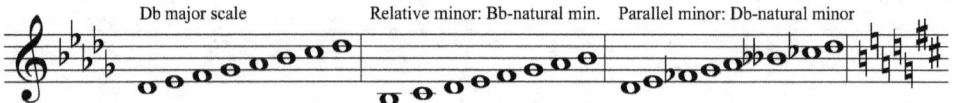

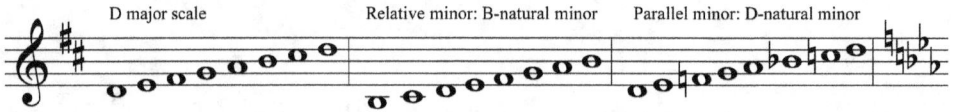

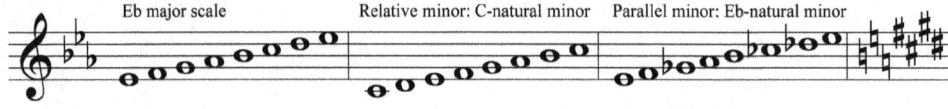

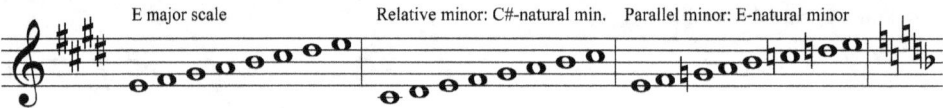

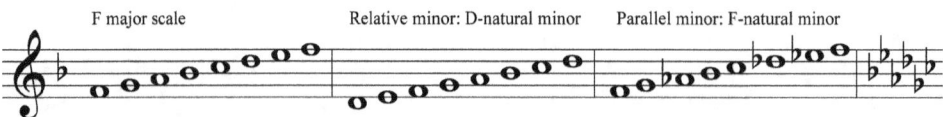

Appendix

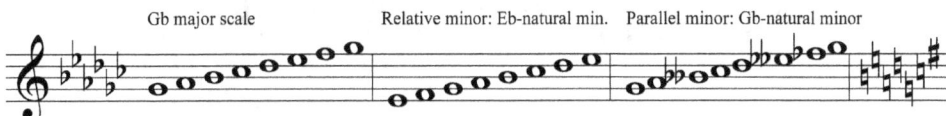

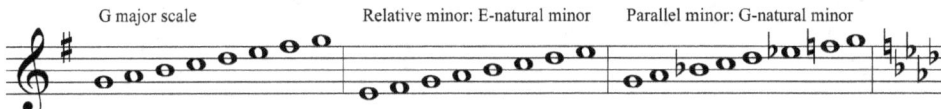

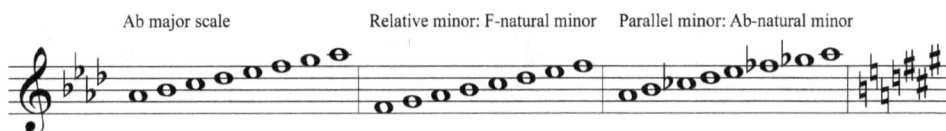

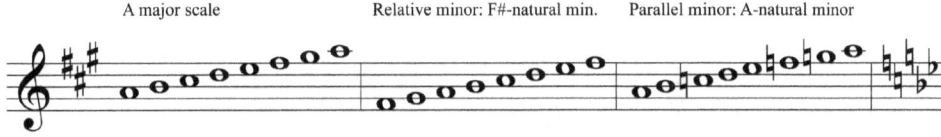

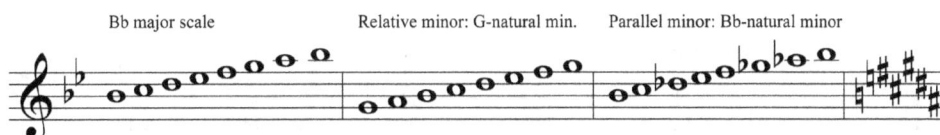

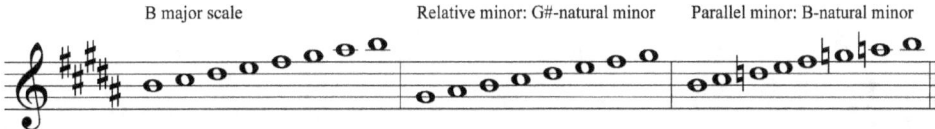

Common Chord Symbols

Appendix

Common Chord Progressions in Minor

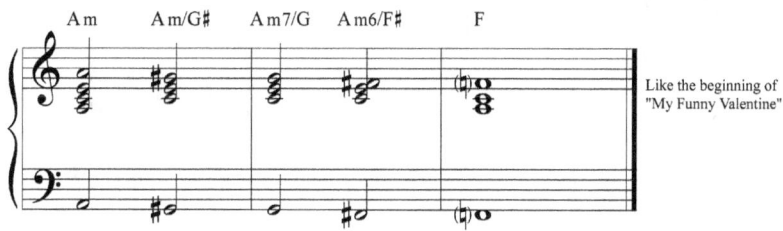

Like the beginning of "My Funny Valentine"

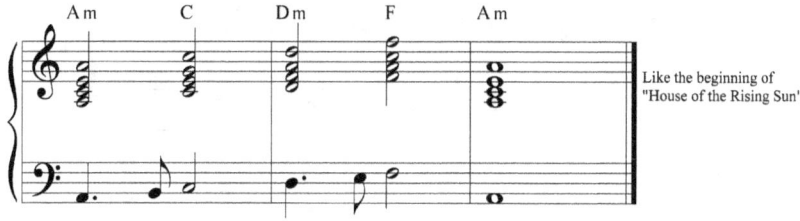

Like the beginning of "House of the Rising Sun"

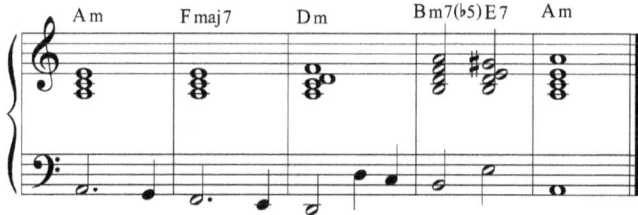

Common Chord Progressions in Major

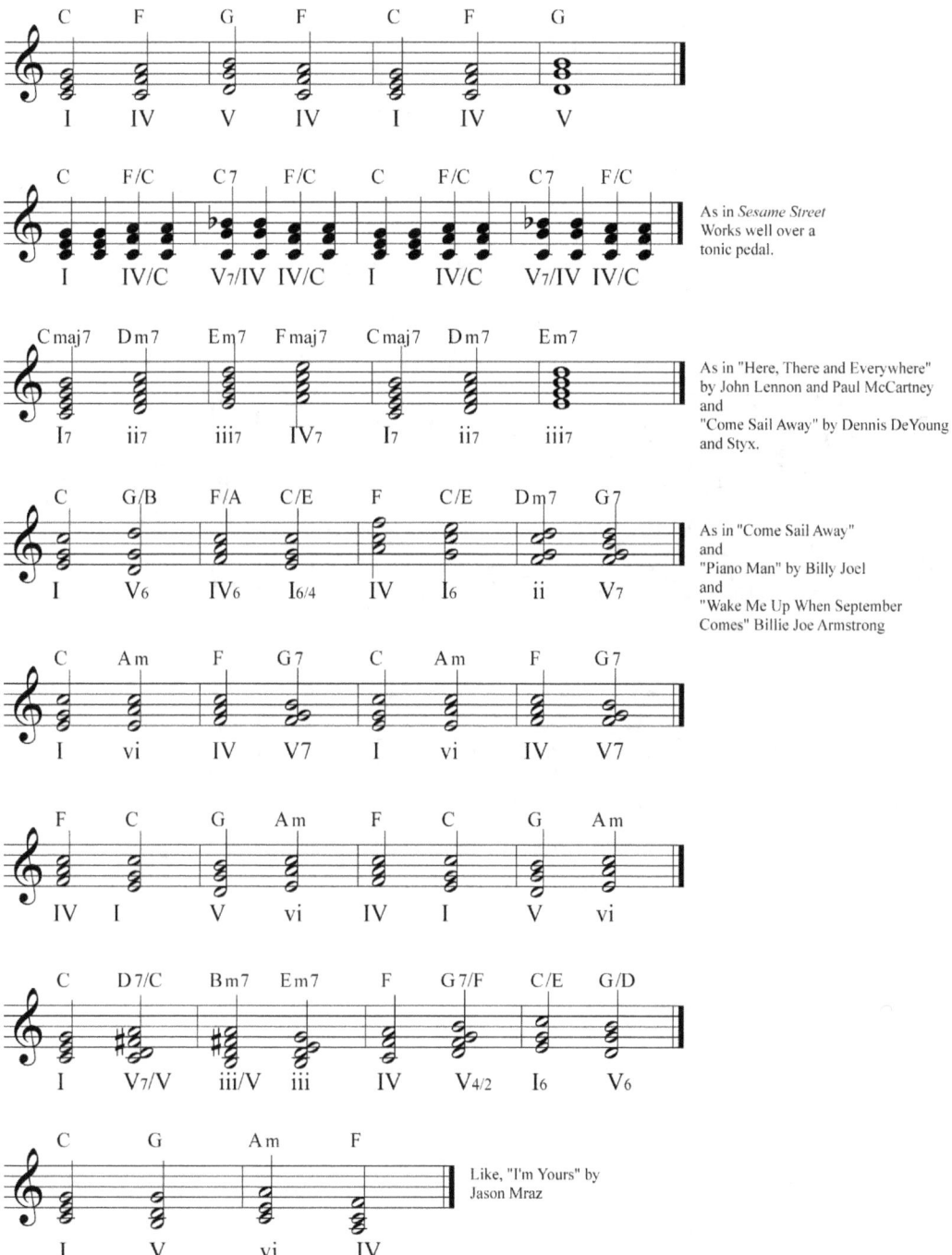

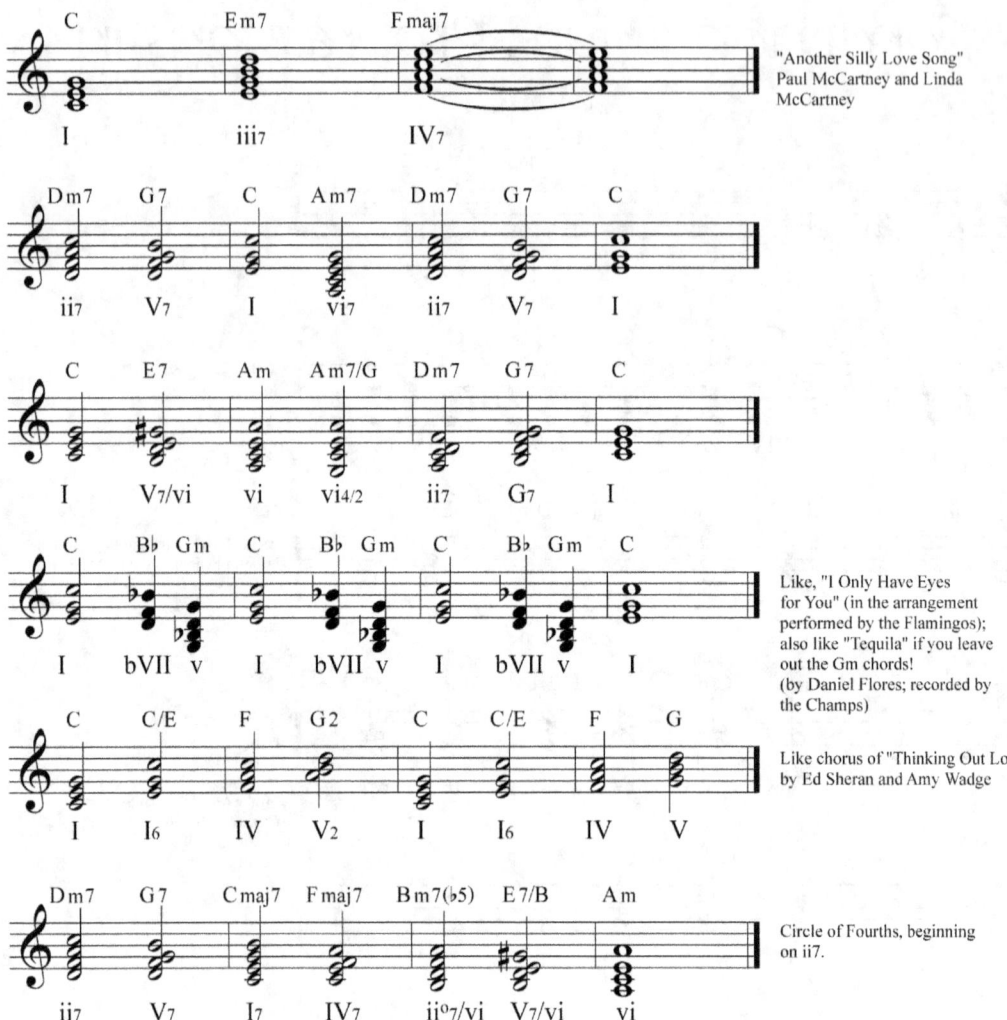

Glossary

Term	Definition
added note chord	A triad plus an extra added pitch, most often a second, fourth, sixth, ninth, eleventh or thirteenth above the root. Pitches added above the seventh are sometimes called extensions.
aeolian mode	One of the eight modes of the medieval Roman Catholic Church, originally spanning the octave from a to a^1 with its intervals following the pattern: whole step, half step, whole step, whole step, half step, whole step, whole step.
album	A collection of recorded music
alliteration	The same sound or letter at the beginning of, adjacent to, or near each other.
anacrusis	One or more notes that occur before the first metrically strong beat of a musical phrase. Also called a pick-up note.
andante	A tempo indication of music instructing the performer to play a piece or section of a piece of music at a "walking speed," that is, moderately slow, from about 76 to 108 beats per minute.
antecedent	The first of two complementary phrases of music followed by a consequent phrase; also called the question, with the consequent called the answer.
anthem	An inspirational song that becomes identified with and emblematic of an entity: a country, a corporation, a product, etc. Also, a religious song with a Biblical text sung as part of a church service.

Term	Definition
arpeggio	A manner of performing chords in a horizontal manner, rather than vertically. The notes of the chord are played one after another, either ascending or descending.
assonance	When two words that are in proximity share the same vowel sound but start with different consonant sounds.
atonal	See "twelve-tone system"
augmented	Intervals: when a perfect or major interval is made larger by one half step. Harmony: a major triad whose chord fifth is raised one half step.
augmented triad	An augmented triad is built by stacking two major thirds, one on top of the other; a major third within the interval of an augmented fifth. The augmented triad can be seen occurring naturally in the triad constructed of diatonic thirds that is built on scale step III of the ascending melodic minor scale. For instance, E flat, G, B in C melodic minor
authentic cadence	A harmonic progression, V – I.
binary form	A composition made up of two interdependent periods.
The Blank Page	The most frightening aspect of a professional life in a creative occupation.
block chord	Three or more pitches, usually thirds, stacked one on another and played simultaneously.
blue notes	The purposeful singing a bit flat of scale degrees three and seven.
Blues Form	A single-period strophic song form of twelve or sixteen measures. Its melody is typically composed using the blues or jazz scale and is harmonized using the primary chords of the major or minor key, each with an added minor seventh.
blues scale	Also called the jazz scale. One of several six-, seven-, eight or nine-note pitch collection. It distinctively features alternate versions of scale degree three, four and seven.
borrowed	Also called modal mixture or modal interchange. The process of harmonizing a melody with a chord found in the parallel minor or major key. For instance, using the minor subdominant in a major key.
bridge	An inconsequential phrase that is placed between two more significant sections of music. Bridges do not include musical or lyrical material that is highly developed or that adds significantly to the development of the song. Often in stylistic contrast to the verse and chorus periods.

Glossary

Term	Definition
buyout production music library model	A recorded anthology of (usually) instrumental music produced for exclusive use in broadcast and marketing productions licensed with a one-time fee that yields no residual payments.
cadence	A melodic or harmonic configuration that creates a sense of resolution.
call-and-response	A compositional and performance technique where one artist or group of performers will present a musical fragment that will be either replicated or responded to by a second artist or group of performers.
choir music	Also, choral music. Music composed for an ensemble of singers.
chord	Three or more pitches arranged vertically and sounded more or less simultaneously.
chord chart	Indicates the simplified rhythm of the chord changes in slash notation
chord fifth	Also, simply, the fifth. The interval of a fifth above the root in a triad.
chord of resolution	The culmination of a cadence; in a melodic cadence, the note of resolution.
chord substitution	The replacement of certain chords with others that the arranger deems to be more appropriate for the assignment at hand, reharmonization.
chord third	Also, the third. The middle voice of a triad in root position and close voicing. The interval of a third above the chord root.
chord symbol notation/chord symbols	Abbreviations used by pop and jazz musicians to indicate harmonic accompaniment in song lead sheets.
chorus	A period that recurs sung each time with the same lyrics. The chorus lyric contains the title of the song. Also known as the refrain, hammer, sing-along, and channel.
chromatic alterations	Scale steps are chromatically altered when they are raised or lowered by a semitone.
chromatic harmony	See "modal mixture"
chromatic scale	A scale that divides an octave into semitones or half steps.
Circle of Fifths	A pedagogic and musical organization of keys and chords in tonal music where the tonics are organized a circle beginning with C and moving clockwise through the sharp keys and counterclockwise through the flat keys.
circular phrase	A phrase that begins and ends on a tonic harmony.
Classical Period	Music that was popular from about 1750 through 1825.

Term	Definition
coda/codetta	A section of music added at the end of a composition whose sole purpose is to announce the song's conclusion. A codetta is a diminutive version of a coda.
color tones	Non-functional pitches added to chords.
Columbia Harmony (also called the Pilgrim's Musical Companion)	The anthology written by Charles Spilman and Benjamin Shaw.
consequent	The second of two complementary phrases; also called the answer.
consonant intervals	Intervals of major and minor thirds, perfect fifths, and major and minor sixths.
counterpoint	A secondary melodic line that is interdependent on both the melody and the harmony.
deceptive resolution	A harmonic progression where the chord of resolution is something other than what might be expected (e.g. V7 - bVI)
development	The compositional process of variation in melody, rhythm, and harmony.
diatonic chords	Chords composed exclusively of major or minor scale tones stacked in thirds.
diatonic scale	Diatonic scales are seven-note collections where each letter of the musical alphabet (A, B, C, D, E, F, G) represents only a single pitch, all pitches are adjacent, and the interval between adjacent pitches is either a semitone or a whole tone. The notes of diatonic scales are easily represented by the white keys of the piano keyboard. Diatonic scales include the natural minor, major, and the six church modes (Dorian, Phrygian, Lydian, mixolydian, and Aeolian), as distinct from the chromatic scale that employs only semitones
diegetic music	Music in a film that appears to be emanating from some element of the action on the screen (e.g., the music that appears to come from the on-screen radio or orchestra).
diminished	A minor or perfect interval when made smaller by one half step is said to be diminished.
diminished triad	A minor third within a diminished fifth. The triad built on the seventh degree of the major scale, or the supertonic of the minor scale. The diminished triad is constructed by stacking intervals of a minor third, one on top the other.
dissonant intervals	Intervals of a second, fourth or seventh.
dodecaphonic	See "twelve tone system"

Glossary

Term	Definition
dominant preparatory chords	The chords that resolve to the dominant, most often the chord of the supertonic or the subdominant, but also the diminished seventh chord constructed on the half step below the dominant ant the major triad (or dominant seventh chord) built on the flatted sixth.
Dorian mode	One of the eight modes of the medieval Roman Catholic Church, originally spanning the octave from d to d¹ with its intervals following the pattern: whole step, half step, whole step, whole step, whole step, half step, whole step.
double period	A pairing of two separate, but interdependent, musical utterances where each is a phrase of music that is experienced as complete and requiring no further resolution.
downbeat	The colloquial name given to the first beat of a measure.
dyad	A two-note chord. In pop music, a power chord composed of a triad without the third.
end rhyme	See "rhyme-scheme"
enharmonically equivalent	Pitches that are named differently but represent the same frequency. For example, A♭ and G♯.
environmental music	Background music played by in shopping malls, restaurants, and at workplaces.
first inversion	A chord with its third in the bass.
folk	Music that has come down to us through the years as part of an oral tradition passed from one generation to the next, whose author is unknown.
form	Within the context of our present study, the term is used to define the order, repetition, and development of musical phrases.
full rhyme	See "ordinary rhyme"
grand rights	Performance rights granted by the composer and lyricist to the producers of musical theater and operatic works.
Great American Songbook	Also called, "standards," the name given to the loosely defined collection of songs created for Broadway and Hollywood musical of the 1930s, '40s and '50s.
guerrilla marketing	Innovative, unconventional, and low-cost marketing techniques aimed at obtaining maximum exposure for a product.
half cadence	A harmonic progression that resolves on the dominant.
half rhyme	Word pairs that end with the same consonant, but do not share the same preceding vowel sound.
harmonic intervals	Intervals that occur simultaneously (vertically).

Term	Definition
Harmonice musices odhecaton	The first collection of music printed entirely from movable type. Published by Ottaviano Petrucci (1466-1539) of Venice in 1501.
historical bar form	A form of musical composition that follows the formal musical design, AAB.
hook	In pop music (especially recordings), any short lyrical, melodic, or rhythmic fragment that provides a composition or recording a distinctively unique and memorable sonic point of reference.
imperfect rhyme	See "half rhyme".
intellectual property	The product of an artistic endeavor. In the music business, songs and recordings are construed as intellectual property. Like other kinds of property, intellectual property can be owned, sold, rented, stolen, or given away.
internal rhyme	See "rhyme-scheme".
intertextual	For our purposes, the interrelationship between one piece of music and another, understanding that all music references some other preexisting piece of music.
interval	The distance between two pitches when counting on the musical alphabet.
introductory verse	A rambling sixteen- to thirty-two measure period whose lyric establishes a context for the song that is to follow. The introductory verse sets the stage for the singer to unfold the story of the song proper.
Ionian mode	A scale whose organization of tones and semitones follows the same pattern as the major scale, e.g., the collection of pitches from C3 to C4.
jazz-scale	See "blues-scale".
jingle production houses	Companies market the works of their employees who are charged with composing and producing recorded music for advertising and marketing.
key of the moment	See "temporary tonic".
leading tone	The seventh degree of a scale; one semitone below scale degree one.
lead sheet	Musical manuscript indicating melody, harmony (in chord symbol notation), and lyrics.
lining out	A tradition of choral recitation, where the leader reads a line and the congregation repeats it in unison, or where the leader sings a line that is then repeated. Also called call-and-response.
Locrian mode	A scalar collection whose interval relationship mimics the diatonic collection from b to b¹, with pitches organized as follows: half step,

Glossary

Term	Definition
	whole step, whole step, half step, whole step, whole step, whole step.
Lydian mode	One of the eight modes of the medieval Roman Catholic Church, originally spanning the octave from a to a1 with its intervals following the pattern: whole step, whole step, whole step, half step, whole step, whole step, half step.
lyrical form	The way lyrics are constructed regarding their rhyme scheme.
lyrical hook	A short memorable word phrase.
major pentatonic scale	A five-note scale whose intervals follow the pattern: whole step, whole step, minor third, whole step, minor third.
major seventh	A musical interval composed of eleven semitones; the interval that spans from the tonic to the leading tone. The name also can apply to the major triad with an added interval of a major seventh above the root
major third	An interval of 4 half steps.
measure	Also called a bar. A unit of time in music determined by the prevailing meter signature and represented in manuscript as the space between two bar lines.
mechanical license	A legal agreement issued by a publisher that grants a record company permission to record a composition published by the publisher.
mechanical royalty	The fee paid by a record company to a publisher for the license of their intellectual property.
mediant	Scale degree three.
melisma	A single syllable accompanied by a group of more than a one note.
melodic cadence	See "cadence"
melodic contour	The shape of a melody, specifically, how it moves higher and lower.
melodic development	Modifying a melody over time.
melodic intervals	Intervals that occur in succession
melodic motive/hook	A short, rhythmically impressive, and memorable melodic fragment.
melodic rhythm	The rhythm of the melody.
metadata	The term used to describe copyright ownership information of recordings and the musical compositions therein contained.
meter	Music occurs in time that is measured by beats, an even succession of metrical pulses, like the sound that is made when one marches. The

Term	Definition
	pulses are organized in groups, most commonly in groups of two, three or four. Other groupings, including five, six, seven, nine, and twelve, are also found in Western music.
meter signature	Also called the time signature. The fractional number that is placed at the beginning of the composition or section thereof. The denominator of the time signature indicates the basic note value of the meter (what note value receives the basic beat of the piece). The numerator indicates the number of note values in a measure (the number of beats found in each measure).
middle rhyme	See "rhyme-scheme"
minor pentatonic scale	A five-note scale whose intervals follow the pattern: minor third, whole step, whole step, minor third, whole step.
minor-sixth	An interval that spans eight semitones. For instance, A to F, or C to A♭.
minor third	An interval of three half steps.
mixolydian mode	One of the eight modes of the medieval Roman Catholic Church, originally spanning the octave from g to g¹ with its intervals following the pattern: whole step, whole step, half step, whole step, whole step, half step, whole step.
modal	Music based on the Gregorian modes (as opposed to major, minor, or other scales), including the Dorian, Phrygian, Lydian, mixolydian, and Aeolian.
modal mixture	Harmonization borrowed from the parallel mode, also called "modal mixture."
moderato	A moderate tempo between andante (a walking tempo) and allegro (fast).
musical alphabet	A, B, C, D, E, F, G, etc.
musical analysis	The dissection of a composition regarding its melody, harmony, rhythm and how these parts interact and relate.
musical annuity	Substantial royalty payments received from a copyright for the rest of the writer's life.
musical form	The architecture of a composition.
musical period	A complete musical statement in tonal music that ends in a harmonic cadence that requires no immediate further resolution.
musical phrase	A unit of music that is self-contained. It is heard as a complete musical statement with a beginning, middle and end, concluding with a final harmonic and melodic cadence that requires no further resolution. A phrase in music is analogous to a clause in language.

Glossary

Term	Definition
musicals	A play or movie where the action is moved forward through singing and dancing. Made popular in the 20th century in England and the U.S., musical theater is related to operetta, comic opera, and the revue.
numerical size	Intervals are measured in terms of their numerical size, that is, the number of letter names the two tones span when counting on the musical alphabet.
octave (perfect octave)	An interval of 11 half steps, for instance from middle C to the C eight scale steps higher.
Olney Hymns	A collection in which the Reverend John Newton's poem, "Amazing Grace," was first published in 1779.
opening phrase	A musical phrase whose final cadence resolves on the dominant.
ordinary rhyme	Two words or the final syllables of two words, that are sung or said exactly alike.
passing tone	In melodic writing, an intermediary note, either diatonic or chromatic, between two scalar pitches.
pentatonic scale	Any of several five note scales, most commonly following the same ordering as the black keys of the piano beginning on either the E♭ (for the minor pentatonic), or the G♭ (for the major pentatonic).
perfect authentic cadence	The harmonic progression of dominant to tonic where both chords are in root position and the chord of resolution (I) has the tonic in the highest voice.
perfect consonances	Intervals of perfect octaves and perfect fifths.
performance royalties	Fees collected by a PRO and paid to the copyright owner for the public performance of a composition. Fees are shared equally by the writers and the publisher.
Performing Rights Organizations (PROs)	Organizations that collect and distribute performance fees to publishers and writers. In the U.S. these include ASCAP, BMI, SESAC, GMO, or PMR.
period	A complete musical thought roughly equivalent to a paragraph in written language that typically includes an antecedent and consequent phrase.
Phrygian mode	One of the five original modes of the Roman Church, its pitches proceed stepwise as: half, whole, whole, whole, half, whole, whole.
pillar/primary chords	The tonic, subdominant, and dominant harmonies of the tonal system. The I, IV and V chords.

Term	Definition
pitch	Term used to describe musical sounds vibrating at well-defined frequencies (as opposed to noise).
polysyllabic rhyme	Word pairs where the last two or three syllables match exactly.
pop music	Any of many genres that are successful in the commercial marketplace, including country, folk, jazz, adult contemporary, R&B, and rock.
Pop Song Binary Form	One of three binary form configurations. Usually thirty-two measures long, divided into two distinct sixteen-measure periods. Each sixteen-measure period consists of two balanced eight measure phrases, labeled A, B and C. Each eight-measure phrase, A, B and C, is commonly divided into two four-measure sub-phrases, where the A-phrase repeats at the beginning of the second period.
power chords	In rock and pop music – a dyad performed on an electric guitar consisting of the root and the fifth of the underlying harmony.
pre-chorus	In a contemporary pop song, a four-to-eight measure phrase that precedes and leads the listener to the chorus.
production	Referring to the artistic musical activities that transpire in the creation of a commercial recording.
production music library	A collection of music produced and licensed by its publisher for exclusive use background music in broadcast commercials, television programs, educational, motivational, and corporate films. The compositions in a production music library are not licensed for use in entertainment, like commercially released recordings.
prosody	The rhythm of language with specific attention to how syllables are accented.
push marketing	A form of marketing where an advertiser creates demand for a product or service through repeated media advertising. This contrasts with "pull marketing," where demand for a product or service is the result of buyers perceived needs.
quality	The sonic characteristic assigned to define further an interval's nature, including major, minor, perfect, augmented, and diminished.
quartal harmony	Harmony based on combinations of fourths rather than thirds (tertian harmony).
radio station IDs / shotgun announcements / sweepers	Very short musical logos designed to be a quickly recognizable sonic identification for a radio or television station or network.
recitation tone/reciting tone	In liturgical chant, a pitch that is repeated during the singing of a long phrase of chant.

Glossary

Term	Definition
relative major	In minor keys, the key constructed on the mediant and that shares the same key signature.
relative minor	In major keys, the key whose root is the submediant of the major key and that shares the same key signature. For instance, G major and E minor, or F major and D minor.
remote key	A key other than the relative key, the key of the dominant or the subdominant.
rhyme scheme	The pattern of the rhyming words of a poem or song lyric. When lyricists place rhymes at the end of a line of text, this is called an end rhyme or terminal rhyme. When a lyricist rhymes a word in the middle of a line of text with the last word of a line or if two words in the middle of a line rhyme, it is called an internal rhyme or a middle rhyme.
riff / lick	Melodic, rhythmic, or harmonic motives that occur in the accompaniment; hooks.
root	The pitch upon which a chord is constructed.
root position	A chord voiced with its root in the bass.
Rounded Binary Form	A form of compositional organization consisting of two periods, thus the binary designation, where the first period recurs after the playing of the second period. This yields a formal structure, ABA.
rhythm track	In a recording, the part performed by the piano, bass, drums, guitar, and percussion.
sawaal-javaab	Literally "call and response" in classical music of North India.
scale	The organization of a pitch collection from lowest to highest.
secondary dominant	A preparatory chord that functions as the dominant seventh of a target chord.
second inversion	A chord voiced with its fifth in the bass.
semitone (half step)	Also, a half step. The smallest interval in Western music, represented by any two adjacent keys on a piano keyboard. For instance, D to E♭, or B to C.
slant rhyme	See "half rhyme."
slash notation	Shorthand musical notation that indicates rhythm only.
spirituals	A form of religious folk song first sung by African Americans in the southern United States. Also called revival and camp meeting songs. Spirituals date back to the early part of the 19th century.
standards	The jargon used by musicians to call songs that are often performed and often recorded by many musicians. Also called "evergreens." The

Term	Definition
	loosely defined collection of songs in the so called, "Great American Songbook."
stop chorus	A performance style in which the rhythm section plays only the first beat of each measure while a musician plays an improvised solo.
strophic form	A single-period form characterized by lyrics that change from verse to verse over an unvaried melody.
sub-phrase	A short phrase, usually four measures long, within a phrase.
supertonic	Scale degree two.
supertonic triad	A triad built on scale degree two, the supertonic.
synchronization royalties	Fees paid by the producer to the copyright owner when a piece of music is licensed for use as part of a motion picture soundtrack.
tempo	The rate of speed at which music unfolds.
temporary tonic	A harmony that temporarily functions as the tonic in a larger composition.
terminal-rhyme	See "rhyme-scheme"
tessitura	The pitch range of a composition or a section of a composition.
The Great White Way	The colloquial name for New York City's Broadway theater district.
third inversion	A chord voiced with its seventh in the bass.
time signature	The fractional number placed at the beginning of the composition or section thereof. The denominator of the time signature indicates the basic note value of the meter (what note value receives the basic beat of the piece). The numerator indicates the number of note values in a measure (the number of beats found in each measure).
tonic triad	A chord built on the first degree of the scale, where scale degree one (the tonic) is the root of the chord.
transpose	Shifting from one key center to another while retaining all the melodic and harmonic intervallic relationships.
triad	A three-note chord, in the tonal system, composed of thirds.
tritone	The interval of an augmented fourth or diminished fifth; the span of three whole steps. Tritones are heard as dissonant in all cultures.
tritone substitution	In reharmonization, using a substitute chord whose root is a tritone away from the true dominant chord for which it is the substitute. The two chords, the original and its tritone substitute, always contain the same tritone in its composition, though the notes of the interval are spelled enharmonically.

Glossary

Term	Definition
troubadour / trouvérs	Noblemen singers and songwriters from southern France and northeast Spain who lived from about 1100 to 1300. The troubadours and trouvérs composed the first vernacular lyric songs of Europe.
twelve-tone system	As distinct from the tonal system, the twelve-tone or dodecaphonic system uses a serial ordering of all twelve chromatic pitches, uniquely formed for each composition.
Twentieth-Century Bar Form	The most common musical form of the first half of the Twentieth-Century, Twentieth-Century Bar Form closely resembles the formal design of the rounded binary form: AABA.
unison	The interval formed by two playing's of the same pitch; the simultaneous performance of a musical line.
verse	A period that complements and leads to the chorus. Verses are usually in strophic form, where the lyrics change from verse to verse, but the melody remains the same.
Verse/Chorus	Double period songs that feature a strophic verse and a chorus that repeats exactly.
Virginia Harmony	The collection in which "New Britain," (the musical setting for John Newton's text, "Amazing Grace"), first appeared.
work-for-hire	A legal agreement wherein a creative agrees to perform or compose as part of his employment without further compensation.

References

Music Examples
(cited in order of appearance)

YESTERDAY, John Lennon and Paul McCartney, © 1965 SONY/ATV Tunes, LLC dba ATV OBO ATV (Northern Songs Catalog).

THE GIRL FROM IPANEMA, V. de Moraes, N. Gimbel, and A.C. JOBIM, © 1962 Words West, LLC/Songs of Universal, Inc.

YOUR CHEATIN' HEART, Hank Williams, © 1953 Sony/ATV Acuff Rose Music.

PIANO MAN, Billy Joel, © 1973 Almo Music Corp./OBO Joelsongs.

WAKE ME UP WHEN SEPTEMBER ENDS, Billie Joe Armstrong & Green Day, © 2003 WB Music Corp. /OBO Green Daze Music.

BRISTOL STOMP, David Appell and Kal Mann, © 1961 Spirit Two Music/OBO Kal Mann Music.

BLUE MOON Lorenz Hart and Richard Rodgers, © 1935 EMI Robins Catalog, Inc.

CAROLINA IN MY MIND, James Taylor, © 1968 EMI Blackwood Music, Inc., EMI April Music, Inc. OBO Country Road Music.

WHAT A WONDERFUL WORLD, G. D. Weiss, George Douglas, and B. Thiele, © 1967 Range Road Music, Inc., Quartet Music, Inc., Imagen Sounds OBO Abilene Music, LLC.

AUTUMN LEAVES, J. Kosma, J. Mercer, J., and J. Prévert, © 1945 SDRM, Morley Music Co. /OBO Enoch & Cie.

DINDI, A. de Oliveira, R. Gilbert, and A. C. Jobim, © 1966 Ipanema Music, Corcovado Music Corp.

DAYS OF WINE AND ROSES, H. Mancini, and J. Mercer, © 1962 W. B. Music Corp.

GONE WITH THE WIND, H. Magidson and A. Wrubel, © 1937 Bourne Co.

I SHOULD CARE, S. Cahn, A. Stordahl and P. Weston © 1944 SGA OBO Stordahl Music Publishing Co., Hanover Music Corp.

I ONLY HAVE EYES FOR YOU, A. Dubin and H. Warren © 1934 W. B. Music Corp.

CHAIN OF FOOLS, D. Covay, © 1967 Springtime Music, Inc., Warner-Tamerlane Publishing OBO Pronto Music, Fourteenth Hour Music, Inc.

BE THANKFUL FOR WHAT YOU GOT, Wm. DeVaughn, © 1972 Music Sales Corp., OBO American Dream Music Co., Delicious Apple Music.

AMERICAN WOMAN, Randy Bachman, Burton Cummings, Gary Peterson, Michael Kale, © 1970 Bug Music OBO Shillelagh Music.

AMAZING GRACE, Text by John Newton, Music by Anonymous, public domain

BACKWATER BLUES, Huddie William Ledbetter, public domain

SUNNY, Bobby Hebb, © 1965, 1966, 1971 Portable Music Company, Inc.

I JUST CALLED TO SAY I LOVE YOU, Stevie Wonder, © 1984 Jobete Music Co, Inc., Black Bull Music

THE GAMBLER, Donald Schlitz, ©1977 Sony/ATV Tunes LLC

HOW SWEET IT IS, Eddie Holland, Lamont Dozier, Brian Holland, © 1964, 1978 Jobete Music Co., Inc.

AT THE HOP, Arthur Singer, John Madara, David White, © 1957 Arc Music Corporation and Six Continents Music Publishing, Inc.

YOU'VE GOT A FRIEND, Carol King, © 1971, Colgems-EMI Music, Inc.

ROAR, Lukasz Gottwald, Bonnie McKee, Katy Perry, Martin Max, Henry Russell Walter, © 2013 Kobalt Music Publishing Limited/Warner/Chappell North American Limited

SHAKE IT OFF, Bryan Michael Cox, Jermaine Dupri, Johnta Austin, Mariah Carey, ©2005 W.B.M. Music Corp., Noontime South, Inc., Babyboy's Little Publishing Company, EMI April Music, Inc., Shaniah Cymone Music, Chrysalis Music, Naked Under My Clothes Music, Songs of Universal, Inc. and Rye Songs

JEREMY, Jeff Ament, Eddie Vedder, © 1991 Universal-Polygram International Publishing, Inc. Scribing C-ment Songs, Innocent Bystander.

JEANNIE WITH THE LIGHT BROWN HAIR, Stephen C. Foster, public domain

MY FUNNY VALENTINE, Lorenz Hart, Richard Rodgers, © 1937 Chappell & Co.

GENTLE HEART, Louis Anthony deLise, © 2014 Print Music Source

HERE'S THAT RAINY DAY, Jimmy Van Heusen, Johnny Burke, © 1949, 1953 Burke & Van Heusen, Inc, assigned to Bourne Co. and Dorsey Bros.

MY ROMANCE, Richard Rodgers, Lorenz Hart, © 1935 T. B. Harms Co.

WE DIDN'T START THE FIRE, Billy Joel, © 1989 Joelsongs

NICK & ME, Louis Anthony deLise & Phillip C. Hartman, © 2014 Bocage Music Publishing, LLC

A FINE ROMANCE, Jerome Kern & Dorothy Fields, © 1936 Universal Music Publishing Group

HELP, John Lennon and Paul McCartney, © 1965 Northern Songs, Limited

I CAN'T GIVE YOU ANYTHING BUT LOVE, Jimmy McHugh & Dorothy Fields, © 1928 Shapiro Bernstein & Co. Inc. O/B/o Aldi Music

EVERYTHING HAPPENS TO ME, Tom Adair & Matt Dennis, © 1941 Dorsey Brothers Music

Periodicals

Custodero, L.A. (2006), Singing Practices in 10 Families with Young Children. *JRME*, Vol. 54. No. 1 pp. 37-56.

Hohmann, A., Rüber, T., Schlaug, G., Wan, C.Y. (2010 April 1), The Therapeutic Effects of Singing in Neurological Disorders. *Music Perception*, 27(4):287-295.

Ingham, Tim. (2018), A Million New Tracks Are Being Uploaded to Streaming Service Napster Every 6 Weeks. *MUSICBUSINESS Worldwide*; June 10, 2018 edition. (https://www.musicbusinessworldwide.com/a-million-tracks-are-being-uploaded-to-streaming-service-napster-every-6-weeks/)

Inman, D. (2011), Industry Spotlight: The Harry Fox Agency. *The American Songwriter*.

Rorem, N. (1974), Why I Write as I Do. *American Music Center's Symposium on Contemporary Music*, City University of New York. *Tempo Magazine*.

Tavern, Mark (2019), Songwriters, Mark Your Calendars: January 1, 2021. Retrieved from *DJBOOTH* (https://djbooth.net/features/2019-07-12-songwriters-mark-your-calendars-royalty-collection/) 23 July 2019.

Tolbert, E. (2001), Music and meaning: An evolutionary story. *Psychology of Music*, 29 (1), 84-94.

Texts

Abbs, Peter and Richardson, John (1990). The Forms of Poetry: A Practical Study Guide. Cambridge University Press.

Aldwell, E., & Schachter, C. (1989). *Harmony and Voice Leading* (2nd ed.). New York: Harcourt Brace Jovanovich College Publishers.

Baskerville, D., & Baskerville, T. (2010). *Music Business Handbook and Career Guide* (9th ed.). Thousand Oaks, CA: Sage Publications, Inc.

Caldwallader, A., & Gagné., D. (1998). *Analysis of Tonal Music: A Schenkerian Approach*. New York: Oxford University Press.

Davis, S. (1985). *The Craft of Lyric Writing*. Cincinnati, OH: Writer's Digest Books.

Feld, S., & Neuman, D. M. (1984). *Sound and Sentiment: Birds, Weeping, Poetics, and Song in Kaluli Expression*. Durham, NC: Duke University Press.

Frank, Robert J., (2010) *Theory on the Web*, http://smu.edu/totw/melody.htm

Grout, D.J., Palisca, C. (2001). *A History of Western Music* (6th ed.). New York: W. W. Norton & Company, Inc.

The Harvard Dictionary of Music, (4th ed.). ISBN 0-674-01163-5 © 1986, 2003 The Belknap Press of Harvard Univ Press

Hugh, F. (1975). *The World of Entertainment: Hollywood's Greatest Musicals*. New York: Avon Books.

Jackson, G.P. (Ed.) (1964). *Spiritual Folk Songs of Early America*

Jaffe, Andrew. (1983). *Jazz Theory*. Dubuque, IA: Wm. C. Brown Company Publishers.

Klein, M.L. (2005). *Intertextuality in Western Art Music*. Bloomington, IN: Indiana University Press.

Laitz, S.G. (2008). *The Complete Musician* (2nd ed.). New York: Oxford University Press.

Levitin, D. J. (2006). *This is Your Brain on Music*. New York, NY: Plume Books.

Lomax, A., Asch, M. (Eds.) (1962) *The Leadbelly Songbook*. New York: Oak Publications.

Orem, P. W. (1924). *Theory and Composition of Music*, Theodore Presser Co. Phila.

Pattison, P. (1991). *Songwriting: Essential Guide to Lyric Form and Structure*. Boston: Berklee Press.

Pere, B. (2010). *Songcrafters' Coloring Book.* Mystic, CT: Creative Songwriting Academy Press.

Pinsky, R. and Dietz, M. (2006). *An Invitation to Poetry.* W. W. Norton & Co.

Tolbert, E. (2001). *Music and meaning: An evolutionary story.* Psychology of Music, 29(1), 84-94.

Turek, R. (2007). *Theory for Today's Musician.* New York: McGraw-Hill.

Webb, J. (1998). *Tunesmith: Inside the Art of Songwriting.* New York: Hyperion.

Finale® Owner's Manual (2014). Eden Prairie, MN: Make Music

Interviews

William DeVaughn, E-mail Interview, 30 June 2019. Hit songwriter and performer, Ft. Washington, MD

David Ivory, E-mail Interview, 24 June 2019; Grammy-nominated engineer, producer, songwriter, and Director of Sound Recording and Music Technology, Montgomery County Community College, Blue Bell, PA

Lori Landew, Partner and Co-Chair, Fox Rothschild, LLP. Philadelphia, PA.

Joseph Renzetti, E-mail Interview, 15 June 2019; Academy Award-winning composer and arranger of many top-ten hit records. New York, NY. *www.JoeRenzetti.net*

Bernard Max Resnick, Esq., E-mail Interview, 20 May 2019 – 1 June 2019; Bernard M. Resnick, Esq., P.C., Bala Cynwyd, PA. *www.BernardResnick.com*

Erik Sabo, Esq., E-mail Interview, 02 Aug 2019; Music Industry Professor, Saint Joseph's University, Philadelphia, PA.

Stephanie Seiple, E-mail Interview, 4 & 10 June 2019; Vice President of Business Development, Crank Media Intelligence, Philadelphia, PA

Jonathan Sprout, E-mail Interview, 19 & 20 June 2019; Grammy-nominated songwriter and performer, Sprout Recordings, Southampton, PA. *www.JonSprout.com*

Tess Taylor, E-mail Interview, 29 & 30 June 2019; President, National Association of Record Industry Professionals; *NARIP.com*, @NARIP, Los Angeles, CA

Websites

- Harry Fox Agency - http://www.harryfox.com
- Mood Media - http://www.moodmedia.com
- ASCAP - http://www.ascap.com/about
- BMI - http://www.bmi.com/about
- SESAC - http://www.sesac.com/About/About.aspx
- NARAS - http://www.grammy.org
- MLC – http://www.supportthemlc.com
- National Association of Broadcasters (NAB) - http://www.nab.org/
- Alphabet Song - http://en.wikipedia.org/wiki/Alphabet_song
- Tin Pan Alley - http://en.wikipedia.org/wiki/Tin_Pan_Alley
- Great American Songbook - http://en.wikipedia.org/wiki/Great_American_Songbook
- Songwriters Guild of America - http://www.songwritersguild.com
- Minstrels - https://en.wikipedia.org/wiki/Minstrel

Index

Index of Terms

---A---

album, 169, 221
Amazon Music, 178
anacrusis, 54, 57, 221
anthem, 172, 221
Apple Music, 178
atonal. See twelve-tone system

---B---

bassline, 23
    passing tone, 31

beat, 14
Billboard magazine, 12, 29, 93, 100, 199
blue notes, 8, 74, 222
bridge, 100, 115
buyout music, 171, 223

---C---

cadence, 223
    authentic, 37, 50, 59, 130, 222, 229
    deceptive, 37
    deceptive resolution, 224
    half, 50, 225
    harmonic, 55
    melodic, 51, 55

call-and-response, 75, 223
channel. See chorus
children's music, 173
choir music, 175, 223
chords, 3, 17, 223
    added note, 17, 21, 221
    arpeggio, 17, 24, 222
    augmented, 222
    block, 17, 222
    broken. See chords: arpeggio
    building, 17
    chord chart, 22, 223
    color, 76, 224
    diatonic, 17, 224
    diminished, 19, 224
    dominant, 28
    dominant preparatory, 51, 225
    dyad, 28, 225, 230
    fifth, 17, 223
    inversion, 24
        first, 27, 225
        second, 231
        third, 232
    leading tone, 13, 36, 226
    major, 19
    major seventh, 12
    mediant, 33, 63
    minor, 19
    naming, 18
    pillar. See chords:tonic
    power. See chords:dyad
    primary, 20, 229
    progressions, 3, 14, 23
    quality, 18
    resolution, 51, 223
    root, 17, 231
    secondary dominant, 231
    subdominant, 28
    submediant, 28, 31, 63
    substitution, 63, 223
    supertonic, 18, 30
    symbol notation, 223
    third, 17, 223
    tonic, 18, 21, 232
    triad. See triad

chorus, 91, 104, 157, 223,
    lyrics, 92
    stop, 232

chromatic
    collection, 11
    scales, 11

Circle of Fifths, 58, 223
Classical Period, 49, 51, 223
coda, 124, 224
codetta, 107, 124
color tone, 21
Columbia Harmony, 224
contour
    melodic, 3, 53, 58, 59, 227

copyright
    law, 160
    notice, 190

counterpoint
    harmonic, 224
    melodic, 224

---D---

development, 224
    harmonic, 3
    melodic, 3, 60, 227

diegetic music, 163, 224
dodecaphonic. See twelve tone system
downbeat, 147, 225

---E---

enharmonic equivalence, 7, 225
environmental music, 175, 225

---F---

Facebook, 178
fake books, 207
form, 3, 47, 53, 225
    AAB, 112
    AABA, 111, 113
    Bar, 112
    Binary, 222
    Blues, 46, 73, 78, 222
    chart of, 147
    Double Period, 46, 225
    historical bar, 226
    lyrical, 53, 227
    musical, 228
    Pop Song Binary, 46, 129, 130, 230
    Rounded Binary, 115, 231
    Single Period, 46, 73
    spiritual, 74
    strophic, 51, 73, 77, 232
    Twentieth-Century Bar, 46, 60, 111, 113, 143, 233
    Verse/Chorus, 46, 87, 233

Index

---G---

German augmented sixth chord, 135
grand rights, 174, 225
Great American Songbook, 111, 225
guerrilla marketing, 192, 225

---H---

hammer. See chorus
Harmonice musices odhecaton, 159, 226
harmony, 3, 17, 57
   cadence, 55
   chromatic. See modal mixture
   counterpoint, 224
   dominant, 113
   intervals, 8, 225
   motion, 3, 51, 53, 59, 115, 130, 209
   quartal, 230
   rhythm, 14, 47, 62
Harry Fox Agency, 189
hook, 226
   lyrical, 61, 93, 116, 227
   melodic, 61, 93

---I---

intellectual property, 158, 226
intertextuality, 26, 226
intervals, 4, 226
   augmented, 5, 7, 222
   chart of, 5
   compound, 8
   consonance, 12, 224
   diminished, 5, 7, 224
   dissonance, 12, 58, 224
   harmonic, 8, 225
   imperfect, 12
   major, 5
   major seventh, 227
   major third, 227
   melodic, 8, 227
   minor, 5
   minor sixth, 228
   notation, 6
   octave, 4, 229
   perfect, 5, 7, 229
   quality, 230
   simple, 8
   tritone, 58, 232
   unison, 233
ISRC, 191
ISWC, 191

---J---

jingles, 171, 226
Jobs in Music
   arranger, 180
   music conductor, 182
   music contractor, 182
   music copyist, 181
   professional manager, 180
   record producer, 182
   song doctor, 180
   studio musicians, 181
   studio singers, 181

---K---

key of the moment. See temporary tonic
key-of-the-moment, 34
Kindie Rock, 173

---L---

law
   copyright, 160
   entertainment, 184
lead sheet, 22, 226
license, 161
   mechanical, 161, 227
   performance, 161
   synchronization, 161
lining out, 52, 75, 226
list songs, 133
lyrics, 139
   alliteration, 150, 221
   assonance, 81, 149, 222
   hook, 61
   rhythm, 55, 141

---M---

master recording, 191
measure, 53, 73, 227
Mechanical Licensing Collective, 161
Meistersingers, 112
   Bar, 112
melisma, 67, 227
melody, 1, 51, 67
   cadence, 55
   contour, 3, 53, 58, 59, 227
   counterpoint, 224
   development, 3, 60, 227
   folk, 52, 225
   gestures, 3
   hook, 61
   intervals, 8, 227
   motion, 59
   motive, 47, 62, 141, 227
   passing tone, 229
   rhythm, 14, 47, 53, 113, 141, 227
metadata, 191, 227
meter, 3, 15, 47, 53, 227
meter signature, 228, See time signature
Minnesinger, 112
modal mixture, 28, 135, 222, 228
motion
   harmonic, 3, 51, 53, 59, 115, 130, 209
   melodic, 59
motive
   melodic, 47, 62, 141, 227
music publishers, 158
musical alphabet, 228
musical analysis, 47, 228
musical annuity, 159, 228
musical period, 228
musical phrase, 54
musicals, 174, 229

---N---

NARIP, 195
Nashville Songwriters Association, 165
numerical size, 229

---O---

Olney Hymns, 229
outro. See codetta

---P---

parallel construction, 129
passing chord, 35

Performing Rights Organization, 162, 175, 229
- *ASCAP, 162, 179, 188*
- *BMI, 68, 162, 179, 188*
- *GMO, 162, 188*
- *PMR, 162, 188*
- *SESAC, 162, 179, 188*

Performing Rights Organizations, 159
period, 229
Philadelphia Volunteer Lawyers for the Arts, 185
phrases, 3, 47, 228
- *antecedent, 50, 80, 81, 221*
- *bridge, 222*
- *circular, 63, 113, 223*
- *consequent, 50, 80, 224*
- *opening, 58, 229*
- *sub-phrase, 51, 88, 232*

pick-up note. See anacrusis
pitch, 3, 229
pop music, 230
pre-chorus, 100, 104, 230
production, 1, 230
production music, 170, 230
prosody, 53, 65, 146, 230
publishing, 159
pulse, 14
push marketing, 158, 230

---R---

radio station id, 172, 230
radio-ready, 188
recitation tones, 91, 230
refrain. See chorus
reharmonization, 63
remote key, 120, 231
rhymes
- *half, 148, 225*
- *imperfect, 148*
- *ordinary, 229*
- *polysyllabic, 149, 230*
- *scheme, 53, 64, 150, 231*
- *slant, 148*

rhythm, 3, 14, 103
- *harmonic, 14, 47, 62*
- *lyrical, 55, 141*
- *melodic, 14, 47, 53, 113, 141, 227*

rhythm track, 38, 231
riff, 231
Rorem, Ned, 153
royalty, 161
- *mechanical, 161, 169, 227*
- *performance, 161, 162, 229*
- *synchronization, 170, 195, 232*

---S---

sawaal-javaab, 231, See call-and-response
scales, 9, 11, 231
- *Aeolian, 11, 221*
- *blues, 222*
- *chromatic, 10, 11, 223*
- *diatonic, 9, 224*
- *Dorian, 11, 225*
- *Ionian, 226*
- *Locrian, 226*
- *Lydian, 11, 135, 227*
- *major, 9, 20, 118, 230*
- *mediant, 227*
- *minor, 9, 20, 118, 231*
- *mixolydian, 11, 228*
- *modal, 228*
- *pentatonic, 11, 58, 227, 228, 229*
- *Phrygian, 11, 229*
- *supertonic, 232*

secondary dominant, 31, 35
self-publishing, 186
semitone, 4, 11, 231
shotgun announcements, 172
sing-along. See chorus
slash notation, 23, 231
SoundExchange, 163, 189
spirituals, 231
split agreement, 187
Spotify, 163, 178
standards, 231
sweepers, 172

---T---

tempo, 3, 14, 47, 232
- *adagio, 14*
- *andante, 54, 221*
- *moderato, 54, 228*
- *presto, 14*

temporary tonic, 31, 97, 232
tessitura, 107, 232
The Blank Page, 143, 222
The Great White Way, 174, 232
The Recording Academy, 165, 179
TIDAL, 178
time signature, 53, 232
Tin Pan Alley, 88
tone tendency, 23
transposition, 60, 232
triad, 17, 232
- *augmented, 222*
- *diminished, 19, 224*
- *major, 19*
- *minor, 19*
- *supertonic, 18*
- *tonic, 18, 232*

tritone substitution, 135, 232
troubadour, 112, 233
trouvéres, 112
twelve-bar blues, 73, 78
twelve-tone system, 233

---V---

verses, 91, 115, 233
- *introductory, 123, 226*
- *plain & fancy, 89, 120*
- *rap & sung, 89, 90*

Vimeo, 178
Virginia Harmony, 233
voices, 17

---W---

work-for-hire, 168, 233

---Y---

YouTube, 178

Index

Songwriters, Composers, and Lyricists

---A---

Adair, Tom, 149
Ament, Jeff, 106
Andrews, Tyler, 90
Appell, David, 29
Armstrong, Billie Joe, 28, 115
Austin, Johntá, 106

---B---

Bacharach, Burt, 16
Bachman, Randy, 38
Badu, Erykah, 90
Bassett, Dave, 104
Bazillion, Eric, 154
Beal, Joe, 125
Becker, Walter, 88
Bennett, Tony, 127
Berg, Alban, 12
Bonfá, Luiz, 136
Boothe, Jim, 125
Brecht, Bertolt, 71
Brothers Jr., Kerry, 89
Brown, James, 143
Brubeck, Dave, 61
Budo, 90
Burke, Johnny, 131
Burke, Sonny, 11

---C---

Cahn, Sammy, 37
Cannon, Hughie, 136
Capurro, Giovanni, 87
Carey, Mariah, 106
Carrell, James P., 52
Cash, Johnny, 71
Chase, Gilbert, 52
Churchill, Frank, 136
Clarkson, Kelly, 89
Coleman, Ornette, 12
Covay, Don, 38
Cowper, William, 52
Cox, Bryan Michael, 106
Cummings, Burton, 38

---D---

Dahlheimer, Patrick, 89
Darin, Bobby, 68
David, Hal, 16
Davis, Miles, 90
de Moraes, Vinícius, 13
de Oliveira, Aloysio, 35
Dennis, Matt, 149
Desmond, Paul, 61
DeVaughn, William, 38, 154, 204
DeYoung, Dennis, 97
di Capua, Eduardo, 87
Dixon, Mort, 125, 150
Dopps, Tyler, 90
Dubin, Al, 37, 136
Dupri, Jermaine, 106
Dylan, Bob, 88

---E---

Eco, Umberto, 144
Eli, Bobby, 154

---F---

Fagan, Donald, 88
Flea, 103
Foster, Stephen, 87, 113
Frusciante, J.A., 103

---G---

Gambel, Kenneth, 61
Gaudio, Bob, 88, 95
Gaye, Marvin, 95
Gershwin, George, 125, 136
Gershwin, Ira, 125, 136
Gilbert, Ray, 35
Gimbel, Norman, 13
Goffin, Gerry, 115
Gordon, Mack, 125, 136
Greenwood, Lee, 172
Grey, Skyler, 90
Grohl, Dave, 89

---H---

Hale, Lzzy, 104, 154
Hampton, Lionel, 11
Handy, W.C., 75
Harbach, Otto, 136
Hardin, Phillip, 143
Harry, George, 89
Hart, Lorenz, 30, 115
Hazard, Robert, 154
Hebb, Bobby, 68
Henderson, Ray, 125, 150
Hill, Lauryn, 90
Hodges, Dave, 89
Huff, Leon, 61

---J---

Jackson, Anthony, 61
Jobim, Antônio Carlos, 13, 35
Joel, Billy, 98, 115
Jones, Isham, 136

---K---

Kahn, Gus, 136
Kale, Jim, 38
Kern, Jerome, 136
Keys, Alicia, 89
Kiedis, A., 103
King, Carole, 88, 100, 115
Kosma, Joseph, 34
Kowalczyk, Ed, 89
Krall, Diana, 127

---L---

LaBelle, Patti, 154
Lada Gaga, 149
Lamm, Robert, 98
Lead Belly. See Ledbetter, Huddie William
Ledbetter, Huddie William, 71, 78, 81
Lennon, John, 13, 26, 31, 36, 87, 88, 98, 115
Lewis, Sam M., 125
Lightfoot, Gordon, 71

---M---

Macklemore, 90
Madara, John, 98

Magidson, Herb, 36
Mancini, Henry, 35, 131
Mandel, Johnny, 136
Mann, Kal, 29
Marks, Gerald, 32, 136
McCartney, Paul, 13, 26, 31, 36, 87, 88, 98, 115
McHugh, Jimmy, 149
McKee, Ben, 91
Mel Tormé, 127
Mendel, Nate, 89
Mercer, Johnny, 11, 34, 35, 131, 136
Miller, Jimmy, 88
Monk, Thelonious, 115
Moody, Ben, 89
Morey, Larry, 136

---N---

Newton, John, 52, 75

---P---

Pankow, James, 98
Pere, Bill, 133
Perry, Katy, 104
Perry, Linda, 87
Peterson, Garry, 38
Petrucci, Ottaviano, 159
Platzman, Daniel, 91

Porter, Cole, 125
Prévert, Jacques, 34

---R---

Raksin, David, 136
Renzetti, Joseph, 68, 164
Reynolds, Dan, 91
Robinson, Smokey, 61
Rodgers, Richard, 30, 115
Rogers, Kenny, 93

---S---

Schlitz, Donald, 93
Sedaka, Neil, 88
Sermon, Wayne, 91
Shaw, Benjamin, 52
Sigman, Carl, 136
Simons, Seymour, 32, 136
Smear, Pat, 89
Smith, Bessie, 78
Smith, C., 103
Spilman, Charles, 52
Sprout, Jonathan, 173
Stefani Germanotta. See Lady Gaga
Sting, 87
Stordahl, Alex, 37

---T---

Taylor, James, 30, 88, 95, 100, 115
Thiele, Bob, 33
Tranter, Justin, 91

---V---

Valli, Frankie, 61, 88
Van Heusen, Jimmy, 131, 136
Vetter, Eddie, 106

---W---

Wand, Hart, 75
Warren, Harry, 37, 125, 136
Waters, Roger, 15
Webb, Jimmy, 71, 98
Weill, Kurt, 71
Weiss, George David, 33
Weston, Paul, 37
White, David, 98
White, Ronald, 61
Williams, Hank, 20
Williams, Joe, 127
Winwood, Steve, 88
Wonder, Stevie, 87, 92
Wrubel, Allie, 36

---Y---

Young, Joe, 125

www.ingramcontent.com/pod-product-compliance
Lightning Source LLC
Chambersburg PA
CBHW051148290426
44108CB00019B/2646